CHANCERS

CHANCERS

Addiction, Prison, Recovery, Love:
One Couple's Memoir

Susan Stellin
and
Graham MacIndoe

BALLANTINE BOOKS

NEW YORK

Published in the United States by Ballantine Books, an imprint of
Random House, a division of Penguin Random House LLC, New York.

BALLANTINE and the HOUSE colophon are registered
trademarks of Penguin Random House LLC.

LIBRARY OF CONGRESS CATALOGING-IN-PUBLICATION DATA
Names: Stellin, Susan, author. | MacIndoe, Graham, author.
Title: Chancers : addiction, prison, recovery, love: one couple's memoir /
Susan Stellin and Graham MacIndoe.
Description: First edition. | New York : Ballantine Books, 2016.
Identifiers: LCCN 2016003606 | ISBN 9781101882740 (hardback) | ISBN
9781101882757 (ebook)
Subjects: LCSH: Stellin, Susan. | MacIndoe, Graham | Drug addicts—United
States—Biography. | Drug addicts—Rehabilitation—United States—
Biography. | Drug addicts—Family relationships. | BISAC: BIOGRAPHY &
AUTOBIOGRAPHY / Personal Memoirs. | PSYCHOLOGY /
Psychopathology / Addiction. | FAMILY & RELATIONSHIPS /
Love & Romance.
Classification: LCC HV5805.S75 A3 2016 (print) | LCC HV5805.S75
(ebook) | DDC 363.29092/2—dc23
LC record available at http://lccn.loc.gov/2016003606

Printed in the United States of America on acid-free paper

randomhousebooks.com

2 4 6 8 9 7 5 3 1

FIRST EDITION

For Liam

AUTHORS' NOTE

Any memoir is subjective, and this one is no exception, but the events described in the following pages did actually happen. We did not invent scenes or characters, although we did change most people's names—except for public figures and Graham's son, because he asked us to use his real name. In order to reconstruct situations and conversations, we relied on email messages, letters, notes, court documents, and input from people who appear in the book, but in some places, the dialogue is based solely on our memories. Some of the letters and email messages quoted have been condensed or edited slightly for clarity. We are grateful for the permission we received to include this correspondence, and for our families' willingness to expose parts of their lives alongside ours.

"I think we are well advised to keep on nodding terms with the people we used to be, whether we find them attractive company or not. Otherwise they turn up unannounced and surprise us, come hammering on the mind's door at 4 A.M. of a bad night and demand to know who deserted them, who betrayed them, who is going to make amends."

—Joan Didion, "On Keeping a Notebook"

PROLOGUE

January 2011
York County Prison, Pennsylvania

I'm sitting in a rental car outside a prison in Pennsylvania, where my ex-boyfriend is being held by the Department of Homeland Security. It's a frigid day in January, the winter back-to-back blizzards buried the Northeast, but I've driven down from Brooklyn during a break in the storms, arriving just as the light is starting to fade.

By 5 P.M., the parking lot where I'm waiting has turned ominous, prison floodlights interrogating a landscape of black and gray.

Inside, Graham can't see daylight, a frequent complaint during the five months he's been a prisoner here. The only windows in the dorm are up near the ceiling—too high for any kind of view. He once described how the inmates would stand against the wall whenever a strip of sunlight entered at an angle. As the sun lowered, the light moved higher on the wall, the men following it with their faces until it was out of reach.

Hearing stories like this has made me appreciate the things you take for granted when you're free.

Last summer, I'd watch the sun set across the East River as I ran along the Brooklyn waterfront, newly conflicted about the Statue of Liberty in the distance. In the fall, I noticed the leaves swirling around the sidewalk, stopping to pick one up so I could share the seasonal shift with Graham. At home I set the leaf on a piece of paper and carefully traced around the edges, knowing I couldn't send him the real thing. Technically, inmates aren't allowed to receive drawings—one of many rules I had to learn—but my tracing made it through the mailroom. Many letters didn't.

The ones that did were often tough to read.

"I just wish I could breathe some fresh air, feel the wind, smell the trees, feel the sun or the rain on my skin," Graham wrote to me, just after he arrived at the Pennsylvania prison. *"Every day here is very painful, lonely and long—no matter what you do to break it up, there's a limit to how you can use up 16 hours a day with nothing to do."*

I was sympathetic to his complaints—shocked, really, at how he and the other prisoners were treated. But after five months of helping him and fighting for his release, I'm worn down by the whole ordeal. It has also taken a toll on me.

My cellphone rings. The noise seems louder in the car, startling me as I fumble to answer quickly. I can tell from the number that it's Graham, which means I can't call him back if I miss it.

"You have a call from an inmate at York County Prison," the familiar recording begins. "Press one to accept the charges, press two to decline. . . ."

I hold the phone closer to make sure I press the right button, anxious because Graham shouldn't be calling me now. He should be in a van heading to the parking lot, or busy dealing with paperwork, or changing out of his prison uniform into street clothes. I'm here to pick him up because he's supposed to be released.

"They haven't called my name yet!" Graham shouts. I move the phone a little farther from my ear. "It's after five and they haven't called my name! They've called other names—ages ago— but not mine. I can't fucking believe it, what is going on?"

"Don't yell," I tell him, reflexively worried—even now—that he'll once again lose phone privileges. "I'm in the car, in the parking lot. The van isn't here yet."

By now I'm an expert at remaining calm, offering support, being optimistic. Back when we were together, Graham looked on the bright side and I imagined every possible worst-case scenario, but I'm starting to panic, too. I've made this trip once before—and drove home alone when Graham didn't get released—so this time I told our lawyer I wasn't leaving Brooklyn until the paperwork had actually been signed.

"Go get your man," he'd said, when he called earlier today. "The judge just signed the order. They're going to release Graham before six."

I look at the clock glowing on the dashboard: It's 5:13.

"Everybody is asking why I'm still here," Graham says. "I have no idea, no one has told me a fucking thing. I'm just sitting here waiting—all fucking day, watching the clock. I cannae take this anymore."

Graham's Scottish accent is always stronger when he's venting, despite living in Brooklyn for almost twenty years.

"Go talk to your counselor," I suggest. "Maybe he can find out what's going on. The visiting area is closed so I can't do much out here."

What I don't tell him is that I don't want to leave the car in case I miss the white van I'm expecting, hoping it's just running late. The paralegal had warned me that if I wasn't *right there* to collect Graham when the van brought him to the parking lot, he'd be driven to the bus station and dropped off—with no coat, no ID, and no money.

That is one of the cruelties of a system operating in the shadows of the law: Even though Graham was picked up by Homeland Security in New York City last August, it's his responsibility to get back home.

Not that he has a home to return to. He lost his house during his downward spiral toward prison, so he's going to stay with me until he sorts things out.

Thinking about how that cohabitation is going to work makes my anxiety kick into a higher gear. We broke up fours years ago and reconnected when I found out Graham was locked up. That news came as a relief—I thought he was dead when he disappeared—but I had no idea what I was getting into when I finally tracked him down.

Nearly half a year later, setting Graham free has practically become a full-time job. I didn't expect to fall back in love with him, and we've sort of danced around what's going to happen once he's out. Until a few days ago, we weren't even sure he'd get released from prison—theoretically, any moment now.

It's almost six when I notice headlights coming up the road, but it's too dark to tell if it's a van and too soon after Graham's call for him to possibly be inside. At this point, I know the prison bureaucracy moves at a glacial pace, so there's no way Graham made it from his dorm to the curb in half an hour.

As the headlights arc toward the parking lot, completing a right turn, my heart drops: It's definitely a white van. I try to summon a shred of hope as I open the car door.

By the time I shuffle across the icy pavement, the van has parked, engine idling. An officer dressed all in black is standing next to the side door, already calling out names. One by one, a few men stumble out—I wonder how that must feel, after months or years of dreaming about this day. But no one is stopping for a long hug or a deep breath of fresh air; family members steer the men toward cars that are still running, mindful of how easily freedom can be snatched away.

I count three—no, four—prisoners who have been released, try to calculate how many seats might be left in the van. As the officer starts to slide the door closed, I step forward and say, "Wait!"

"I'm here to pick someone up," I tell him, trying to sound confident, assertive. But when I say Graham's name, there's a doubtful question mark at the end.

"He's not on the list," the officer says, barely glancing at his clipboard.

In that moment, I feel an unworthy kinship with the victims of authoritarian regimes, well aware that my sense of persecution is at odds with the suburban setting: There's a mall with a Gap and a food court across the street, I have a room at a nearby Hampton Inn.

I explain that Graham is supposed to be released today, that the judge signed the order, that I've driven to Pennsylvania *twice* to pick him up, that this is wrongful imprisonment. My outrage is no match for the power of a functionary who couldn't care less.

"You'll have to work it out on Tuesday," the officer tells me, slamming the van door. "Monday is a holiday, so no one who can help you will be in until then."

I want to scream every obscenity I can think of, grab his shoulders and shake him, unload all the frustration of the past half year. But I just stand there shivering as he climbs back into the van. He doesn't give a shit about me—I'm no one to him.

After he drives off, I'm not ready to concede defeat, so I spend another hour outside the prison, shouting at guards through intercoms, calling our lawyer in New York, pleading with night shift employees entering the building to help me. But there's nothing anyone can do. Graham is not on the list.

Part One

WE

"The obscure we see eventually,
the completely apparent takes longer."
—Edward R. Murrow

CHAPTER ONE

Summer 2002
Montauk, New York

When Graham and I first met, in the summer of 2002, it definitely wasn't love at first sight. We were both part of a group of loosely connected friends who shared a beach house in Montauk, which at that point was still the affordable, laid-back alternative to the Hamptons. As one friend put it: In the Hamptons, you wore a sweater draped over your shoulders; in Montauk, you tied a hoodie around your waist. In either case, it was a way to escape New York City when the heat became oppressive.

About a dozen of us rented a house just uphill from the beach, alternating weekends according to a schedule plotted out at the beginning of the summer—and then promptly abandoned. I had signed up for four weekends, thinking I'd overlap with my sister and a few friends, but as everyone's plans shifted, I ended up spending two of those weekends with people I didn't really know.

That was partly the point of doing a share house—mixing it up a bit, maybe indulging in a summer romance—but our group was pretty tame by beach house standards. Most of us were in our thirties, working in advertising, media, photography, or film. I was thirty-three and doing well as a freelance writer, but I wasn't having much luck finding a partner.

The memories I have of that summer are like slides clicking around a circular tray in an old projector, images that are a bit fuzzy on the screen lit up in my mind. But the first time I met Graham, there's no doubt he made an impression. A thirty-nine-year-old Scotsman, he was gregarious and self-confident, if a bit cocky about his success as a photographer. Lean and energetic, he talked practically nonstop—funny anecdotes about the people whose portraits he'd taken and frank opinions about American culture. His girlfriend, Liz, was twenty-five and much more aloof, so they struck me as an odd match as a couple.

That weekend, I remember staying up late with Graham and his English friend Tom, empty beer bottles on the kitchen table outnumbering the housemates who had drifted off to bed— including Liz. At first glance, the scene might've seemed like typical Saturday night excess, but their banter had a bittersweet context. Tom's wife had died of cancer a few years earlier, leaving him to raise their young son, and he was moving back to London to be closer to his family. Graham was divorced and had an eleven-year-old son who was spending the summer with his grandparents in Scotland. It was one of the last weekends Graham and Tom would be together on the same side of the Atlantic.

I lingered long after I stopped drinking, just taking in the intensity of their friendship—laughter that brought tears, a crescendo of voices competing to make a point, a shared history weighed down by the ballast of pain and parenting. I had a wide circle of friends, relationships nurtured in the absence of kids or a husband, but this raucous expression of affection felt foreign, a brand of British boisterousness I hadn't been exposed to reading novels by Jane Austen and Virginia Woolf. It reminded me of the late nights my old boyfriend Ethan and I spent with friends when we were living in Argentina—that unfiltered passion I associated more with Latin America than Britain.

When I finally left the table, it felt like stepping away from a campfire, their voices receding but not quite fading as I walked down the hall. Even after I settled into a twin bed with damp sheets, I could still hear Graham and Tom in the kitchen, arguing about politics or art or the details of some long-ago road trip. It was the soundtrack of an impending end, when suddenly everything and nothing else mattered.

Later that summer, my friend Scott and I tagged along with Graham and Liz to an art opening in East Hampton, riding in Graham's red Volkswagen with music blaring. The Guild Hall gallery scene was a blur of cocktail party mingling and art-crowd conversation, all the high heels and sundresses making me self-conscious about my jeans and flip-flops. Afterward, the exhibition curator invited us back to the house where he was staying, a stately colonial overlooking Town Pond. We had more drinks on the deck of his garret apartment; other people stopped by and left. I was starving, but eating didn't seem to be on anyone else's agenda.

By the time Graham was ready to call it a night, it occurred to me that we were all too drunk to drive, but I was too tired to raise the issue—all I wanted to do was sleep. On the way back to Montauk, the car windows rolled down to let in a sobering, exhilarating rush of air, I knew that it was a reckless ride, that I was throwing my usual caution to the wind. But by that summer after 9/11, my concept of danger had shifted: After a year of reading and writing about the survivors and victims of that attack, I didn't really see the point of calculating risk. It was the kind of thing I did as a teenager in Michigan, riding in cars with boys who shouldn't have been behind the wheel.

The last scenes I remember from Montauk are actually captured on film; Scott took pictures Labor Day weekend and gave me copies of his prints. It was cold and windy but Graham's son, Liam, was back from Scotland and they decided to go for a swim, so a few of us followed them down to the beach. We were wearing fleece jackets and sweaters, but Graham and Liam stripped to their shorts, diving into the foamy fury of waves. As soon as they popped up, the current carried them in a line parallel to the shore—two slim bodies no match for the rough sea. They paddled and splashed back to land, ran toward us, then dove in again. Over and over, their bare feet slapping the wet sand as they ran past.

I grew up around lakes—swimming ever since I was two—but

I never quite embraced the ocean. On a windy day, I found the unpredictability of the waves unnerving. But Liam seemed to be loving it; he and Graham were both laughing and trying to get the rest of us to join in, but none of us were tempted to leave our perch on a dry berm of sand. We were content to be watching; Graham and Liam were living. There was a part of me that envied them, that adrenaline rush of getting carried away.

Graham had bought Liam a kite, and later that day, Scott took a photo of me helping them put it together on the beach. The string was horribly tangled and I offered to straighten it out, suggesting that my female fingernails would slide more easily between the knots. But Liam quickly grew bored and Graham soon sided with him: It was a cheap kite, it wasn't worth the effort, they'd find something else to do. Long after they gave up, I was still hunched over the tangled mess—I always thrived on having a challenge to complete.

Eventually, my persistence paid off: The kite flew. There's a photo of Graham with his head thrown back, his arms spread wide along the string, guiding the kite against the wind. It must've been late in the day because Graham is silhouetted against a cloudy sky, a dusky shadow as the sun struggled to announce its descent.

And that's it. Like clicking through the slides of my 1970s childhood, it feels like there must be more, that surely other images are buried in a box, waiting to summon memories that are missing.

Graham insists that I wore a red bikini that summer, but I've never owned a red bikini; in the photos Scott took, I'm wearing a red hooded sweater with denim shorts, my legs tan after a summer in the sun. Graham remembers the party in East Hampton, the late nights with Tom, and swimming with Liam that stormy Labor Day weekend. But I barely made a dent in his consciousness—one admittedly clouded by liquor—and after September, I can't say that I thought much about him. He had a girlfriend and I was interested in someone else by then.

At some point that fall, Scott told me that Graham and Liz were getting married; Scott was invited to their wedding at Graham's brownstone in Brooklyn. My initial reaction was, *"How come you got invited and I didn't?"* But that sentiment was short-lived. Scott had been friendly with Liz, and with me she always kept a cool distance, although I did wonder if she was going to regret what she was getting herself into. Graham's drinking was in that zone approaching problematic—maybe fun to be around when he was the life of the party, but not so pleasant to deal with day after day.

Scott was not one to gossip or make catty comments about the odds of a marriage lasting, so his report on the wedding was characteristically succinct: It was a fun party, Graham's parents and his brother flew over from Scotland, his sister and her family came from Ireland, a few friends from London made the trip. The closest he got to dishing was a comment about how much everyone drank.

The only other contact I had with Graham was the cc list of a few group emails: messages to settle unpaid bills and a couple of invites to parties that Graham and Liz didn't attend. There was some talk of organizing another rental for the following summer, but it never came together. Prices in Montauk were starting to creep up, a few housemates had moved away, and others had lost interest in the group dynamic—including me. After three summers of dealing with the personalities of different share houses, I'd had my fill of negotiating room assignments and dinner plans.

As a freelance writer, I was shifting from covering technology to writing about travel—mostly for *The New York Times*—and the new beat meant I could expense the cost of some trips. That fall, I flew out to California to write an article about Point Reyes;

toward the end of winter, I went to Brazil for a feature about Búzios, a resort town near Rio de Janeiro. My flight left New York at 10:20 P.M. on March 19, just minutes after George W. Bush announced that the United States was invading Iraq.

By the time the plane landed the war had started, so it was an awkward time to be an American abroad. Years earlier, Ethan and I had spent six weeks traveling around Brazil, getting a warm welcome pretty much everywhere we went. But in 2003, with bombs raining down on Baghdad, the reception from the locals was chilly. Everyone kept asking what the hell the U.S. was doing—a taxi driver, a waitress, other travelers. It was the first time I felt deeply uncomfortable about where I was from.

After I flew back to New York, I wrote an article about the beaches and nightlife in Búzios, describing the waves lapping against the seawall and the palm fronds rustling outside my hotel window. But what I remember most about that trip was an acute sense of shame. It left me with the nagging feeling that I was writing about the wrong things. I wanted to make a change, but I couldn't afford to turn down the travel assignments that were coming my way.

In 2004, an agent approached me about writing a travel book; within a few months, I had signed a deal. It was a guide to planning, booking, and troubleshooting a trip in a do-it-yourself era— not the kind of book that makes a major impact or wins any awards, but it was a useful topic and it meant I didn't have to constantly scramble for work. I just didn't realize how much of my life it would consume. For the next year, pretty much all I did was write.

CHAPTER TWO

January 2005
Upper West Side, Manhattan

In January 2005, after having no contact with Graham for three and a half years, I dug up his email address and sent him a message. The subject line said: *long time, no Montauk swims.*

"It's Susan, formerly of the Montauk share house a few summers ago," I wrote. *"I'm attaching a photo to refresh your memory, which also serves a second purpose: I need to get a more professional photo taken because I'm writing a book."*

In the picture I sent, I'm wearing a red turtleneck sweater with my curly hair piled up in a loose bun. Despite my slightly parted lips and weirdly come-hither look, I wasn't trying to seduce Graham—it was the only close-up I could find on my computer. I sent it mostly because I wasn't sure Graham would recognize my name.

Without confirming that suspicion, he wrote back saying he was *"just in from a shoot for the Guardian in London"* and had been *"away for a month over xmas all over the globe."* But he'd be happy to take my picture and would give me a call.

That would be the first time Graham promised to call, and then didn't.

There wasn't really a rush to get a photo taken, so I let it drop as I got consumed by writing the book. (Lesson learned: Get an author photo taken before you've got dark circles under your eyes from staring at a computer screen for a year, and don't wait until your summer tan fades to a dull winter pallor.)

By December, I was under the gun to submit a head shot to my publisher, so I decided to try Graham again—despite my sister's unenthusiastic response when I asked what she thought of his photos. After looking at his website, she told me she didn't think he made people look attractive, and that his lighting was a little harsh.

Since she had met Graham at the share house in Montauk, I wondered if her opinion of his work was clouded by his boisterous behavior that summer. Still, I clicked through his online portfolio again—mostly portraits of authors and artists and musicians, along with photos from ad campaigns for clients like IBM and ESPN.

In some sense, my sister was right: These were not glamorous images, highlighting perfect makeup and flawless skin. But I didn't want to look like I was auditioning for a bit part on Broadway, or trying to get a date on Match.com. I wanted to look like the people in Graham's pictures: self-assured and authentic, not trying to be somebody they weren't. Besides, I was sort of curious to see him again.

So as much as it was a practical decision to contact Graham—I couldn't afford any of the photographers my friends recommended—I didn't choose him entirely on a whim. There was even a fair amount of deliberation behind the breezy follow-up email I sent.

"So I never did anything about a photo," I wrote. *"I don't suppose you're in town and have time in the next couple of weeks to shoot a writer who isn't quite as famous as your usual subjects?"*

This time, Graham did call. At first, I had a hard time understanding his accent—the Scottish way he rolled the *r* in his name, and said "cannae" instead of "can't." He suggested I come by his house in Brooklyn, instructing me to exit the subway from "the ass end of the train." When I asked about his rate, I was relieved to hear that he'd only charge me for his expenses.

The day we'd agreed on, two weeks before Christmas, he answered the door half-dressed, his brown hair a bit disheveled. Clearly, he had forgotten our plan.

"Is this a bad time?" I asked.

Graham was still buttoning his shirt, a vintage western pattern, and his wool pants were falling down—not a style statement so much as a size mismatch. He looked thinner than I remembered, but still had a rough-around-the-edges charm.

"I couldn't find a belt," he said, abandoning the shirt buttons to hike up his trousers. "Sorry, I just woke up."

It was one o'clock on a Saturday afternoon.

"Did I get the time wrong?" I asked, knowing perfectly well that I hadn't. "I can come back later—I'll go get a coffee or something. Or we can do this another day if now isn't a good time."

"No, it's fine. I was up late, scanning some photos I had to send to London."

"Oh, I thought maybe you'd had a rough night," I joked, thinking about the time Graham and Tom had kept half of the Montauk house awake.

"I gave up drinking," Graham said, quick to correct my assumption. He held open the door as I stepped over the mail scattered near the entrance, shoes climbing up the wall in a pile. "Do you want coffee? Actually, I might not have any coffee. I can make you a cup of tea."

"That would be great," I said, hoping I hadn't offended him with my comment. I wasn't much of a tea drinker but the house felt chilly, like the heat hadn't been turned on yet for the winter.

Graham lived in a brownstone he bought back when taxi drivers wouldn't take passengers to the outer boroughs, renovating the parlor floor so it was one big open room. It felt more like a loft than a nineteenth-century home—sort of an artist's studio with a kitchen at one end. As we waited for the kettle to boil, I looked at the photographs on the walls: a nighttime view out an airplane

window, a shot of two gas storage tanks just as one was exploding, and a picture of a tiny soccer field surrounded by tall buildings.

"Did you take these?" I asked.

"The big prints, not the black-and-white ones. That one of the
row houses in Edinburgh I picked up at the Chelsea flea market.
It's an albumen print from the 1860s."

"I've never been to Scotland," I said, feeling a bit awkward,
wondering if Liz was still asleep downstairs. But it turned out she
and Graham had split up.

Before he snapped a single photo, while my tea was still warm,
Graham summed up the previous three years of his life: He had
gotten married, then divorced, fell into a funk, took time off from
work. But he had quit drinking, he assured me—even went to
rehab to get sober. I knew plenty of people in recovery, so this
confession didn't set off alarms. If anything, it seemed like a positive sign.

Every time he disappeared to the basement to fetch more film
or a different light, I perused all the collections on his shelves—
photography books and record albums mixed with stoop sale and
trash night finds: piles of sunglasses, punk band pins, Scottish trin-
kets, and little windup toys. It was the opposite of my sparsely
decorated apartment, which didn't give much away—except for
shelves full of books. I was drawn to Graham's world, full of personality and art and clutter.

He teased me about the sweaters I'd brought for the photo
shoot, rejecting my admittedly plain choices. "No turtlenecks—
necks are sexy," he said. "Not a cardigan—unless you want to
look like a librarian. . . . Do you have anything that's not black or
gray?" (The J.Crew V-neck we settled on was navy.)

I gave him a hard time about his unconventional lighting meth-
ods: fluorescent tubes I thought would make my pale skin look
purple, aluminum foil he rolled out on the table in front of me—to

bounce light up under my eyes. Even though I expressed my reservations in a playful manner, my sister's comment hovered like a cartoon thought bubble at the back of my mind.

"I know I said I liked how natural people look in your pictures," I told Graham. "But please don't make me look *too* real."

"Well, I could smear some Vaseline on my lens and give you a nice soft-focus look, but I think you look pretty good. Just give me a smile that says, 'Buy my book!'"

After hours of flirtatious banter, and more photos than I suspect Graham really needed to take, he suggested we go get something to eat. That didn't seem like a typical way to wrap up a photo shoot, but I was enjoying being with him so off we went to Smith Street—Graham narrating a monologue almost the entire way.

He had settled in Brooklyn when he moved to New York in 1992, working at a photography gallery after getting his MFA from the Royal College of Art in London. He and his first wife, Anna, shared custody of Liam (who was now fifteen); she lived in their old brownstone a few blocks away.

It was tough to break in once Graham got going on a topic, but I managed to squeeze in a few details about my life. After graduating from Stanford University, I taught English in Argentina for two years, then got hired by an Internet start-up in San Francisco. A job at *The New York Times* website brought me east, just before the dot-com boom went bust. Luckily, I'd cashed in my stock options for the down payment on an apartment in Manhattan, but I didn't love where I lived—surrounded by chain stores on the Upper West Side.

"You should move to Brooklyn," Graham said. "Before it gets too expensive. All there used to be along this street was a dodgy bar, a diner, and a couple of delis, but now it's becoming like Soho."

Bypassing a French bistro and other restaurants he deemed too trendy, Graham chose a tiny Spanish place with Formica tables and bright lights. He revealed that he was "sort of" a vegetarian and ordered a salad; I polished off a steak burrito. Since he wasn't charging me for the photo, I insisted on paying for the meal.

It was dark by the time he walked me to the subway, offering to wait with me until the train came. Before I passed through the turnstile, he surprised me with a kiss—an impulsive swoop toward my lips that I didn't quite know how to interpret. It was more forward than an Italian cheek kiss, but too quick of a peck to be sure it was a romantic gesture.

"Do you think that's a Scottish thing?" I asked my friend Sara, calling her as soon as I got off the train. She told me I was being an idiot—of course he'd made a move—but I wasn't entirely convinced. I wasn't used to being hit on so quickly.

The next day, I got my answer. *"I had a nice time Saturday,"* Graham emailed me. *"We should jump on a plane to Vegas and hit the desert for a few days."* We had joked about using some of Graham's frequent flier miles to fly somewhere sunny—I'd get a tan, then he'd retake my photo. But in case he thought I might actually take him up on that offer, I replied saying Vegas was a little too far to travel, so he invited me to a friend's Christmas party instead. *"I hate going to things like that alone and I'd really like to go w/you if that's ok. Sort of like an uncomplicated date!!"*

That was a reference to a story he'd told me about a woman who had propositioned him, promising "uncomplicated" sex. I was a little surprised when he revealed that he wasn't a one-night-stand type of guy; it didn't track with his flirtatious behavior.

"I think a transcript of Saturday's conversation would confirm that your life is definitely not uncomplicated," I wrote back. *"Where/what time is the party?"*

Graham never followed up about the Christmas party, but after he got his film processed he invited me over to his house to choose a photo. Carefully scrutinizing the contact sheets, I had a hard time hiding my disappointment: His lighting tricks were no match for my raccoon eyes. Even though I looked young for my age, with freckles and reddish-brown curly hair, you could tell I'd spent too much time in front of a computer.

"That's what Photoshop is for," Graham promised. "A little dodging to lighten the shadows under your eyes, some work with the healing brush to smooth out a few wrinkles."

"I hope you're not planning on charging me extra for that," I joked. "Remember—you already told me you're still learning digital retouching."

After flipping through the contact sheets a second time, I marked a couple of photos with the yellow-arrowed stickers Graham gave me. It all felt very old school, with a loupe and the rolls of film scattered on the table. Graham hadn't yet made the transition to the digital era—he'd taken my portrait with a 1970s Hasselblad, one of those cameras you hold at your waist, looking down into the lens. I wished I'd looked closer at the Polaroids he shot to test the lighting, telling him I should've at least tried to tame my wild hair.

"Listen, I think you look brilliant," he said. "But if you don't like any of these, we can try again. You're not gonna hurt my feelings if you tell me they're all crap."

"No, they're fine," I insisted. "One of these will work. I just didn't realize how tired I look. And my hair always seems so messy in pictures."

"I like your hair," Graham said.

We were sitting next to each other at a long pine table made by one of his friends. Our knees were touching; I wondered if he was going to kiss me, couldn't decide if I wanted him to or not. I was attracted to him, but sitting for a portrait and then getting hit on by the photographer seemed like such a cliché, and I didn't want to be one of those gullible girls if Graham was that kind of guy. But then his phone buzzed—it was always beeping or buzzing. He picked it up to read a text. With that momentary distraction, the charged moment between us passed.

"I have something for you," I said, reaching into my bag for the books I'd bought for him: *The Year of Magical Thinking,* by Joan Didion; *The Namesake,* by Jhumpa Lahiri; and *The Kite Runner,* by Khaled Hosseini.

While he was taking my picture, Graham had asked which authors I liked, saying he mostly picked up books his neighbors left outside for anyone to take—but there was usually a reason they were giving them away.

"You didn't have to get me anything," Graham said. "I only asked because you're a writer and I figured you've read things I haven't. I could've gotten them myself—I was going to ask you to email me the names."

"I wanted to give you something, for taking my picture," I said, suddenly self-conscious about the gift. Maybe it came across as a bit condescending, like I thought he should be more well-read.

Graham was flipping through the books like a boy who didn't expect a present at Christmas—the way he carefully turned the pages, his head bowed in concentration. I got the sense that he wasn't used to being on the receiving end of anyone's generosity, at least not lately.

"Thank you," he said, in a quieter voice than usual. "I've got something for you, too."

"You already gave me something," I protested. "You took my picture!"

But Graham was already clomping down the stairs, rummaging around one of the bedrooms on the floor below. I could hear him opening and closing drawers, a closet door banging shut, more footsteps—as if he'd descended one more level, to the basement. When he finally resurfaced, he was holding something up, triumphant about whatever he'd found.

"Close your eyes," he said.

I did, playing along. After more rustling, and what sounded like paper being cut, he placed a small object in my hand, his fingertips brushing my palm.

"You can open them now."

I was holding a blue plastic cone with a white rectangle connected to a key chain at one end. I had no idea what it was.

"Look," Graham said, grabbing it out of my hand. He held it up to my eye: It was a toy photo viewer, with my picture lit up inside.

"I think I look better this way," I said, genuinely touched by his gesture. "I like the tiny version of me."

"I prefer the big version of you," Graham said, not missing a beat.

There was something refreshing about how direct he was—I wondered if that was a Scottish trait, or if he just blurted out whatever popped into his head. But I still hadn't made up my mind about how I felt about him, and I wasn't going to decide that night: The transit workers were threatening to strike starting at midnight, so I wanted to get home while I could still catch a train.

"I should probably get going," I said. "It sounds like there really might be a strike."

"You could always get stuck in Brooklyn . . . Liam is staying at his mum's house tonight."

"Except I'm flying to Michigan tomorrow morning, remember? I told you—I'm going to see my family for Christmas."

"Oh, right. I forgot about that." Graham wasn't any better than me at hiding his disappointment.

Standing up to get my coat, I suddenly felt bad about leaving, insisting I'd be fine walking to the subway alone. The route to the quickest train meant passing by the housing projects Graham had warned me about. "Drug dealers hang out there," he'd said. "Just watch your back."

I gave him a hug at the door and thanked him again for taking my photo. He thanked me for the books and gave me a polite peck on the cheek. When I turned around to wave from the sidewalk, he'd already gone back inside. For a moment, I regretted rejecting his offer to walk me to the train.

The street was dark and the wind blew back the hood of my coat. Pulling it up over my head, I snapped the flap tight under my chin, checked my watch—10:20—and hustled toward the subway. Waiting on the platform, I took the photo viewer out of my pocket and looked at my picture again.

I had plenty of reservations about getting involved with Graham—mostly, his two divorces and the prospect of dating a guy with a teenage son. I liked him, but I wasn't sure I wanted to deal with all that baggage. He had talked a lot about his messy breakup with Liz, so I wasn't sure he'd really put that behind him.

But no one had ever pursued me as intensely as Graham did, through a flurry of emails and text messages he sent while I was away: updates about his bathroom renovation (*"I bet you'll want to submerge yourself in warm soapy water the minute you see it!"*), synonyms for the word *yuppie* (despite his working-class up-bringing, I told him owning a brownstone meant he had to embrace his bourgeois status), and many suggestions that we test my travel skills by jetting around the world (*"We could take your book and see if it works!"*).

I was used to men who had their pick of available women, so Graham's full-court press was definitely flattering. And there was certainly something appealing about his Scottish charm. Sending a few flirty messages of my own while I was away for Christmas— dropping hints that I hoped to see him again—I decided it couldn't hurt to see where this went.

When I got back to New York, I surprised Graham by showing up at his door.

———

IT WAS AFTER midnight on New Year's Eve—really, New Year's Day—by the time I stumbled over to Graham's house. Fueled by champagne and the depressing moment when all the single people watch all the couples kiss, I had walked there after leaving a party at a friend's house ten blocks away.

His front door was open and I could see lights on inside, but I hesitated on the sidewalk across the street. I hadn't told him exactly when I was flying back from Michigan, and now I was having second thoughts about my last-minute surprise. Why would anyone leave their front door wide open late at night, in January, with drunken revelers wandering around?

There were shades covering the windows, but I thought I could see people inside—maybe the heat was cranking so they were letting in some cool air. Or I could just interpret it as a sign: The door is open, all you have to do is walk through.

My New Year's resolve was wavering and I was freezing. If I was going to do this, I had to make a move. Just then I saw Graham through the doorframe, at the far end of the room—I quickly ducked behind a tree. But I was facing a long subway ride to get home, with no chance of catching a cab. The thought of that journey, combined with the effect of too much champagne, propelled me across the street and up the stairs.

Graham's back was turned, so I made it through the door and across the room without him noticing my entrance. Standing behind him, I reached around and covered his eyes with my hands. The shock of my cold fingers may have startled him more than my presence, and as he spun around, I barely finished saying "Happy New Year" before he kissed me—this time leaving no doubt about his intentions. His enthusiastic reaction overcame any of mine.

Later, I asked him why he'd left his door open.

"I was waiting on first footers," he said.

"First footers?"

"In Scotland, when people walk by and see your door open you welcome them in and ring in the New Year."

What he neglected to mention about this tradition was that ideally, the first person to enter your home after midnight on January 1 was supposed to be a tall, dark-haired man bearing gifts for good luck. Blonds, redheads, and women should be sent away, lest they bring misfortune to the household.

Unaware of this superstition, I spent the night and most of the next day.

In the haze of that alcohol-tinted first sleepover, I chose to overlook a few details that clashed with my idea of a grown-up life. There was no food in the refrigerator, Graham's bedding looked like it had been discarded from a college dorm room, and the general housekeeping could be summed up with the word *disarray*.

He apologized for the clutter in an email he sent just after I left, with the subject line *www.you&me.com*.

> *You completely took me by surprise last night - smarty*
> *pants! I'm still thinking about it 'coz it was the last thing I*
> *expected and I got a bit embarased coz I'm Not really used*
> *to that sort of thoughtfulness these days. and sorry it was*
> *messy and I was a bit scatterbrained . . . It was a treat to*
> *wake up with you this morning.*
> *G xxxxx*

I attributed the messiness to bachelorhood and the part-time presence of his teenage son. Any other reservations I pushed aside. I had just spent the past year holed up writing a book—I was ready for a break. Getting involved with Graham wasn't a fling, but it was definitely some kind of escape.

———

AT FIRST, OURS was an obsessive, indulgent connection, which excluded the rest of the world. If I woke up craving a chocolate croissant, Graham would bike to every bakery in the neighborhood until he found one, returning with lukewarm cups of coffee and a bouquet of some budding vine, chosen because it didn't look like flowers. He never wanted to be ordinary—which was a big part of his appeal.

He had just renovated his bathroom and put in a claw-foot tub, which we christened with hot baths for two after scouring nearby stores for bubbles. He paid attention to details like candles and music and pieces of colored fabric thrown over a lampshade to create a mood. I made sure we had clean towels.

But I had my spontaneous moments. One night, late, it snowed. We had just taken a bath and were in the kitchen making tea, naked except for our towels. There was enough snow on the back deck to make snow angels, I pointed out. He dared me, so I stepped into the frigid air, stretched out in the fresh powder, and spread my arms and legs wide to create wings and a skirt.

The snow was still falling, swirling through the light shining on the deck and melting on my skin, now barely covered. Laughing, tingling, alive, I got up and dashed inside. Graham was standing by the stove, warming his towel over the flame. When he turned toward me holding the corners wide to wrap me up, he didn't realize it had caught fire—until I shrieked and threw it outside.

I was caught up in his intensity, but I hadn't completely abandoned myself.

"Tell me you love me," he said, lying on top of me but not looking at me, his breath warming the place where my neck sloped into my shoulder. I kissed him instead; it was too soon for those words. Too soon for me, at least—we'd only been dating a couple of weeks. Graham had no reservations about how he felt.

When I was at my apartment, he would email me photos of himself, self-portraits that were childishly sentimental yet professionally composed. In one he was holding a heart over his chest that he'd cut out of construction paper. In another, he'd written our initials in black marker on his arm. At my desk one morning, I clicked to play a song he'd sent just after I left Brooklyn: "Nobody Does It Better," the Radiohead version. My whole body flushed, still lit up from the previous night.

"Couch? Floor? Bed?" Graham would whisper in my ear, kissing me at the door when I arrived at his house. It became a routine, each of us adding increasingly uncomfortable options to the list.

"Table?"

"Stairway?"

"Desk?"

"Sink?"

Our clothes were usually off before either of us said much else.

Music became a way Graham communicated whatever he was feeling, making me CDs labeled with themes for all the songs he chose. "S Is for Suzie," featuring twenty-six songs with my name in the title, or a mix called "Scottish Minute," a reference to Graham's tendency to show up late when we had plans—with songs like "Wait a Minute" by Ray J and Lil' Kim.

I wasn't sure if Graham was more interested in expanding my musical tastes—as a teenager, he took the overnight bus to London to see punk bands; my first concert was Air Supply—or if he wanted me to glean some deeper meaning from each collection he made. One CD was an eclectic mash-up of artists: Nouvelle Vague singing "This Is Not a Love Song" by Public Image, followed by Johnny Cash covering U2's "One."

I expressed my affection by cooking for Graham—lasagna, risotto, cookies, and pies—and by commuting back and forth to Brooklyn, more than an hour each way. I preferred staying at Graham's house, and so did he, but I worked better at mine. My book was coming out soon and I was busy dealing with the galleys, so it's fair to say that Graham was a welcome distraction at a stressful time.

He tried to be sensitive to the boundaries I set up, determined to keep one foot firmly planted in my other world of deadlines and responsibilities and bills. But each message he sent chipped away at my walls. *"Let me know if you're tied up with work and stuff later or if you want me to kiss you,"* he wrote.

"Both," I wanted to reply. I liked all the attention, but I wished Graham would slow down. A long email, titled *"this n that,"* summed up how he was feeling about our future together—just a few weeks after I showed up at his door.

He wrote it late one night at his computer upstairs, printing out a copy and slipping it under my pillow when he finally came to bed. I was already asleep, barely registering his body nestling up against mine, so I read it when I woke up the next day. The time stamp on the email version was 4:46 A.M.

okay, don't know what to say so straight up......i wasn't really expecting this. yes i definately led you on, flirted, peppered phone calls and conversations with wee inuendos. basically i got a real crush on you and i liked it. i love your company, your humor, the way you talk to me......almost everything but now i'm getting scared 'coz i don't know what you want......I know you plan on travelling after being tied down with the book for so long - that's great you deserve it. i just don't wanna fall in love ('coz it'll happen) then watch you head off - but more so i don't want to make you sacrifice anything that you've been thinking of doing. i don't really know what your thinking so i'm throwing my cards on the table - early on. of course I want to be with you i feel fucking great with you - it feels like we've been together ages.......actually i'm at the point of almost deleting this and coming to bed but i won't 'coz it's important-ish. i could really simplify this.

*susan calls graham for pic
graham obliges and flirts with susan
susan falls for graham
graham's already fallen for susan
susan is on graham's mind
graham is a bit confused about relationship when
he should really just relax and see what happens.
susan needs to tell graham this in a nice but
assertive way (if she wants).*

i think you'll know what i mean. I don't want someone so good coming into my life only to leave again. unless i can work on taking it as it comes - and not to give or expect too much too soon. i've had a long time off and got comfortable in that space but now i realize how much better it can be.

and don't think i'm expecting a vow of commitment or anything like that. i'm just trying vainly to let out what's on my mind in a more coherent manner than if I blurted it out.....i'm sure you've pretty much guessed all this so you can throw it back at me or give me some constructive critisism whatever you fancy - i can take it.

*love,
graham*

He'd added handwritten notes to the copy he printed out, and some of the words were highlighted with little question marks—

where his email program's spell checker had suggested replacements. It made Graham's letter seem even more vulnerable and earnest.

Still, I was touched by everything he wrote. Despite his tattooed arms and rough Scottish accent, Graham had a schoolgirl's sensitivity—all these feelings swirling around, sometimes spilling over or misunderstood. I was attracted to that passion, but wondered if I could navigate such intense emotions over the long haul. My temperament was much more even-keeled.

"Thank you," I told him, after reading the printout he'd given me. We were still in bed, Graham pressed tight against me.

"Sorry for the weird formatting," he said. "And all the typos—I'm not a good speller. I know I'm probably saying too much and you're gonna tell me it's too soon. . . ."

I kissed him to stop him from talking—a rare time when that actually worked.

"You don't have to apologize," I said. "It's a beautiful note. But I wish you wouldn't worry about me selling my apartment and moving. First of all, I'm not as impulsive as you, so if I ever do anything like that you'll have plenty of notice."

That made Graham smile. He had called me the least impulsive person he'd ever met, which annoyed me at first, but I knew it was probably true.

"And when I said I wanted to travel—of course I'd rather be traveling than stuck at home in front of a computer. But I've got a book coming out so it's not like I'm going to take off anytime soon."

"We should go somewhere," Graham said, seizing the opportunity to press his case for a vacation—or a holiday, as he called it. "I keep telling you, I've got all these miles on United—we could fly business class. We'll pick somewhere warm, lie on the beach, get a tan. Maybe find you a red bikini."

"Business class?" I joked. "You really are a yuppie. I might have to find someone to travel with who's a little more down-to-earth."

After years of interviewing people, I was good at redirecting conversations, so I was relieved when Graham didn't press me to respond to his note right away. Because as much as I appreciated all the heartfelt things he wrote, I *wasn't* entirely comfortable with the cards he was throwing on the table. Even though he'd quit drinking, I still wasn't sure what had led him into rehab—or whether that problem was likely to rear its head again. So I felt like I needed to communicate that, gently, when I replied to his message later that night.

Back at my apartment, I probably spent as much time as he did carefully crafting my email, beginning with a reference to the song "Collide," by Howie Day.

> *Don't dis my not-so-edgy musical tastes, and don't take the lyrics too literally, but the idea of two people colliding is sort of how I feel about all this. I didn't really see it coming either, but I guess there was a moment when I felt like I'd regret it more if I didn't take that leap and see what happened, even though I knew it wasn't going to be uncomplicated, and that your world is much more chaotic than mine.*

> *You might worry that I'm going to sell my apartment and buy a one-way ticket to Thailand (not likely). I worry that I'm going to show up some day and find the Graham I knew in Montauk (not all bad, but you were obnoxious when drunk) or the Graham I'm probably lucky I didn't know whenever you hit bottom. For all your openness, you've never really talked about what made you decide to put your life back on track.*

> *But you have to give me credit for believing that you are trying to do that—and believing that you can. I feel like I reconnected with you somewhere on the path to rebuilding*

*your life, but that's also nervous-making because you seem
really vulnerable right now. It's really intoxicating to be on
the receiving end of all that attention, but I don't want to
take advantage of your generosity or feel like you're doing
things because of me, because that puts a lot of responsibility on me.*

*I guess the last thing I want to say is that even though I
can't promise that this is forever (and you can't either), I
think it's worth taking a chance. So here's what I'm supposed to tell you: just relax and see what happens. Having a
stress-free solo life has its benefits, but then you'd be missing out on snow angels at 5:00 a.m. And I'd be missing out
on all the good things I've gotten since entering Graham's
world . . . not the least of which is remembering what it
feels like to get so close to someone that when they're
across the room that's too far away.*

xo,
-s-

Even then, I knew Graham would notice that I didn't use the
word *love*. But I was relieved when he wrote back saying, *"It's
probably about the nicest, most honest letter I've ever got. I won't
go on except to say 'thank you' and I'll relax and we'll just take it
as it comes. No seeing other people though—can't do that one.
Also, I'll tell you whatever you want—I've not hidden or lied
about anything."*

It was hard to imagine Graham keeping much to himself. The
nights we were apart, usually during the week, we'd talk on the
phone for hours. Or rather, Graham would do most of the talking
and I'd listen, the battery of my cellphone heating up as he described whatever he'd done that day: scanning negatives for his

website, replacing the faucet in his kitchen sink, painting a book-shelf he'd found. He was in an industrious phase, hoping to impress me with all his accomplishments, but he got sidetracked easily—in life, and on the phone.

A discussion about his website would lead to a story about the friend who was helping him with the redesign, a bass player in a band that was about to become famous. Which would remind him of the first few times he saw them play, in small bars on the Lower East Side, but now they were playing concerts all over the world. That would segue into an anecdote about the time he took Michael Jackson's portrait—Graham had a picture on his refrigerator of the two of them, their arms casually slung around each other's shoulders. And then he'd promise to send me a song he'd just thought of, "All I Want," by Joni Mitchell, which I had on a cassette somewhere but he wanted me to listen to it again, and really pay attention to the lyrics.

Instead, after we hung up, I got an email saying, *"Just listening to your slightly exasperated breathing, occasional sighs and sweet voice makes me want to be naked with you."*

The Joni Mitchell song arrived in my inbox a couple of days later, when he remembered he'd been meaning to send it. I actually didn't need to listen it; my friends and I had played that album in college so I already knew the lyrics—about love bringing out the best in us—and I already knew that's how Graham felt.

Although I loved all the emails he sent, loved listening to him talk, his stories and jokes spilling out like a waterfall fed by some infinite source, I had trouble keeping up with the flow. He had a lot of time on his hands, I told myself—and tried to tell him, explaining why my messages were less frequent, sometimes curt. He was taking time off after a few years of well-paid assignments, but I had to work.

The truth is, I was a bit jealous of his ease with feelings, and his way with words. He was a photographer; he was supposed to be the visual one. I made my living as a writer; I should've been more expressive.

But I couldn't always find the right words when I needed them; like a photograph developing in a darkroom, I needed time before I could reveal myself. And to some degree, I was holding back because of everything he'd told me about his past—the drinking, some drug use, a stint in rehab, a bad breakup.

I can't say I was certain he'd put all of that behind him, but I did believe him when he said he'd never lie to me. Graham held back so little, I didn't think he was capable of hiding anything.

And so, worn down by his pleas that we go away somewhere, I relented. In late January, barely a month after we first got together, we booked a trip to Hawaii—using Graham's miles.

Honestly, when he picked up the phone to call United, I thought there was *no way* he'd come up with free tickets to Honolulu, over Valentine's Day, booking just two weeks in advance. But he was smiling as he told the representative that he wanted to surprise his wife with a holiday, spinning out some tale about an anniversary, his Scottish accent working its usual charm.

When he put his hand over the receiver and told me she'd found two seats in business class, leaving on February 11, how could I possibly have turned him down?

CHAPTER THREE

February 2006
Kauai, Hawaii

I'm pushing past some tangled vines to get to the edge of the cliff when I hear Susan's voice behind me.

"Don't even think about it," she says, coming up the trail and stopping.

"I just want to get a little closer," I tell her, holding up my camera. "I like how the clouds split the blue of the sky and the blue of the ocean."

"Then use a zoom lens. It's a straight drop down to the Pacific."

I'm not afraid of heights—growing up in Scotland, my pals and I would dare each other to climb just about anything: the sides of quarries, old oak trees, abandoned buildings—but Susan gets vertigo so all week she's been nervous about where I'm taking pictures.

"Alright," I say, backing up through the brush. "I suppose if I fall you're not going to scramble down the cliff and save me."

Susan laughs and pulls me back onto the path. "Like I told you, if you get in trouble swimming I may be able to help you, but I'm not cut out for any rescue missions that involve heights."

That's one of the things I like about her: She's really practical and sensible, then she'll do something impulsive, like surprising me on New Year's Eve. I'd already fallen for her the day I took her picture, flirting with her from the get-go, but she's been kind of hard to read. I was hoping the trip to Hawaii might bring us closer—and it's been brilliant so far. Sun, sand, sex, Susan: all the S's I wanted. But I still get the feeling she's holding back a bit.

After another half hour of ups and downs along the trail, we make it to Hanakapiai Beach, the farthest we can go without a permit. There's a sign nailed to a tree that says, DO NOT GO NEAR THE WATER. UNSEEN CURRENTS HAVE KILLED 82 VISITORS. It's got white painted hash marks counting all the people who have died.

"That's a bit ominous," I say, wondering who's been updating the tally. The ocean is so rough there's nothing but white foam swirling around the rocks—black boulders that are round and smooth from getting pummeled constantly.

Once we eat our packed lunch, I take a few pictures of Susan— quite the outdoor type in her blue Patagonia jacket with a bandana tied around her hair. I like how Susan looks so tiny standing next to some palm trees with the huge cliffs in the background. My dad always says a picture means nothing unless it's got scale.

"You know there are palm trees on the west coast of Scotland," I tell her.

"That sounds like the beginning of one of your jokes."

"It's true. They grow there because of the coconuts brought up by the Gulf Stream. You see them in all these little fishing towns, next to guys in big wool sweaters unloading their boats."

"I'm going to have to google that later," Susan says, looking a bit skeptical as she points to the sky. "Actually, we should start heading back soon. I think we're about to get drenched."

By the time we've packed up and hit the trail, the clouds have rolled in and the rain is really beating down. The streams we crossed earlier are now torrents rushing down the hills and the path is like melted chocolate. I'm using a broken-off branch to keep my balance and Susan is hanging on to me most of the way.

Normally, I don't like getting caught in the rain but in Hawaii it hasn't really bothered me. City rain always feels dirty, but here it's warm and sort of cleansing—like it's washing away all the crap of the past few years.

Back at the condo, I sit naked on the bathroom floor, watching

Susan shower and shave her legs. I love how she's so meticulous, maneuvering the razor around her ankles and pulling it up over her knees. Just as I step in to join her, red mud from the trail dripping down my legs, she grabs a towel and starts drying off.

"Don't go," I tell her, leaning in for a kiss.

"You can try that again after you're clean," she says, teasing me with a quick squeeze before hopping out.

"Listen—between swimming and showering and getting rained on all week, I haven't been this clean in ages."

THE NEXT DAY, we fly to Honolulu and check into a hotel in Waikiki. It's finally sunny out, so within minutes Susan has changed into the blue bikini I bought her and we're heading down to the beach. There are stands renting equipment for every water sport you can imagine—even those Hawaiian outrigger canoes.

After we walk for a while, Susan picks a place to spread out our towels and opens her book, giving me a chance to escape.

"I think I'll pop into town for a bit," I tell her. "I need to buy some more film."

"Really? This might be our last sunny afternoon at the beach. Can't you just buy it at the hotel later?"

"I shoot medium-format film so I have to get it at a photography store. I found one that's not too far from here."

"Okay," Susan says, taking off her T-shirt and wriggling out of her skirt. "But you never know what might happen when you leave your girlfriend alone in a bikini."

"I won't be long," I promise. "Don't let some bronze surfer steal my spot."

But by the time I find the store and get the film, it's been forty-five minutes, so I'm sweating and anxious as I try to work out which direction I should be walking. I've got one more stop before I head back to Susan, who's probably wondering what the fuck happened to me. She left her phone in the hotel room, so I can't call and tell her I got a bit lost.

I look at the directions I scribbled on a piece of paper, decide to turn right, and finally find the street I want. This is definitely not the touristy part of Honolulu. After a few more blocks, I get to the address I wrote down, open the door, and wait for my eyes to adjust.

The girl up front has that Bettie Page look, except with ear gauges and more severe bangs. I ask how long it'll be, telling her I'm in a rush.

"I've got an opening at seven," she says coldly.

"You can't squeeze me in before that? I'm supposed to be meeting my girlfriend and I'm already late."

She tells me she'll check with Nikki, walking over to a skinny girl with bleached blond hair. When she comes back she seems to have warmed up to me a bit. "You're in luck—Nikki can take you in a few minutes. I just need you to sign the consent form and pay up front."

I sign without reading it, hand her the cash, and sit down between a guy wearing a Hawaiian shirt and a woman who looks old enough to be my mum. These tattoo parlors are all the same. I got my first tattoo when it was still illegal in New York—a friend told me about an underground parlor run by two rockabilly guys in the East Village. Now it seems like tattoo parlors are everywhere you go, and even housewives are getting little flowers on their ankles.

I flip through one of the binders full of designs—lots of bluebirds, hearts, and tribal patterns—the sound of tattoo guns buzzing in the background. Once Nikki finishes with her customer, she cleans up her workstation and detours to the bathroom, which takes forever. Just as I'm starting to wonder what the hell she's doing in there—*getting high?*—she comes out and introduces herself.

"I'm sort of in a hurry," I tell her, repeating what I told the Bettie Page girl about my girlfriend waiting. "It's meant to be a surprise for her."

I pull out my drawing—a little *S* intertwined with a 7, Susan's favorite number—and show her where I want to get it tattooed, just above my right wrist. I've got Liam's name on that arm and "Mum and Dad" on the other one, written across a ribbon in the beak of a swallow.

"Well, this shouldn't take too long," Nikki says, walking me over to her chair. I watch as she copies the design onto a transfer and places it on my wrist, relieved that her hands seem steady.

"A little more to your left," I tell her.

"You don't want it centered?"

"No, I like things slightly off-kilter."

She laughs and presses the transfer onto my skin, then prepares the ink for the gun. After a few minutes of stabbing with the needle, it's done.

"How's that?" she asks, smearing the tattoo with a bit of ointment.

"Brilliant, thanks."

"Just keep it out of the sun for a couple days—and the ocean. I hope your girlfriend likes it."

"Me, too," I say, hurrying for the door.

WHEN I GET back to the beach, I spot Susan where I left her a while ago, her head bent over reading her book. She's got a blue sarong wrapped around her shoulders and a floppy hat shadowing her face so she doesn't notice me at first. I plop down next to her, worried that she might be annoyed.

"Sorry I was gone so long—I got something for you!" I tell her, holding my right arm out in front of her, the ointment glistening where it's mixed with sweat.

She doesn't say anything at first, just stares at my wrist for a few seconds, then looks up. "You got a tattoo," she says, sort of confused. "I thought you went to get film?"

"I did get film. I wanted the tattoo to be a surprise. It's an *S*— for Susan—with a seven—your favorite number."

"Oh . . . right. The thing is, I don't really have a favorite number. That's what I told you when you asked the other day, but you kept pressing so I finally said seven."

"Well, lucky seven then. Maybe it'll bring us good luck!"

Susan pushes back the brim of her hat and smiles, but she seems unconvinced.

"Listen, no one has ever gotten a tattoo for me so I'm not sure what to say. I mean, I was sort of hoping you'd get Liz's name removed from your other wrist, but I guess now we'd better stay together or your next girlfriend is going to have to settle for an elbow."

I'm not quite sure how to take this. I *think* she's trying to be funny, but it feels a bit like a jab.

"I've been meaning to look into that," I say, twisting my watch to cover up Liz's name.

"Anyway, thank you," she says, leaning over and kissing my neck. Opening the guidebook on her lap, she points to a map of Waikiki. "Do you remember that pink hotel we walked by earlier? I thought we could stop there on the way back. It's got a bar out front, right by the beach."

"Whatever you want," I tell her, kissing her on the lips this time. "Unless you fancy going back to the hotel first? Maybe chill for a bit and then go out?"

"Later," she says, trapping the hand I'm running up her leg. "I'm starving—I can't go as long as you do without food. You don't mind going to a bar, do you? It's actually more of a restaurant so I don't think it'll be a big drinking scene."

I don't really go to bars anymore—it's a bit boring, not doing the thing everyone else is doing—but I tell Susan I don't mind. We only have a couple of nights left in Hawaii so I want her to have a good time.

By the time we get there, the sun is setting and the bar is lit up with tiki lanterns. The hostess leads us to a table near two chubby guys strumming tiny ukuleles. Susan barely looks at the menu before flagging down a waitress and ordering a mai tai. I decide to try a guavatini, minus the vodka.

"Do you want to split the pupu platter?" she asks.

"What's that? We don't eat pupu in Scotland."

Susan rolls her eyes at my attempt at a joke. "It's a mix of appetizers: barbecued spareribs, fried shrimp, teriyaki chicken, and some sushi."

I don't eat shellfish, pork, or raw fish, but I tell her that's fine. I don't tell her I had a Snickers on the way back from the tattoo parlor so I'm not actually that hungry.

It doesn't take long for the waitress to come back with our drinks—garnished with a pineapple wedge, a cherry, and a little paper umbrella.

"Cheers," Susan says, raising her drink.

"Cheers," I answer, feeling silly clinking my glass of juice.

She finishes her mai tai by the time the food comes, orders another one, and polishes off most of the pupu platter with her second drink. While she goes off in search of a bathroom, I pick at the teriyaki chicken, opening and closing my pink umbrella between bites.

To be honest, it *is* a bit weird being in a bar and not getting drunk. I used to feel like this in pubs in Scotland when I was younger—like I was just biding my time while everyone else was having fun. My brother and sister would tease me 'cause they'd be knocking back pints and I'd be struggling to keep up after a couple of rounds, even pouring my drink into a potted plant once—my sister took the piss out of me for that. But I was running a lot back then, training for races, and hard drinking just didn't fit in with that routine. Plus I didn't like how out of control everyone around me got when they were drunk. It usually led to fighting and I hated that hooligan mentality.

That's why it was a shock to my family when I started drinking heavily later on. I remember visiting my sister when I was in Dublin for a shoot—she had married an Irish doctor and moved there—and one night we all got hammered, listening to records and singing along to eighties bands. My sister didn't give me a hard time, but I could tell she was surprised. She did say something the next morning about me making up for lost time.

Susan isn't much of a drinker, so I don't really mind that she's a bit tipsy tonight—until she pops up behind me, leans over my shoulder, and says, "How about a dance?"

"I don't dance," I tell her. "Especially when I'm sober."

"I don't dance, either, but no one knows us here so who cares if we look ridiculous." She grabs my hand and gives it a tug, so it's pretty clear she's not going to take no for an answer.

The only other couples on the dance floor are about twice our age—mostly Japanese tourists and sunburned Americans with gray hair. It's a bit awkward at first, like school dances when I was thirteen, but once we get into a groove it feels good to hold Susan close. I kiss her ear, then work my way over to her lips. When she kisses me back, her breath smells like rum.

Over her shoulder, I notice two girls in grass skirts swaying back and forth, passing out leis to all the dancing pensioners. I spin Susan around so she can see what's coming our way.

"I can deal with the dancing," I tell her. "I don't mind the hula music. But I really don't want to wear a ring of flowers around my neck."

"You mean you don't want to get lei'd?" she says, cracking up at her own joke.

"Very clever," I say, steering her toward our table. "But I'd rather save that for the hotel."

BACK IN OUR room the AC has been cranking, so Susan slides open the door to the balcony to let in some warm air. I follow her outside, pushing past the curtains flopping around in the breeze. Even though we're on the tenth floor it sounds like the ocean is right below our feet.

She's still wearing her bikini and a miniskirt but her T-shirt is off, the string of her suit tied across her back. As she leans against the railing, I come up behind her and kiss her neck, slipping one hand inside her top. With my other hand, I reach under her skirt.

I'm thinking I'll just get things started and we'll move inside once the room isn't so cold, but she turns around and unzips my shorts, using her toes to push them all the way down. Pulling me toward her, she lifts her skirt and nudges me over against the wall. I'm sort of surprised that she's going for it—I glance at the other balconies, wondering if anyone can see us. But pretty soon her legs are around my waist and I'm trying to hold her up and get her off without losing my balance. At this point, I don't really care who might be watching.

Afterward, we end up in a heap on the balcony, our feet poking through the railing. Susan's head is on my shoulder and her arm is draped across my chest.

"Well, I've learned one thing," I tell her, kissing the top of her head.

"What's that?"

"I'm gonna have to buy you mai tais more often."

"I'm not sure about that," Susan says. "I think I might regret that second one."

We both laugh, but sometimes I do miss it—the way alcohol

lets you loosen up a bit. It just got to the point where I couldn't stop at that nice relaxing buzz.

THE NEXT MORNING we drive up to Oahu's North Shore, stopping in the surfing town where they shot that movie *Endless Summer*. It seems like every other car has a surfboard strapped to the roof, and the ones that don't are VW buses selling some kind of crafts made of shells.

Susan wants to try shave ice—a Hawaiian snow cone—so we line up outside a place she read about online. I tend to be more impulsive when I travel, but I like how she put so much effort into planning our trip. I think it's her way of trying to make it special.

The weather is a bit shitty so we skip the beach and walk around town with our cone. The gray day reminds me of Scotland, the sort of overcast that's good for taking pictures—like a huge softbox that diffuses the light. Pulling out my camera, I ask Susan if I can take her portrait before we move on.

"Really?" she says, wiping her mouth. "My lips must be bright red from the cherry syrup."

"That's alright—they'll match the building I want in the background."

We walk back to the shave ice place and I show Susan where to stand, against a red painted wall with a white-trimmed window. I take a few photos with her staring straight at the lens, then some more with her looking down, sipping the last melted ice with a straw.

"Okay, now step out." After she moves out of the frame I take another picture, keeping the composition exactly the same.

Just before we came to Hawaii I got this idea for a project: "She Loves Me/She Loves Me Not." It's a series of diptychs: The first photo is of Susan standing somewhere—on an empty street, under a light in a parking lot, on the balcony of our hotel. The second one is the same setup, without her in the picture. I wasn't sure how she'd react to the idea, but she's been pretty good about going along with it so far. I think she likes that I'm taking pictures again, and it's not like we haven't talked about my frustrations with her uncertainty.

I need to let her catch up to me, she keeps telling me. Let her get there at her own pace. But sometimes it feels like I have no idea where I stand with her, which is basically what these pictures are about—me wondering if she's going to be in my life or not. In all the photos she's there . . . and then she's gone.

As soon as we get to the resort where we're spending the night, we change into our swimsuits and head to the pool. When Susan booked this place I pictured water slides and hordes of kids running around, but it's actually pretty quiet—maybe because it's still gray and misty. There are just a few other people on deck chairs and a couple of kids who look totally bored.

I jump in and paddle over to a waterfall tumbling into the far side of the pool. The water pummeling my head is colder than I expected—all I can hear is the roar crashing down around me. I wave to Susan to get her to come over, but she shakes her head and points to the Jacuzzi, so I hop out of the pool and ease myself in next to her.

"Fuck, that's boiling."

"Give it a minute," Susan says, already submerged up to her neck. "It's not really that hot."

It's almost dark now, so the spotlights around the pool make everything look like a film set, illuminating the palm trees and leaving us in the shadows. I reach over and grab the camera Susan left on a towel, balance it on the ledge, and set the self-timer. Sliding over next to her, I wait for the flash to go off, then I kiss her.

When I open my eyes it just pops out: "I love you," I say.

Susan turns toward me, puts her arms around my neck, and kisses me. I pull back, waiting.

"You know, I could get used to this," she says. "I wish we could stay here another week."

I don't know how to respond. Susan is asking what I want to do for dinner, rattling off options, but I can't answer. I just sink lower and lower into the Jacuzzi until her voice fades and all I can hear is the hum of the jets. *I'm not gonna get mad,* I tell myself. *I'm not gonna overreact. I'm not gonna ruin the last night of our trip.*

When we get back to the room, while Susan is in the shower, I rummage in my bag, pull out the plastic bottle I've got hidden, and take a small sip. It's just methadone—and not enough to get high—but I'm hoping it's enough to keep any withdrawal symptoms from kicking in.

I don't usually take methadone, but I couldn't exactly run around Hawaii trying to buy heroin, at least not with Susan around, and there was no way I was going to risk bringing drugs on the plane. It's not like I'm a junkie, but I've been using enough that I can't go without it for more than a day without getting dope sick, so I got the methadone to tide me over while we were away. The problem is, I didn't really know how much to take—I probably overdid it at first—and a few days ago I realized I was running low. I'm just hoping I've got enough left so I don't start going into withdrawal tomorrow. I have no idea how I'd explain that to Susan.

I hate that I'm hiding this from her—I kept promising myself I'd get clean before our trip, but I couldn't figure out how to detox without her catching on. And if I tell her now, she'll freak out and leave me and that would send me into a total tailspin. After we get back I'm thinking I can slowly taper off—tell her I've got a job out of town to explain why I can't see her for a while. But it would be a lot easier to kick if I knew she'd still be there for me when the really hard part hit—the brutal depression that feels like it'll never go away. That's the main reason dope is so fucking hard to quit.

ON OUR LAST day in Hawaii, we've got a few hours to kill before our flight so we drive back to Honolulu and stop in Chinatown for lunch. I'm not really hungry—my stomach feels tight, and now I'm getting sniffly with the odd shiver. I decided to save the last few drops of methadone until we head to the airport later, so those first signs of withdrawal are starting to creep in.

By the time we leave the restaurant I'm feeling a bit better—as long as I keep my mind occupied, it's not too bad. As we're walking through Chinatown, I reach over and hold Susan's hand.

"Shit," she says, suddenly stopping.

"What?"

"There's Ethan, across the street."

"You're joking." Before our trip she told me her ex was going to be in Hawaii around the same time as us, but I can't believe we've actually run into him.

"I'm not kidding," she says, pulling me around the corner. "Let's go—I don't think he saw us."

"You're not going to say hi?"

She looks at me like I'm mental. "Are you serious? After your fit when I told you our trips might overlap?"

Even though they were together a long time ago—and he's into men now—I did find the timing a bit suspect. For some reason I pictured him as this Rupert Everett type, the British actor all the girls wish they could turn straight. But now that I've seen him, he doesn't really seem like a threat. He's shorter than me, and looks sort of bookish.

"If you want to talk to him, it's fine with me."

"Are you sure? It feels kind of shitty to sneak away, but if it's going to upset you, it's not worth it."

"It's not going to upset me," I tell her, slightly irritated by the assumption. "Go ahead—I'll wait here, then you can wave me over if it's not too weird."

I hang back and watch her surprise Ethan, who I'm actually a bit curious to meet. Susan hasn't really talked much about their relationship, except to say he was a different person when they were living in Argentina, and that he developed a habit years after they broke up. He's been clean for a while now—all the guys he's traveling with are on some kind of AA retreat. I wonder what she's told him about me.

After a couple of minutes she turns toward me and waves. I try to look relaxed as I cross the street.

Susan introduces me to Ethan, I shake his hand, and he introduces me to the rest of his pals. We all chat about the weather and the beaches, but once they move on to talking about people they know, my mind wanders—until Ethan's sponsor comes over and starts asking me questions. I suddenly feel put on the spot, like he's trying to figure me out. He's looking at me a wee bit too intently.

I'm starting to sweat—Susan notices and hands me a crumpled napkin. I wipe my forehead and the back of my neck, wishing we could wrap up this little reunion, 'cause the stress is just making me sicker.

"I think Graham might be getting the flu," Susan says. "He was fine up until today but he woke up feeling a little queasy."

"That's a bummer," Ethan says, backing away slightly. Now he's looking at me funny, which makes me even more anxious. *What if it's obvious to him and he says something to her?*

Finally Susan says we should probably get going, rattling off all the things we need to do before our flight.

Putting my arm around her shoulder, I tell everyone, "I guarantee you we'll be at the gate long before the plane rolls up."

They all laugh and we do a round of nice-to-meet-you good-byes. On the way back to the car, Susan says, "See, that wasn't so bad."

"What do you mean? I'm the one who said you should talk to him."

"I know, I'm just saying I think it went okay. Didn't you?"

"It was alright. He's not quite what I expected."

"You thought he'd be all buff from the gym? Make you feel like you had to start working out?" Susan stops and puts her hands on my chest—she's always joking that she'll have to break up with me if I get too skinny.

"No . . . well, maybe a little," I admit. "I'm actually thinking of getting back into running. You know, really trying to get fit."

Even as I'm saying it, I know it's a long shot. The last time I ran I was trying to avoid some cops. They had stormed into the projects just as I was leaving so I took off once I was out the door. Luckily they didn't bother chasing me—I only made it a couple of blocks before I had to stop.

"Just don't get obsessive about it," she says. "I can't date a guy who gets up really early to go for long runs, especially if you decide to train for another marathon or something."

"Okay, no marathons," I tell her—one promise I know I can keep. These days it would be a stretch to manage even a mile.

AFTER OUR PLANE takes off, I press my camera against the window and take a few pictures of the ocean, with the coast of Hawaii disappearing below the wing. I started taking photos out of plane windows years ago, when I was traveling all over the world: crossing Siberia on the way to Japan, flying over Africa to London, arriving in New Zealand at dawn—all the islands looked like floating pieces of moss. I've got some great shots looking down on Manhattan, but right now the thought of landing in New York is just depressing.

The more I picture walking into my house, the more the craving kicks in—and it doesn't help that Susan seems ready to get home. She's already making a list of everything she needs to do, scribbling away next to me, but I'm going back to the same dysfunctional routine. I've got bills piling up, no work on the horizon, no agent bringing in big advertising jobs. I used to have one but we fell out, partly because my drinking got out of control, but I also needed some time off after working too much. All the stress was getting to me, and that just made me drink more: a few drinks at dinner, a nightcap at the hotel bar, then a flight with free booze for hours.

No one in my family knew how bad it had gotten until Liz made me call my sister and tell her I had a problem. *It sounds like you're describing an alcoholic,* my sister said, and I told her no, I'd just become a bit too dependent on alcohol. But I asked her not to tell anyone else. I didn't want my parents to worry, and I thought my brother would think I was a loser—getting fucked up in my mid-thirties, instead of in my twenties, when most people party. But eventually everyone found out. In 2004, some friends called my dad and brother and said they needed to straighten me out. So they flew to Geneva when I was there for an assignment, surprised me at the end of the shoot, and told me they were taking me to Scotland to get help. I was a bit pissed off, but I didn't fight it. It was sort of a relief that they finally knew.

Then when we got back to Scotland the hospital wouldn't admit me—I didn't have a doctor's referral, and I wasn't covered by the health service because I didn't live there. I ended up staying with my parents for a few days, making up excuses to get out of the house so I could buy booze in town. I couldn't quit cold turkey 'cause I was terrified of having a seizure—it had happened a few times before when I tried to stop drinking, and it was really scary.

I'm sure my parents knew what was up but they didn't know what else to do. My dad went to the pub, my mum sat in the living room watching the telly, and I holed up in the spare bedroom, staring at the rain lashing against the window. Finally, I couldn't take it anymore—I called the airline and bought a ticket leaving the next day. Once I got back to New York, I picked up right where I'd left off.

Everything sort of snowballed after I got back. Liz had moved out, my career was going off the rails, I basically had a breakdown—ending up in the hospital, trying to detox and get my head straight. A couple of months later I went to a pricey rehab in California for twenty-eight days, a total waste of money and time. The whole notion of abstinence was just too overwhelming. The first thing I did on the flight back to New York was have a drink—I figured I just needed to drink more sensibly. It wasn't until after I realized Liz wasn't coming back that I finally did quit drinking, more or less on my own.

That's sort of how I ended up with a drug habit. I'd been using cocaine to clear my head after drinking too much, and then a friend introduced me to crack—a way more intense rush, with no messy nosebleeds. Eventually I added heroin to the mix. I should've known better, but that first hit was fucking brilliant. I remember thinking, *This must be what people think heaven is like—I wish I could stay like this forever.* Once I discovered dope, I didn't really need to drink: The high lasted longer and I didn't smell like booze or slur my words. To be honest, a heroin habit is easier to hide— but not so easy to quit. I'd gotten divorced (again!), I was trying to climb out of a dark hole, and suddenly Susan showed up at my door. I was pretty up front with her about my past, but obviously there were some things I left out. I didn't want to scare her away.

And now she's sitting next to me, planning for her book re- lease, which makes me feel even worse about my stalled career. I wish I could have a drink, just to take the edge off—the flight attendant is coming down the aisle with her cart. She's passing out little bottles to a guy a couple of rows ahead of us, I can practically smell the Jack Daniel's from here. That sound of miniature bottle tops cracking open, ice rattling in plastic cups, and liquor being poured reminds me of so many boozy flights. Before she gets to our row, I put away my camera, push my seat back, and close my eyes. Better not to even look.

THE FIRST THING I do when I get home is go straight out and cop. For a second on the plane, I thought maybe I wouldn't—I had this idea that I could just white-knuckle it and deal with the withdrawal on my own. But by the time I get to Brooklyn, I'm too sick to fight the cravings, and walking into my empty house makes any thought of trying to get clean disappear. I get cash from the ATM at the deli around the corner and head over to the projects—quicker than waiting for a dealer.

Once I've gotten myself straight, I download our holiday pictures to my computer—Susan coming out of the ocean in her bikini, the two of us sitting by a canal in Honolulu, me kissing her on the beach in Kauai. We look so happy together I feel like biking up to her apartment and surprising her, but it's freezing out so she'd probably think I was mental.

Instead, I email her some of the best photos and upload the rest to an online album, sending her the link. It's after 1 A.M. when I finally get a message back—short and to the point: "*Hmm . . . this link doesn't work. Don't worry about sending any more pics tonite. I'm going to sleeeeeep. Miss you already!*"

Well, at least she misses me, but I wish she were here. It's gonna be weird sleeping alone again. After staying up most of the night—back to my bad habits—I finally crash on the couch. I don't wake up until I hear the front door bang and Liam burst in. At first I panic, wondering if I've left any drugs lying around, then I relax when I see that I didn't.

"Hi, sunshine," I say, standing up and giving him a hug. I used to hum that Stevie Wonder song to him when he was a baby: *You are the sunshine of my life. . . .* Now that he's almost six feet tall, wearing cargo pants and a hoodie—with no coat, even in February—that nickname doesn't quite fit. But I can't let go of it, and I am always happy to see him.

"Hey, Dad. How was your trip?"

"Brilliant. What's up with you? Is your mum away?"

He usually spends weekends with me and stays with her during the week, but she travels for work so sometimes things get shuffled around.

"No, she's in town. I just came by to pick up some books."

"Oh really?" I ask, ruffling his thick curly hair. "You were here *studying* while I was gone?"

"Actually, I wasn't over here at all," he says, grabbing my shoulders and grinning. "They're library books I left here. I need them for a project that's due tomorrow."

"Well, I'm glad to see you're not leaving things till the last minute."

I try to get him to open up about his classes and what else he's been doing, but he dodges my questions, asking me about Hawaii instead. So I show him some of the photos and we talk about what he wants to do for spring break—then I remember a message I got from one of his teachers.

"By the way, how come I got a call about you missing class?"

"I dunno. . . . When was it? I haven't skipped any classes—it must be a mistake."

His defensiveness reminds me of my own attitude as a teenager—at his age I was constantly getting in trouble. But Liam doesn't have that same rebellious streak so I don't want to be too hard on him, especially since we haven't spent as much time together since Susan started coming around.

"We can talk about it later," I tell him, deciding to let it drop. "Do you want to do something this weekend? We could go to the arcade in Chinatown."

"Maybe. Can Jason stay over on Saturday?"

Normally I wouldn't mind—Jason is like a brother to him, he's also an only child. But right now it feels like Liam is playing me so I'm a bit reluctant to give up some of our weekend time.

"Let me see if Susan is going to be here," I say, reaching for the phone buzzing in my pocket. "But it'd be nice if we could hang out at some point."

"We will," he says. Sensing my distraction, he kisses my cheek and disappears downstairs to his room. A few minutes later he leaves through the door under the stoop, shouting, "Bye, Dad!" as it slams. His quick exit makes me wonder if he really did come by to get books, but there's no point going to the front window to check. He was on his skateboard so he'll be halfway to his mother's house by now—or wherever he was headed so fast.

I feel like I never quite know what's going on with him, not like I did when he was collecting Pokémon cards and begging me to buy him a Game Boy. Some of that's my fault—I know my drinking was hard on him, and bouncing between two parents must be a pain in the ass. He seems to like Susan, which is a relief, but it's got to be weird when your dad is totally caught up in a new relationship just as the main thing on your mind is girls.

I've tried to let him know he can talk to me about anything—we've had conversations about peer pressure and contraception and respect, all things I never talked about with my parents. At least I know he's gotten the message about safe sex. The night Susan came by to look at the contact sheets for her book photo, Liam told me he'd left something for me under a pile of magazines, "just in case." Turns out it was a condom. He had an assignment to buy condoms for a sex ed class—to get over being embarrassed, I guess—so he passed one off to me.

He's very protective of me that way, and I'm probably too lax with him. I know he's been through a lot, so I try to make it up to him by not being one of those tough dads. I suppose it makes things easier for me as well. I give him space so he'll give me space, I don't challenge him so he doesn't challenge me. It's a pattern we fell into when I was drinking too much.

But he's fifteen now, with a life of his own, going out a lot more with his pals. I sometimes wonder if I'm cutting him too much slack—just as he's starting to push back a bit. He's mentioned my late nights, the fact that I haven't been working lately, the friends that have drifted away. And now with Susan in the picture, I've got both of them keeping tabs on me. Things are starting to get a lot more complex.

CHAPTER FOUR

March 2006
Upper West Side, Manhattan

When I looked at the photos Graham took of us in Hawaii, I thought of Duane Michals—a photographer who writes captions to go along with his pictures. In one, a couple is sitting on the edge of a bed, entwined but fully clothed. The text says: "This photograph is my proof. There was that afternoon, when things were still good between us. And she embraced me, and we were so happy. . . ."

Our pictures reminded me of that image. We were happy. Things were good. The photos proved it.

There were lots of shots of us together—holding hands on the beach in Kauai, side by side in a hot tub on the North Shore. But the ones that became my proof were the photos I took of Graham: tan, healthy, smiling in the saturated light just before sunset.

In one of my favorite pictures, he's walking ahead of me toward the surf, his arms outstretched in a perfect T, his camera slung over his shoulder. It's a moment of pure bliss, like he wanted to gather up every ray of sunlight, every drop of salty mist, embrace the whole horizon and pull it close.

It had rained and water had collected in a dip in the beach behind him, so I was trying to capture his reflection when I took the photo. But I only caught part of it—an arm, his head, and his torso. Later, I noticed that it looked like the wet sand was wiping away the rest of the reflection, as if already erasing the moment.

———

AS SOON AS we got back to New York, I had to put our relationship on the back burner and turn my attention to work. The trip
had been great, just what I needed—well, except for our last day
in Honolulu. I thought Graham had gotten some kind of stomach
bug, but that didn't really explain his anxious mood. I assumed he
was also in a funk about our vacation ending; I was, too. The difference was, I brushed it off and moved on.

My book was due out in just over a month, so I didn't have
much time to think about anything else. I was busy sending out
emails, building a website, and trying to drum up publicity, contacting every writer and editor I knew. Since I was a freelancer, ten
days off had put a dent in my income, so I was also hustling for
work.

Graham understood why I was holed up in my home office; I
was actually surprised by how supportive he was of my book. It
was a travel planning guide, not an exposé about some injustice in
the world, but he threw himself into the promotional frenzy as if
I'd written a future bestseller: designing posters he planned to
paste up all over the city, printing copies of the cover on T-shirts,
and sending me links to potential reviewers. I was almost embarrassed by all the effort.

To me, his photography seemed like more of an art form in the
hierarchy of creative pursuits, at least compared to the type of
journalism I'd done—mostly, advice about technology and travel.
But he viewed writing as the tougher endeavor, expressing the difference in a way I'd remember whenever I couldn't string together
a coherent sequence of words.

"I've got the whole world to make a picture," he told me. "You
only have twenty-six letters."

The fact that he wasn't taking many pictures seemed to weigh
on him, so I was trying to encourage him to kick-start his own
career. But he resisted the return to reality, hoping to follow up our
Hawaiian holiday with another escape. Four days after we got

back, he started asking about planning a trip to Nevada, then suggested we visit a friend of his in Japan.

Trying to recapture our tropical romance, he rode his bike up to my apartment one wintry night, presenting me with two coconuts and a box of cocktail umbrellas. It turns out street vendors aren't just showing off for tourists when they thwack at a coconut with a machete; we tried every knife in my kitchen before Graham finally resorted to drilling a hole in one end. I liked that he was handy—unlike most New York men—but power tools didn't quite spark the mood he envisioned, so I made hot chocolate and we poked our umbrellas into marshmallows instead.

That night, huddled under my down comforter, we made love with most of our clothes on—"socks-on sex," Graham called it. Once I rolled onto my side, he folded his body into the same shape as mine. He always liked falling asleep with me in his arms.

"You know, it's probably raining in Hawaii," I said, watching the snow gathering on the windowsill.

"And the roosters would be waking us up soon," Graham mumbled, already fading.

"And I'd be really sunburned," I pointed out.

"I still wish we never left," he said, adding, "I love you," before drifting off to sleep.

"I think you're pretty great, too," I whispered, squeezing his arm where it crossed over my heart.

But from the way Graham's breathing had settled into a pattern, I could tell he hadn't heard me—lately, he'd been nodding off long before me.

I KNEW IT was becoming a problem that I hadn't told Graham I loved him. Every time he said it, I felt his hopeful anticipation and then the crushing letdown when I couldn't give him the same caught-up-in-the-moment response. I thought going along with his "She loves me/She loves me not" series would diffuse some of that tension—not to mention give him a new project to work on. But after a while, it just seemed to shine a spotlight on the question I hadn't answered.

I told myself it was a timing issue: Graham was more impulsive than me, so it made sense that he'd blurted it out after two weeks. But deep down I knew that wasn't the only reason I was proceeding with caution, so I decided I should tell him why I was holding back. Being a writer, I thought I could explain myself more clearly in an email, so late one night I sat down at my computer and tried.

It took a few paragraphs to wind up to the topic I'd been avoiding, finally addressing it head-on.

> *I'm sorry in advance if this upsets you or makes you feel like you can't get beyond your past, but it's taking me time to trust that you don't currently have a problem with drugs or alcohol—and to figure out whether I can live with the uncertainty that I'll never be sure it won't be a problem again. I know you've been very open with me about your past, and I'm glad you have, but it's still a very unsettling issue to deal with when you're entering into a relationship. That's the main reason I've been trying to slow things down. . . .*

It was probably a mistake to put all that in an email, but I was having a hard time bringing it up in person, or on the phone. It was still that era when people wrote emails as if they were rediscovering the lost art of writing letters, so when I mustered up the courage to share my insecurities, email seemed like a safer way to open the door.

The thing is, I didn't really think Graham was using at that point. I trusted that he wouldn't hide it from me, or that I'd be able to tell. Even though my experience with drugs was limited—

I'd smoked pot, but I'd never tried anything else floating around at parties—I wasn't completely naïve about their effects. And Graham's mood swings sometimes made me wonder what exactly was influencing his highs and lows.

The next morning, he woke me up with a call.

"I got your email," he said, immediately launching into a defense. "And I understand what you're getting at and why you might have some doubts about me, but I don't want my past to dictate what you feel about us being together. I've been really open and honest with you about everything—trust me, the last thing I want is to go down that path again. It was too traumatic and too painful and I can't believe you think I'd hide—"

"I didn't say I thought you were hiding anything from me," I interrupted, still groggy from my sleepless night. "I said it's hard for me to deal with the fact that you might start drinking or using again."

"You said *currently* have a problem."

I rolled over, looking at my alarm clock: 7:23 A.M. Graham must've waited as long as he could before picking up the phone.

"Well, sometimes when I come over there are empty beer bottles on the table. It makes me wonder what you're up to when I'm not around."

"Just because I have people over who have a beer occasionally doesn't mean I'm drinking," Graham said, his voice getting louder, and more emphatic. "You can't really expect me to ditch all of my pals who drink. You drink at my house or when we're out."

That was true. After working hard all week I was usually ready for a drink by the time I got to Graham's place on Friday night. He always said it didn't bother him, but maybe I was being too cavalier.

"If you don't want me to drink when I'm with you I won't," I said, hoping he wouldn't actually take me up on that offer. "But that's not really the issue."

"Then what is the issue? I hate that word. That's such an American thing, having all these *issues*."

I hesitated, trying to figure out how to cross this minefield without Graham exploding.

"I'm sorry, I shouldn't have said 'currently.' The point I was trying to make is that one of the reasons I've wanted to take things slower is that I do sometimes worry about what's going to happen five or ten years from now. People fall off the wagon, they relapse after being clean for decades. You can't pretend it's not a possibility."

I could hear Graham suck in a breath before speaking, delivering his monologue without a pause.

"Listen, Susan—If you're already worrying about what could happen five years from now, there's an endless number of things you can add to the list. I could get knocked off my bike and end up in a coma, some lunatic could push you in front of a train. I just want to love you and for you to love me back. I know we can be happy together but you've got to want it, too. You can't keep dwelling on all the negative things that might happen. Why don't you focus on what's good in your life? What's good about us."

And that's how Graham threw me off the trail: It wasn't his problem we were talking about, it was mine.

By the time we hung up, we had moved on to discussing all the stress in my life—the book, my worries about money, the constant pressure to convince editors to give me work. Graham was reassuring; I cried. I felt bad about putting him on the spot.

Frankly, he was right that I worried too much about worst-case scenarios. "Smile, it might never happen," he'd say, whenever he caught me lost in some gloomy thought. I liked that he made me see things I wanted to change—it meant that he really knew me, and wasn't afraid to speak up. But I did worry about Graham's sobriety over the long haul.

It felt like getting involved with someone whose cancer was in remission: There was always a chance that the tumor could come back with a vengeance. But then again, didn't cancer survivors (or recovering addicts) deserve to be loved?

Ironically, neither of us remembers exactly when I first said, "I love you," or what prompted me to finally utter those words. But it must've happened just after our talk, because a few days later Graham sent me an email saying he wanted to take some more "SLM/SLMN" pictures—our shorthand for his "She loves me . . ." project—ending his message by saying, *"Now it can be SLM . . . SLMLoads."*

And I did love Graham. Maybe I expressed it in a more understated way than he did, but that didn't make my feelings any less real. In fact, I sometimes thought that what I felt was more authentic, because I'd waited until I really meant it. Our gestures of love were just different.

He emailed me pictures of graffiti hearts he found painted on the sides of buildings; I cooked dinner for him, packing up leftovers he could reheat when I wasn't there. He cut up the listings in the arts section of *The New York Times,* presenting me with tiny clippings of things to do when he brought me coffee in bed. But I was the one who followed through and bought tickets—he had ideas, I made plans.

It's not so much that we were opposites who attracted; it's more that each of us was missing something in our lives, and along came someone with the pieces that fit. I wouldn't have filled out an online dating profile and come up with anyone like Graham, and I'm sure he wouldn't have been matched with me. That's partly why I had never embraced those sites. In my mind, falling in love wasn't about meeting someone with all the characteristics you thought you wanted. It was about finding someone you didn't realize you needed—or at least, that's what Graham was for me.

By his birthday in March, we were back on the top of a roller coaster I was learning how to ride. The weekend before he turned forty-three, I went up to the Catskills to visit some friends for a couple of days; Graham stayed home so he could hang out with Liam. I was feeling a little guilty about encroaching on their father-son time, so I thought it might be good to spend the weekend apart. But after I got back on Sunday night, I took the train down to Brooklyn so Graham wouldn't wake up on his birthday alone.

He preempted my presents by giving me a note he'd written, on the kind of lined ledger paper children use when they're learning how to write. The way the penciled words spilled across the page, it's like Graham didn't even notice the lines. I tried not to notice his spelling mistakes.

Well it's my birthday but I want to say that the fact we've made it through 2½ months of ups and downs not having known each other apart from a few days at Montauk is really amazing. I'm very proud of you for even considering taking me on—I feel sort of privilaged that you had time for me even if it was a welcome distraction you were looking for + not some guy talking about his sorry old "this is my life so far." Today I hope is the first of many birthdays—mine and yours—that we will spend together. The best present I could get—for every birthday from now onward—is to be able to look in your eyes and without words know that you love me as much as ever + knowing that I do too. (Love you that is). You're a surprising but beautiful woman, complex but disernable, committed but wary, loving yet strong, smart but not conceited. Honest + understanding + many more attributes that make you that very special you. Somehow in this visual, emotional, geographical cocophoney of everything we bumped into each other. All I can say is brilliant! I love you. Gx

The card I gave Graham wasn't nearly as gushy, but I put a lot of effort into the presents I picked out for him: a vintage shirt I discovered at a thrift store, a photography book he'd mentioned he wanted, and a kitchen stool I found on the street. Graham loved searching for treasures on trash night—I didn't—but the wobbly stool didn't quite meet his standards. Since he'd given me a lingerie *catalog* on my birthday and told me to order whatever I wanted, I figured we both had a learning curve to master.

I did try to mimic his (usually) romantic gestures by starting a list I planned to add to in the coming months. *"Here's the first entry on my list of Things I Like About Graham,"* I wrote in the card I gave him, picturing many birthdays and holidays we'd share.

#1) That I can't imagine ever getting bored with you.

I signed it, *"Love, S."*

FOR A WHILE, things were good between us—the way life feels on the days you later realize you took for granted. We went to galleries and movies, showed each other our favorite places in the city, spent a rainy weekend just lounging in bed. We even talked about our future together, which I was beginning to let myself imagine.

When the bathtub backed up and I insisted we call a plumber—help Graham resisted, sure he could fix it himself—the plumber commented on all the pictures on the walls and asked if we were both photographers.

"I'm a writer, he's a photographer," I said, suddenly seeing our life from the outside looking in. As the plumber talked about wishing he could've been a photographer, I felt like one of those couples other people envy. Free to pursue our creative careers, unburdened by bosses or young kids. Our relationship had its challenges, but I never felt restless or trapped.

A few days later, Graham asked me to move in with him, offering to take back part of the upstairs apartment he leased to renters. He'd been suggesting that since January—a running joke at first, but this time it was a more formal plan.

"The front room can be your office," he said, showing me a drawing he'd sketched on a scrap of paper. "We'll connect it to the living room with one of those circular stairs."

"Too noisy," I pointed out. "I couldn't write listening to you banging around down here."

"So we'll put up a wall—with a door."

"What about a bathroom?" I asked, half in jest. "I'd have to go down two floors every time I needed to pee."

"We could add a bathroom," Graham said, undeterred by the logistical challenge—or the expense.

I secretly coveted that room, which overlooked the tree-lined street, with its stoops and wrought-iron fences. All the windows in my apartment faced brick walls, barely letting in any light. Still, I wasn't ready to take that step.

"You couldn't afford all that," I said, trying to deflect Graham's proposal with humor. "The renovations I'd demand would be *very* expensive."

The truth was, I could barely pay the mortgage on my apartment, carefully tracking every penny I spent. But we'd been dating for just a few months, and moving in together was a big commitment—one I wasn't prepared to make.

"Sometimes I don't know why you're with me," he said, crumpling up his drawing and tossing it across the table.

I grabbed his arm as he started to walk away. "Please don't be like that. I can't just sell my apartment, move in with you, and then be out on the street if we break up."

"See, that's the problem with you—you assume we're not going to stay together."

"Well, you've been divorced *twice* already," I snapped. "Maybe the problem is you rush into relationships that don't work out."

I knew it was a bitchy thing to say, but I couldn't help myself. One of my hesitations about Graham was that if we ever got married, I'd be his *third* wife. That didn't feel like "third time's a charm" to me—it felt more like third place.

"Forget I brought it up," Graham said, yanking his arm free and stomping downstairs.

I was happy to do that, but I knew he'd stew about it for days.

I CAN'T PINPOINT exactly when things began to unravel, but obviously the loose threads were there all along. I just didn't tug at them hard enough—or maybe I tugged at the wrong ones.

There were always sources of friction between us: Graham was disorganized, emotional, and quick-tempered. I was uptight, reserved, and withdrew from conflict. But our differences also complemented each other in positive ways. His optimism lifted my darker moods; my encouragement tempered his bouts of insecurity. I sometimes had trouble picturing us staying together over the long haul, but I couldn't imagine leaving him. Still, it became harder to ignore the signs that something else was creating tension between us.

When I wasn't around, Graham hung out with friends from the housing projects around the corner—people he had photographed and wanted to help out if they needed a favor, he told me. The doorbell would sometimes ring late at night and he'd send whoever it was away, complaining about pals with erratic schedules. He talked about other friends—designers, photographers, musicians—but I never met them.

I worried that the company he was keeping was holding him

back, one foot stuck in his former dysfunctional life. But I didn't want to seem judgmental or controlling, so I didn't suggest he cut those ties. Graham never hid the fact that some of his friends were addicts, or that he'd used drugs during the years when he was drinking. He said he didn't want to turn his back on anyone still struggling to get sober or clean.

"I don't believe in that tough love bullshit," he told me. "That's how people end up dead."

Loyalty was a characteristic we shared, so I accepted that, reluctantly—until fragments of that other life burst into mine.

One Sunday afternoon in late March, I found a syringe in an eyeglass case in Graham's bathroom, just another object I absent-mindedly picked up, expecting to find a pair of vintage frames. But this time, what I discovered drained all the feeling from my limbs. I was numb as I walked up the stairs.

"It's not mine," Graham kept saying, collapsing into heaving sobs when I confronted him. "I don't know where that came from—it could've been anybody who's been over. I don't monitor what people do when they go to the bathroom."

It was the first time I'd seen him cry like that, and as I stood there with the eyeglass case splayed open in my hand, I wavered between instincts I didn't trust in myself. Graham didn't fit the image of a junkie—there were no track marks on the arms I'd kissed. When I sent my mom some of our Hawaii pictures, she wrote back saying he looked "wholesome." Yet there I was holding a needle pointing toward my heart.

"Why should I believe you?" I said, my mouth so dry my tongue kept sticking.

Graham pulled up the left sleeve of his shirt, showed me the inside of his arm. "Because I'm *not using*!" he insisted, practically shouting the last two words.

I was standing as he lay crumpled on the floor, his shoulders shaking as I weighed my decision. *This is what I'd worried about all along.*

But Graham was so adamant—"I need you to believe me, I'm not a junkie," he kept repeating, as I ran through various scenarios in my mind. I'd met some of his friends from the projects—they didn't exactly hide their habits. One of them could've shot up in the bathroom, then left the needle behind. *Besides, if Graham were using heroin, wouldn't I have seen the signs?*

He was slim, but he wasn't gaunt. He was a bit scatterbrained, but his life wasn't unmanageable. We were hardly ever apart for ten days in Hawaii so he couldn't possibly have been getting high. *What if I accused him of lying and I was wrong?*

"You can't let this stuff happen here," I finally said. "You can't put me in this position. And what about Liam—what if he had found it?"

"I know," Graham said, his whole body sagging with relief. "I'm really, really sorry. It won't happen again. I'll tell my pals they can't be bringing that shit into my house."

Then I curled up next to him as he apologized and made promises, the two of us facing each other the way we sometimes slept. Whenever we woke up that way, I thought of lost hikers discovered after a freak snowstorm, their bodies entwined in an embrace of survival as much as passion.

EVEN AS I accepted Graham's explanation for the needle, went to bed with him, and spent the night in his arms, I didn't totally believe that he wasn't hiding something. I just didn't have enough evidence to be sure. It was like that legal standard: I felt like I needed to find him guilty *beyond a reasonable doubt,* and his story seemed plausible to me. Or at least plausible enough to make me doubt whether my suspicions were right.

That made me reluctant to tell anyone else about what I'd found—especially since I'd kept our relationship pretty separate from the rest of my life. At first, I wanted to make up my own mind about Graham before my family or friends weighed in, thinking some people wouldn't approve of my choice.

So I put off telling my parents I was seeing someone until we booked the trip to Hawaii, figuring I should let them know I was going to be gone. My mom was upset that I hadn't filled her in sooner, sending me an email after we talked: *"Couldn't you have just dropped a hint somewhere along the way? Like, I went out with a photographer last night! It just threw me. But I am very happy for you. . . . Remember, all I want is for you to be happy."*

My dad was more blunt about his concerns. "I am a little stressed about the two marriages," he admitted. My parents are Catholic—they go to church every week—so I figured those broken vows might raise a red flag. But I left out the details about Graham's drinking and drug use, emphasizing his savvy purchase of a Brooklyn brownstone instead. Since my mom and dad were both real estate agents, I was hoping Graham's impressive home equity might outweigh his double divorce.

I was mostly worried about my sister's reaction, since she'd met Graham in Montauk and I wasn't sure what kind of impression he'd made. She had moved to Los Angeles before Graham and I started dating, but when she came back to New York for a visit the three of us went out for dinner on the Upper West Side. She thought Graham seemed totally different than he'd been at the beach house—charming and funny, now that he was sober. I remember the two of them bonding over my idiosyncrasies, the way people do when they're trying to find common ground about someone they both know well. Mostly, I was just glad that everyone got along.

I wasn't going to jeopardize that tenuous connection by calling my sister a few weeks later and saying, "Guess what? I found a syringe in Graham's bathroom. He said it's not his but I'm not one hundred percent sure."

Still, I couldn't keep that discovery entirely a secret. It was like a bad dream I had to share with someone, just to get it out of my head.

I ended up confiding in my friend Sara, who had encouraged me to take a chance on Graham right from the start. "I think you really like this guy," she had said, a few weeks after Graham took my picture, when we were out at a bar gossiping over glasses of wine.

The one time she'd met Graham, she didn't notice anything odd about his behavior. *"He's cute, smart, and most of all totally ga ga over you!"* she'd emailed me the next day. So when I told her about finding the needle, I was relieved that she didn't jump to conclusions or pick a side. After we talked, she emailed me links to a few Web pages describing signs of drug use, which was what I needed at that point: a friend who looked out for me, but could still keep an open mind.

I'd already done my own googling—which was only more confusing—so I also called Ethan, thinking he was more informed about drugs. We had broken up and were living on separate coasts by the time he developed a habit, so I didn't know he was using until he told me he'd quit, mostly by embracing AA.

Ethan was not one of those people in recovery who assume they have all the answers about someone else's situation, but he did caution me not to be too gullible or naïve about Graham.

"You can't be guilted into feeling bad about being suspicious," he said, after I described finding the needle. "These are all very reasonable questions."

When I asked if he'd noticed anything unusual about Graham in Hawaii, Ethan didn't take the bait, pointing out that they'd barely spoken. The closest he came to expressing an opinion about what I should do was telling me, "Trust your instincts."

The problem was, my instincts were conflicted—I didn't know what to believe. And Graham kept trying to persuade me to believe him. Since he was always sensitive to even the tiniest shift in my mood, he knew I hadn't put my doubts to rest. So a few days after I found the needle, he sent me a long email, ending with words he hoped would do just that.

I've been way too cavalier about who I've had around and
what's been in my house . . . but I'm not a liar.
If I were using
I wouldn't give you my keys
I wouldn't ask you to move in
I wouldn't tell you all I did
If I was . . .
But I wasn't.
I love you,
Graham

That was the most definitive denial I'd gotten; it was almost like a poem the way he'd broken up the lines.

The thing is, *I wanted to believe him.* I wanted all the things he said to be true. Because if Graham was lying to me about using, that meant he was capable of lying about everything—like telling me I was the "love of his life." In my mind, you couldn't love someone that much and lie about something so big.

Graham's email arrived just as I was getting ready to go meet him in Brooklyn, so I called him to let him know I was walking to the train.

"Do you want anything from Manhattan?" I asked.

"Just you," he said.

A warm, tingly feeling seeped through me, like a puff of air turning the embers of a fire from gray to red. I didn't want to give that up—the way Graham lit up my senses. Not if I didn't have to yet.

OVER THE NEXT few weeks, I registered certain things I didn't quite put together—like a child recognizing the letters of a word without knowing what it means.

Graham started sleeping erratically, staying up half the night one night, then nodding off after dinner the next. He disappeared into the basement for long periods of time; woke up early and went on mysterious errands. His healthy glow from Hawaii gave way to pasty skin and pelvic bones I could feel when we had sex. He was increasingly moody and on edge.

As this other personality emerged, I never knew which side of him to expect, and that made me even more tense.

My book was about to be published and I was planning a party at Graham's house to celebrate, on a Friday night in early April. It was the first time he was meeting my parents, and many of my friends, so I wanted him to make a good impression. That didn't happen.

When I arrived at his house a few hours before the party, hoping to find the floors swept, the bathroom clean, and Graham showered and sharply dressed, everything was a mess. He looked like he'd just woken up, foggy and disheveled, and he couldn't look me in the eye—a guilty reflex that was becoming a habit.

I blew up at him, throwing an empty jar across the room— a rare outburst fueled by disappointment and pent-up anger. He cowered like I was a parent about to hit him, but he didn't say anything in his defense. In some sense, it didn't matter. I knew the answers to all the questions I hadn't been asking.

We worked in a parallel frenzy to clean the house and get everything ready, barely speaking, then spent the evening in a stony standoff, not even bothering to pretend things were okay in front of our guests. After everyone left, I took a half-empty bottle of wine out to the backyard and finished it by myself, sitting in the dark on a broken chair. When I came inside, I found him asleep on the couch with a crack pipe in his fist.

It was a shock but not a surprise—like getting a cancer diagnosis after a battery of tests. As I slid the warm glass pipe from his hand, he opened his eyes just long enough to register that I was standing there, then closed them again. There was no discussion and no apology that night; I tossed and turned alone in Graham's bed.

I think he did that deliberately, that letting me find him was easier than confessing. But I knew even before he admitted it that he must've had a dual habit: heroin and crack.

We were at his house a couple of days later, sitting on the floor, holding hands. Even though I had begged him to be honest with me, I wasn't prepared for what would happen next. He knew it would change everything. I didn't.

But once the words were spoken—entering my consciousness to take up residence in the pit of my stomach, a twitch in my eye, nightmares about crack houses and needles and death—everything solid and knowable in my life gave way to the vortex of his addiction.

CHAPTER FIVE

April 2006
Boerum Hill, Brooklyn

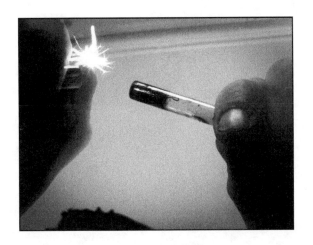

I'm in a daze on the couch—I must've slept here all night. I hear Susan moving around downstairs but I don't want to face her. I'm dreading what she's going to say after finding me with the pipe.

What a fucking disaster. I'm trying hard to remember what happened, but the details come back in bursts of clarity clouded by haziness and denial. After we fought, I figured she knew what was up so I spent most of the party avoiding her, barely talking to her family or any of her pals.

I feel like sneaking out—I'm desperate for a hit—but it's too late for that. I can already hear her footsteps slowly coming up the stairs.

I'm staring at the TV, my reflection distorted in the blank screen, when she stops between me and the door.

"You're not even going to look at me?" she says. Out of the corner of my eye, I can see her bag next to her on the floor.

When I glance up, she doesn't seem pissed off—just disappointed and worried and tired. It hurts so much to see her in pain I have to look away. *I should've split as soon as I woke up.*

"I'm sorry," I say. "I didn't mean to ruin your party."

"It's not about the party, Graham."

"Well, I'm sorry about everything."

I can hear kids' voices outside the window, a scooter bumping over the cracks in the sidewalk—all the neighbors going about their normal day.

"Is that all you're going to say?" she asks.

"What else do you want me to say?"

"I want you to tell me what's been going on. . . . Can you please just be honest?"

At first I don't answer. A flush of shame fills me with a prickly heat. I feel like if I say anything, I'll lose it somehow.

"I can't do this right now," I finally mumble.

"Really? Now isn't a good time for you? How about a few weeks ago when I found the needle in your bathroom, or last month when I told you I was worried about you relapsing, or any of the dozens of times I asked if something was wrong—I guess those were all bad times, too?"

When I don't answer, she asks, "Don't you think I deserve to know?"

I look up at her again, say, "I think it's pretty fucking obvious at this point." I don't mean to snap at her, but the comedown from the crack is making me aggressive. I feel like she's got me backed into a corner.

"Well, it's not clear to me. When did this start? Is this a relapse or have you been using the whole time we've been together? Crack and what else? I'm assuming that needle really was yours."

That sets me off. "What difference does it make? Why do you need the details—when, what, where, why? 'Cause I really don't feel like being interrogated about all my failings. I love you, and I am so fucking sorry, but I just . . ."

I can't finish that thought. I'm not ready to admit all the things she wants me to tell her. I feel physically and emotionally gutted.

"Then I'm leaving," she says, putting on her coat. "My parents are waiting for me at my apartment."

I don't want her to go, but the craving is gnawing away at me—I wish she'd just get it over with so I could go cop.

"Well, we're not done here," she says. "I need to know what the fuck has been going on, but I probably won't be able to talk until my parents leave on Monday."

"Alright" is all I can manage. I don't get up and she doesn't come over to kiss me. When the door slams, part of me is relieved that she's gone.

I dig through my pockets for the pipe but I can't remember if Susan took it or I hid it. I stick my hand down between the cushions, then stand up and pull all the pillows and cushions off the couch. *Fuck.* I'll have to buy another one at the deli—$2.50 for a lighter, a screen, and a pipe, slipped across the counter in a brown paper bag.

I find my phone, scroll through my contacts, start making calls. "I'll be there in five," I say, once I connect. Then I hang up and head out the door.

WHEN I GET back I call Liam—he slept at a friend's house after leaving the party. He sounds distracted but says he'll be home later and asks if I'm having dinner with Susan and her family tonight.

"I don't know," I say, a rush of guilt sweeping through me. "She went back uptown to meet her parents so I'm not sure what's going on. But if you want to have some pals round that's fine."

After hanging up, I smoke some more crack, then send Susan a flurry of text messages. I just need to reach out to her—I'm not thinking too much about what I type. My emotions are all over the place, my mind is racing. I've got that crack-induced confidence that I can fix things.

If I just let her know how bad I feel, how much I love her, that I don't want her to leave me, then maybe we can get over this and move on. *Didn't she say something about us not being done?*

I try to cling to that feeling, even as the comedown kicks in, about ten minutes after the high. That's what makes you keep smoking—it's like when you've got a cake and you keep cutting off little bits, after telling yourself you're only gonna eat one slice.

Heroin is different—once the initial rush passes, you can function for hours without needing it again. So you shoot up to fight the comedown from crack, and smoke crack to wake up when you're nodding. It's a constant juggling act, mixing uppers and downers, but the world seems perfect when you get it just right.

LATER THAT AFTERNOON I get an email from Susan. She's going to dinner and a movie with her parents, then they want to go to church in the morning so she doesn't know when she'll be able to talk.

"*Not quite sure how to interpret some of the messages you sent,*" she says. "*Please don't go off the deep end!*"

I don't know how to take that. I'm surprised she still gives a fuck about me, but I'm worried about what she's telling her family. Picturing her talking to them makes me angry—I don't want everyone to know. I feel like calling and telling her not to say anything, but I'm sure that wouldn't go over too well.

In a way, it's sort of a relief that her parents are still here. It gives me some space to try and work out what to do next. Not that my options are looking good.

I was really hoping I could nip this in the bud before Susan caught on. But after she found that needle, started asking questions and getting suspicious, I knew I was running out of time. Even though she's a bit naïve about drugs, she's not stupid—sooner or later she was gonna figure things out. I'd tell her I was late because the subway got delayed, or that I was going out early to get coffee and muffins, but I could tell she didn't always believe me. She'd say, "Let's just make breakfast here"—like she was testing me, to see if I'd find another reason to leave the house.

It's not that I don't want to quit—I just don't know how the fuck to go about it. It's like trying to organize some major event without anyone knowing. It can take a week to detox—which I can do on my own, I've done it before. But it's painful and messy, so I wouldn't want Liam or Susan to see me like that. Then I'd still need some kind of rehab, so how am I supposed to explain disappearing for a month? Plus I don't have insurance—and even if I did, rehab probably wouldn't be covered. I don't want to pay a fortune for some half-assed program that didn't work for me the first time around.

They're all excuses, I know, but it's not as easy as people think. There's *wanting* to quit, then there's actually making it happen. And not just for twenty-eight days—for the rest of my life.

As the reality of the situation sinks in, I have no idea what to do. I pace around the house, racking my brain for some way to get Susan back. But I can't concentrate, my mind is spinning. I can't even figure out how I'm gonna get through the next few hours.

It's a relief when Liam rolls in with a couple of pals. They pile into the living room pulling videogames out of their backpacks, bragging about who's got the highest scores and arguing about which game to play. For some reason all the noise calms me down—explosions and gunfire mixed with whoops and groans.

Across the room I sit down at my computer and type *"rehab detox new york"* into Google. I open a few links, skimming the descriptions of all the programs that pop up: *"7-day guaranteed drug detox . . . All you have to do is want to stop—we'll teach you how. . . . In-patient rehab—comfortable, effective, cheap . . . 88% success rate at six months."* I feel like I'm shopping for a car or picking a retirement plan—everyone is selling the perfect recovery package. But if it were that easy, it would've worked for me when I did it before.

I'm scribbling names and phone numbers on a piece of paper when Liam comes up behind me—I quickly pull up some photos on the screen.

"Hey, Dad. Can we order something to eat?"

"How about pizza?" I say, scanning his face, trying to figure out what he saw. "If you're hungry now, I think there's some cheese and crackers left from the party."

"Cool," he says, grabbing the phone. "Have you got any cash or do you want me to put it on your card?"

I pull some crumpled bills from my pocket and give him more than enough. Once he heads back to the couch with a menu, I re-open the Web page I was looking at—hopeful promises about recovery, testimonials from past residents, and photos of happy, healthy-looking people on a beach. It's all bullshit. The rehab I went to was totally depressing, with fluorescent lights, ugly couches, and a bunch of addicts smoking like fiends.

As I read through the program rules listed on one site—*no phones, no TV, no reading material except the Bible*—my enthusiasm for recovery starts to wane. I open up Craigslist instead, wondering if there's anything I can offload to help pay for this, maybe a camera or a few of my photography books. I've got a first edition of *The Americans,* signed by Robert Frank, but I don't think I could part with that. Or I could sell some of my prints—the Weegee should be worth a few grand.

After Liam's friends leave and he goes to bed, I pick up the pizza boxes and pile them on the counter, taking a few bites from the only slice left. My mouth is so dry I can hardly chew.

The silence of the house and the loneliness bring the craving back with a vengeance. I still have a couple of little rocks in the basement, and whatever residue is left in the pipe. I'm not going to get rid of it, so I might as well smoke it—then there won't be anything left to tempt me tomorrow.

The thought of the hit is so intense I can practically feel it before I'm halfway down the stairs. *This is it,* I promise myself. *After tonight, I'm done.*

———

ON SUNDAY MORNING, the dope sickness is slowly seeping in, those first little shivers making my skin crawl. I have to fight hard not to run out and cop. "Call someone in recovery," my rehab counselor used to say. "Reach out."

I'm not sure how talking to someone can take away this craving, but I try my friend Andy—he's been clean for a while now. He doesn't pick up so I send him a text: *"Call me. Need to talk."*

A few minutes later my phone buzzes. It's a message from a dealer asking, *"You good?"* I hesitate before shoving it back in my pocket. I wish I could turn it off but I'm still hoping Susan or Andy might call.

I'm looking out the window, watching my neighbors work on their garden, trying to block everything else out, when I hear Liam stumble up the stairs. I'd almost forgotten he was still here.

"You look like you're half-asleep," I tell him.

"Maybe because you woke me up in the middle of the night banging around."

"Sorry, I couldn't sleep so I thought I'd do some scanning."

He opens the fridge but it's practically empty—everything got eaten at the party.

"There's not much in the way of food," I say, feeling bad I didn't at least buy cereal and milk for him. "Do you want to go out for breakfast?"

"No, I've got too much homework. All my school stuff is at Mom's so I'm going to head back over there."

"You don't want to go to the diner first?" I'm not really hungry, but I'm desperate to get out of the house.

"I'll get something at Mom's," Liam says, filling a glass with water and gulping it down. "Aren't you hanging out with Susan today?"

I clear my throat and take a sip of cold tea from a mug sitting on the counter. "Maybe later. Her parents wanted to go to church this morning, but you know that's not really my thing."

"Is everything okay with you guys?"

"Yeah," I say, wondering if he noticed the tension at the party. "Susan wanted to spend time with her family while they're here. She doesn't see them that often so I thought I'd give them some space."

He looks like he's not totally buying that, so I'm relieved when he doesn't press me. I don't want to lie to him, but the thought of telling him the truth is too much for me to handle right now. When Liz left me, she never said a word to Liam—after being in his life for years. Susan hasn't been around that long, but I know he likes her so he'll be disappointed if she just disappears, too.

Besides, he's got schoolwork to focus on, and final exams coming up. The last thing I want is for him to be worrying about me.

AFTER LIAM LEAVES, I go down to the basement and rummage around until I find some AA leaflets I picked up after my stint in rehab. I don't know why I hung on to them—I didn't go to meetings that often—but I circle one that's starting soon at a church not far away.

I'm a bit shaky on my feet so I decide to walk instead of riding my bike. By the time I get there, I'm fifteen minutes late. I don't really want to go in—I can't face all those sober eyes looking at me, judging me—so I walk to the other side of the street and lean against a wall. I'm thinking I'll wait until they take a break, then I'll slip in with everybody else.

For a while I just stand there, staring at the blue and white AA pendant hanging on the door. I'm picturing them all sitting there doing their shares—someone is probably saying, "I know God has a path for me," which always makes me want to ask, "Really? His path was to fuck up your life for twenty years before deciding it was time for you to get clean?" Then there's usually some annoying guy boasting about his drinking days—like if he thought he could get away with it, he'd still be doing it, but he can't and it's obvious he totally resents that.

The more I think about it, the less I want to go in and listen to all that bullshit—the self-righteous speeches and mindless slogans, as if AA is the only way anyone can quit. I wait around until a few people come out of the church for a smoke. Now is my chance to duck in and take a seat. But I don't. When they go back inside, I just walk away.

Back at home I don't know what to do with myself. I play some records, surf the Web, watch TV. But I'm craving crack so badly and I'm so stressed about Susan I can't focus on anything else. I'm sure she's going to break up with me—why wouldn't she? I've lied and hidden so much, I can't think of anything that would convince her to stick around. Even if I said it was just a relapse, there's no way she'd ever believe me.

I grab my jacket and walk to the deli around the corner, buy a pint of ice cream and a pile of candy, then eat it all while flipping through crap on TV. The sugar rush helps a little—filling the emptiness in my stomach. I just have to get through the night, make it to the next day. But the buzzing of my phone is like a trigger. I wish I could throw it out the window but I need it in case Susan calls. I check again. . . . It's not her.

I start to cry. There's no buildup, no warning—just tears I can't seem to stop and a harsh lump in my throat that makes me wince every time I swallow. When it finally passes, I wipe my eyes on my shirt and fumble in my pockets for what's left of my cash. One more time won't make a difference at this point.

CHAPTER SIX

April 2006
Upper West Side, Manhattan

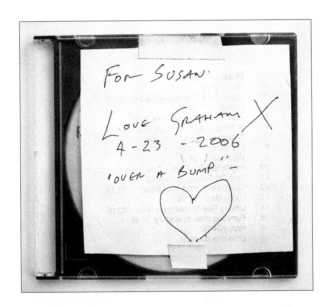

As a reporter, I always carried a notebook with me, mostly to write down to-do lists, story ideas, or quotes from interviews when I didn't have my laptop. But the week after my book party, I took notes while I was on the phone with Graham.

I'm not sure why. Up until that point, I'd only jotted down the occasional pithy comment he shared. (*"If it's big and in color, it's art. If it's small and in black and white, it's photography."*) I think I was afraid I wouldn't remember the details of our conversation, after we hung up and I sat there trying to process everything he said. Graham hadn't revealed much when I saw him on Monday, after my parents left—other than admitting he'd been using again. But I already knew that. As soon as I saw the crack pipe in his hand, I knew the needle I'd found in the bathroom was his. What I wanted was answers, explanations, a *full confession,* so I hoped he'd open up more on the phone, when he didn't have to see my reaction.

I suppose the notes were also a way for me to vet his story later, a habit after years of checking facts. "Addicts lie," Ethan had told me, so matter-of-factly it was like he was describing the sun coming up every day, a law of nature that couldn't be changed. I resisted the immutability of his assertion; I believed Graham still had a moral compass that just needed to be realigned—despite all the evidence that kept proving Ethan was right.

Before this call, Graham had assured me that he'd been going to meetings "every day" since my party, at an institute in Manhattan that offered an alternative to AA. But when I looked up their website to learn more about their approach, I discovered they didn't host daily meetings, like he'd said. Each time I caught Graham in a lie, it didn't feel like I was dealing with an addict who couldn't help covering up his habit. It felt like a personal betrayal.

This is what I wrote down while we talked, along with the questions I asked:

Why should I trust you?

You've got to be able to trust me. I need you not to second-guess it or doubt it, because it's really unfair.

When did this start?

Three or four weeks ago. I don't know why. I had started using, being what everybody thinks I am. Shit and useless. I got scared that I was really going to relapse.

So this isn't a relapse?

I didn't f'ing relapse—relapsing is when you go back to where you were before.

Did you think about telling me?

Yeah, until I saw you and then I couldn't. I'm sorry—I didn't want to be a disappointment to you. I'm really scared that I'll lose you.

Why did you lie about going to meetings every day?

I wanted you to think I was being good. I didn't want you to know I was f'ing sitting around feeling sorry for myself. I went to one meeting but I left halfway through. On Sunday, when Liam was at his mom's.

What drugs have you been using?

I smoked some crack. I used a little heroin.

With who?
Myself. Just me.

How many times?
Maybe a dozen. I was doing it to try and come down.

When I was with you?
I just did it when I was on my own. I never used at your house. It's so fucking scary. Even when you haven't used in two or three days, you're getting that need.

Did you ever share needles?
No. Of course not.

Were you using in Hawaii?
No. I didn't f'ing use when I was away—that's hard you know.

Was there some kind of trigger?
After my birthday, we weren't getting on. I was wanting too much and I wasn't getting what I wanted. I just felt low and lonely.

So did you see it coming?
There's no fucking knowing when it's gonna happen. It's way more complex than that.

THE FIRST TIME I read those notes, I was surprised at how dispassionate they make me seem—as if I were interviewing a source for an article, trying not to miss a good quote or an important fact. "It was like you weren't even talking about a relationship that you were in," Graham said. (I wrote that down as well.)

In some sense, I was still reeling from the revelation that he'd been hiding his habit from me—experiencing a low-grade version of shock, sort of numb and detached. I had bottled up my reaction during the weekend I spent with my parents after the party; I didn't want to tell them I'd found Graham with a crack pipe, so I just said we'd had a fight and they didn't pry.

By the time I went back to Graham's house on Monday, I was too worried about him overdosing to really be angry. He looked so devastated and vulnerable—like the façade he'd been hiding behind had completely shattered. It was probably the moment I felt closest to him, even though we hardly spoke the whole time I was there. We just sat on the floor in his bedroom, crying and holding hands. It was like something bad had happened to both of us, and neither of us had any idea how to fix it.

I knew he thought I'd gone over there to break up with him. Earlier in the day, he'd sent me an email saying, *"What you probably want to say I understand, but if that's the case can I just accept it and maybe you can do your bit in a day or two—when I'm a wee bit more able to look at you?"* But the truth is, I hadn't made up my mind about what I was going to do.

"What I need most from you is to know what's going on," I wrote back. *"And don't assume you know how I'm going to react because I don't know. I'm not coming over with an agenda, or a speech or a brick to throw at your head. I understand that you're in a vulnerable place and I don't intend to push you over the edge. You should know by now that I don't do things rashly."*

In the end, I decided not to leave him—mostly because I thought it was just a relapse, even though Graham resisted that word. He told me he'd started using after his birthday in March, and I accepted that because that's when I first felt like something was wrong. Back then, I had a limited understanding of addiction and only a vague sense of the grip it had on Graham. I thought that this—like any problem—could be solved with a plan, and that faced with the prospect of losing me, surely Graham would be motivated to get clean.

I had a harder time admitting that I didn't want to face losing him. Even though I'd been single for years, and didn't always mind being unattached, I knew it would be different after being with Graham. Maybe some of his passion was fueled by the excesses of a compulsive personality—or the influence of drugs—but I was sure that I'd never find anyone who loved me as intensely as he did. Graham was like a lightning rod for feelings, and when I was with him, the current flowed through me.

IN SOME WAYS, our relationship actually got better after Graham's secret was out in the open. The stress of all that hiding and lying faded to the background for a while, and so did another source of tension between us—Graham's insecurity about my love. He stopped worrying about that because I didn't leave.

"Susie, you've really shown me something quite extraordinary in you," he wrote—one of many apologetic messages that filled my inbox. *"I can never ever question your love for me as long as we live."*

Another email arrived with the subject line *"Your United Airlines Relationship Mending Trip."* Graham had forwarded a list of last-minute discounts on United, highlighting a cheap fare from New York to Osaka, Japan. He had edited the text to read, *"Dear Graham MacIndoe and Susan Stellin, It's about time you guys took a break and spent some quality time together about ½ way round the world. Do it now or forever kick yourself!"*

Of course, I had a different agenda for mending our relationship woes. If I was going to stick around and help Graham deal with his drug problem, I wanted him to commit to two things: an addiction support group for him and some kind of counseling for us. Reluctantly, he agreed to both conditions.

I didn't insist on rehab because he'd already done one of those programs, and it didn't seem like another month away would help him stay clean once he got home. Besides, I thought this was a temporary setback, one many addicts experienced at some point. "Relapse is part of recovery," addiction experts often warned. But I left it up to Graham to figure out what kind of support he'd embrace; he was resistant when I suggested AA.

"I don't believe in that whole God thing," he told me, working himself up to a familiar rant. "That's really a problem for me. I know they talk about your 'higher power' or 'God as you understand him,' but I want to be the one in control of my recovery. I don't want to turn it over to a fictitious guy in the sky or some imaginary being I've invented."

"I get that," I said. "But can't you just take what's useful to you from the meetings and ignore whatever isn't helpful?"

"Yeah, but people sit there talking about white light moments and thanking God for bringing them recovery and it just pisses me off. Why would God save some junkie who fucked over everyone in his life and ignore all the kids getting killed all over the world? God's got a lot to answer for if he's gonna save me and let some innocent kid die."

"So what do you want to do?" I countered. "You keep rejecting everything I suggest. You don't think you need an outpatient program, you don't want to see a therapist who specializes in addiction, you don't want to go to AA. . . . What does that leave, Graham?"

"I don't know, I have to think about it."

"Well you agreed to try *something,* so you'd better come up with an answer."

A couple of days later, Graham left me a note saying, "I have to consider the AA option." I'm sure he relented mostly because he didn't want to make the effort to find another support group— and AA was convenient and free.

He was even less enthusiastic about seeing a couples counselor, telling me he'd "talked circles around all the counselors in rehab" and didn't want to spend a fortune rehashing all of our fights. Even though therapy had been my idea, I had my own reservations about how much it would help.

The only time I'd seen a shrink was when I lived in San Francisco in the mid-1990s, before the dot-com boom went bust. I was working for an Internet company that paid mostly with stock options, so I could only afford a grad student who charged clients a discounted rate. But all we ended up talking about was the latest drama at the office, so I quit and rejoined my colleagues at a local bar after work, where we all complained about our difficult bosses.

In other words, that brush with therapy left me with mixed feelings about the process. It also left a lot of stones unturned.

When I called David, a couples counselor a friend had recommended, he explained that he was an integrative therapist, mixing psychodynamic training with a cognitive behavioral approach. I had no idea what that meant, so I asked how much he talked during sessions. I figured Graham might steamroll anyone who was too passive.

"I'm not silent," David assured me. "I like to address each person's way of doing things."

We booked an appointment for the following Monday, an impulsive decision for me. I had done more research when I bought a new printer.

Our first session didn't get off to a great start. Graham was late meeting me for our appointment in Manhattan, arriving sweaty and agitated as he locked up his bike. While we waited for the elevator, he reminded me that he was only doing this because I'd insisted, and he didn't see how discussing our problems would accomplish anything except reopen fresh wounds.

But I was convinced that he'd never truly be free of his habit if he didn't address the emptiness he kept talking about, which he was clearly trying to fill with drugs—or love. If there was any upside for me, it was having a mediator who could weigh in on our fights. Graham was an addict—and he'd lied to me about it—so I assumed David would take my side. I had the moral high ground.

As we took our places on David's well-worn leather couch—not sitting too close together (that would seem clingy) or too far apart (that would seem cold)—I tried to break the ice with a joke. "We may be the first couple to see a therapist after only being together for four months!"

David smiled as he jotted something down on his notepad. I wondered if he'd written "uses humor as a defense," or just remembered an errand he needed to run.

Despite his resistance, Graham was more open to the process than I expected, giving long, detailed responses to David's questions about how we got together, what he liked about me, and when he first started using drugs. But there was definitely an edge to some of his answers—like when David asked, "Can you tell me about the first memory you have of your mother?"

"You sound like that guy in *Blade Runner*," Graham said, slightly aggressive. "You know, when he's giving Leon the test to figure out if he's human or a replicant and he asks him to describe his mother, to see if he can provoke some kind of emotional response. So Leon pulls out a gun and says, 'I'll tell you about my mother'—then shoots the guy giving the test."

I shrank back into the couch as I looked over at David, who was looking at Graham like he wanted to press some kind of hidden alarm.

"But I get what you're asking," Graham continued, totally nonplussed. "So my first memory of my mother is probably when I was about three and she came and woke me up one night because a house across the street had caught fire. We watched it from the window—the chimney and the roof were on fire and there were sparks shooting everywhere and fire trucks trying to put it out. My dad was working the night shift so he wasn't home. He worked in the coal mines then, alternating day shifts one week and night shifts the next week, so my mum was home alone a lot with me and my baby brother—my sister wasn't born. So my mum would wake me up sometimes just to keep her company or watch the telly with her. I remember one time when she woke me up to watch Iggy Pop on the BBC's late-night music program, *The Old Grey Whistle Test,* but that was later on when I was older. . . ."

While Graham was talking, all I could think about was my answer—and the fact that I couldn't come up with one. I could picture lots of photos from my childhood, like one of my brother and sister and me sitting on the dock with our mom, all of us in bathing suits she had sewn. She was fashionably skinny in her red, white, and blue bikini, with big sunglasses à la Jackie O.

But talking about a photo felt like failing the test. It wasn't actually a memory of an event; it was a snapshot I'd looked at many times in an album. I broke out in a sweat, wondering why I couldn't remember my childhood the way Graham did—with all these vivid details and emotions. *Did this mean he was human and I was not?* Flipping through a mental calendar, all my memories were linked to photos: first day of school . . . Halloween costumes . . . Christmas morning . . . Easter dresses. . . .

"I've got one," I interrupted, as if I'd just beaten a game show buzzer. "In the spring, my mom would always point out when the crocuses she'd planted started popping up in front of our house. I'd come home from school and she'd show me the green leaves poking through the ground. She grew up on a farm so she liked to garden."

David looked at me like he was waiting for me to say something else. When I didn't, he asked, "Did you help your mom with the garden?"

"We always had chores so I remember pulling up weeds, but I think my mom mostly planted the flowers."

I shifted on the couch, uncomfortable about being put on the spot. Maybe I had passed the test, but my answer clearly would've gotten a lower grade than Graham's richly evocative response.

That's why I never quite understood Graham's resistance to therapy—I preferred staying in the background, observing other people's lives, but he loved having an audience listen to him ramble on and on. In fact, at one point during our initial phone call with David, he had asked Graham, "Do you always talk this way?"

Graham thought he meant the Scottish accent, but David corrected him: "No, I mean so fast and for so long that no one can interrupt you."

Yes, that was pretty much how Graham talked when he was engaged with a topic. Between his verbal onslaught and my guarded parrying, David clearly had his work cut out for him, but we did leave his office more optimistic than when we arrived. Graham's mood had lifted and my curiosity was piqued; David was much sharper than the last therapist I'd seen.

"We both felt good about this morning's session," I emailed David later that afternoon, when I wrote to schedule our next appointment. *"That seems like a weird thing to say after discussing uncomfortable topics, but I think this is going to be helpful—for both of us."*

ONCE THE INITIAL crisis had passed, I felt like my life had split onto two parallel tracks. On one set of rails, I lived a normal existence—doing radio interviews for my book, talking to editors about assignments, going to yoga classes and dinners with friends. On the other set of rails, I was consumed by Graham's struggle. It wasn't always easy to jump between trains.

I believed he really was trying to quit, but I was so naïve about the setbacks and challenges that are part of the process, my suggestions may have hurt more than they helped. I thought that getting clean was mostly a matter of willpower: You finally decided to quit because the negative consequences of using had become unavoidably, painfully clear. I didn't understand that Graham wasn't capable of that kind of rational thinking—at least not about drugs. In his mind, logic didn't have the upper hand.

I had little tolerance for anyone who offered a reality check on my expectations—opinions that weren't always sensitively dispensed. But for the most part, I didn't share many details about our situation with friends or family, except for Ethan. And even with him, I cherry-picked the advice I was willing to accept.

"The time frame for getting better is long," he cautioned. "It's not weeks or months, Sus, it's more like years."

Maybe for you, I thought. *But Graham is different. His whole life has been about beating the odds.*

Graham's rise out of the working class was an immigrant's version of the American dream. He talked his way into art school, landed a New York gallery job, bought a brownstone, got approved for a green card. When he decided to become a commercial photographer, his success was practically instant. In British slang, people might call him a "chancer"—an opportunist or risk taker—although I preferred a more positive spin on that label.

Yes, he was reckless and looked for any angle that might give him an advantage; sure, he relied on his Scottish charm to get him out of a scrape. But I always admired how Graham was willing to take a chance on things most people considered a long shot. In some sense, that was an attitude we shared: Neither of us thought the rules applied to us.

So if anyone could kick heroin and crack, I thought Graham had the determination to do it—and compared to a lot of addicts, he was in a better position to succeed. He had money for treatment, an enviable career, and a girlfriend, son, and family who loved him. I thought he had everything he needed to win that fight.

———

Two weeks after I found Graham with the crack pipe, he gave me another CD he'd made, this one called "Over a Bump." A few of the songs were clearly chosen for their romantic titles ("There's No Me Without You" by the Manhattans, "Lucky Man" by the Verve), but I didn't know what to make of some of his other choices—like "A Mistake" by Fiona Apple, or "Breaking the Habit" by Linkin Park.

If Graham was so focused on getting over a bump, why did he give me a CD with lyrics like *"I'm gonna fuck it up again"* and *"I'll never be alright"*? I wondered why he was sending such a pessimistic message, doubting whether he really could stay clean. But I didn't ask him about it—that's how denial works. You're complicit because sometimes you just don't want to know. It already felt like our relationship revolved around Graham's recovery, and that was starting to weigh me down.

At first I wanted to know everything about what he was going through: what withdrawal felt like, how often he thought about using, and whether it was stressful to pass by the places he used to cop.

"I don't really want to talk about it," he'd say, and I didn't push him. I didn't want to make him dwell on anything that might make him want to use, and by that point, I was tired of talking about drugs. Then once he started embracing AA—not just pretending to go to meetings—there was a different distance between us, something separate about his experience that I couldn't share.

He'd tell me stories about the other addicts he met, elaborate tales of self-destruction that made his own transgressions seem tame. I was glad he was making the effort, and focusing on what was useful to him—an abridged version of AA's twelve-step program.

"I think this could all be condensed into three or four steps," he told me. "If you admit your life is unmanageable, recognize how you've fucked up, and make amends to the people you've hurt, you've pretty much got it covered. The rest seems sort of redundant."

Looking at the brochure he showed me, I couldn't really disagree. AA had helped Ethan and many other people I knew—which is why I'd encouraged Graham to try it—but there were things about the program that bothered me as well. It didn't seem to get at the underlying reasons why people drank or used drugs, and a lot of the slogans struck me as a bit superficial.

After one meeting, Graham sent me an email someone at AA had suggested he write, which sounded like it was plagiarized from a pamphlet. I asked him to try again—this time using his own words. The second draft he emailed me seemed a little more sincere.

Well after a lot of thinking i realise that i really have to get my act together so that you and i can have the oportunity of a brilliant life together. i cant lie or deny - it doesn't fool anyone and is somewhat pathetic - which is a way worse way to be seen than my fear of feeling weak if i say i've slipped. i'm not one for making excuses or blaming others - not parents, friends, timing, surroundings, or fate. i know how lucky i've been and when i think of your love and that i can have it in my life - if I allow it - i realize now that i was being selfish. you've given me this chance to prove myself - which i truely appreciate. i don't want to change into a boring aa person - but i'm feeling pretty ok at the meetings!

To be honest, I didn't want Graham to turn into a boring AA person, either. Our sober social life already seemed more middle-aged than I would've liked. Sometimes I envied other couples who could split a bottle of wine at dinner, or hang out at a bar on a Saturday night. I was trying to drink less around Graham—just the occasional beer or glass of wine—but drinking alone always felt awkward. Graham and I had to find other ways to unwind.

We went bowling, took Liam to Chinatown, watched movies, did some gardening. I planted petunias in neat rows under Graham's overgrown bushes; he bought a little fountain because he thought the sound of running water was calming. We were making progress with David, my book was getting good reviews, and Graham was finally getting serious about looking for work. All in all, things were moving in a positive direction.

Then in May, just as the flowers I'd planted were beginning to bloom, things took a darker turn. Graham started acting secretive and moody again—which put me on high alert. I guessed that he hadn't quit entirely, and became obsessed with confirming or disproving that suspicion.

I looked for the brightly colored bits of plastic used to package small amounts of crack, glassine heroin envelopes, anything resembling a belt. Burned spoons, lighters, syringes, packets of sterile water, nubs of metal mesh—all evidence I searched for relentlessly, even digging through his pockets in the middle of the night when I'd wake up in a panic.

We had vicious fights and teary reconciliations and occasional quiet moments when we were too exhausted to do anything but lie next to each other, a temporary truce in our ongoing battle. At a club listening to a band after an argument, we just stood there holding hands, all the energy in the room running along the V linking my shoulder with his.

"I'm not going to leave you," Graham said at one point. "You're going to have to leave me."

I knew that, but I couldn't make myself take that step. Despite everything, I needed him. He filled my own empty places with his constant attention, calmed my anxieties with his reassuring words and capable hands, showed me possibilities where I only saw limits, lit up my nerve endings, challenged me to take risks.

I also thought he was making progress, and I couldn't let go of the hope that he'd eventually get better. If I could just find the right thing to say or do, I was sure I could nudge him along that path.

THAT FANTASY WAS shattered a week before Memorial Day, not entirely out of the blue. We had gone to an opening for Graham's friend at a gallery in Manhattan, then spent the night at my apartment uptown. The next morning, while I was in the shower, a feeling came over me that I still can't explain.

As if I were a puppet and someone else had control over my movements, I turned off the water, pulled the plastic curtain aside, and stepped up onto the side of the tub. At that height, my eyes were level with the top of the medicine cabinet, which I hadn't looked at or cleaned in years. Lying in the dust, there was something wrapped up in a wad of toilet paper. I reached across and grabbed it, carefully unrolling the tissue. I already knew what I'd find inside.

Still dripping from the shower, I put on a robe and stormed into the bedroom. Graham was sleeping so I had to shake him awake. "Get out!" I screamed. "NOW! Get dressed!" I threw his clothes at him, not even bothering to search the pockets.

"What the fuck . . . ?" he protested, deflecting his shirt from his face. Then he noticed what I was holding in my hand: a syringe, a blackened pipe, and a lighter. His expression shifted from confusion to fear.

"Don't . . . say . . . a fucking . . . word," I spit out. "Just leave!"

He didn't even try to defend himself. Before heading for the door, all he said was "Can I have my kit back?"

"ARE YOU KIDDING ME?!!" I shrieked.

———

"*I FEEL LIKE I can't breathe,*" I wrote in my notebook later that night. "*I feel panicky and trapped. I have to be able to flee. But to where? No word from G. Picture him shooting up, lying half comatose, not feeling the pain I have to feel and it makes me angry. I hate that he has an escape, even though I know it's destroying him. Weirdly, it doesn't seem fair. I took half an Ambien—how is that different? It's already seeping through me, pulling me toward sleep.*"

AFTER I THREW Graham out of my apartment, I reached out to just about everybody I knew. Unlike the first time I found out that he was still using, there wasn't any reason to protect him. Our relationship was over—I didn't care what anyone thought of him anymore.

"*Need break-up coping advice,*" I emailed a friend who had recently been through a split. "*Still in that very shattered period— you know, focusing on the essentials like breathing and eating and not crying during work calls or meetings. With the added bonus that I get to worry whether G. has gone off the deep end and OD'd!*"

Although I cast a wide net, desperate for any kind of connection, Ethan was the main person I turned to for support. This time he was blunt about what he thought I should do.

"Graham shouldn't be in a relationship until he deals with his addiction," he told me.

On some level, I knew that was true, but there was something about it that still felt wrong. Was there any other disease—besides leprosy—that basically condemned people to suffer through it alone?

"The best thing you can do for him is offer to help get him into some kind of treatment program," Ethan said. "But you can't take this on all by yourself. You have to insist that other people are involved."

"I know. . . . It's just that there isn't anyone else he's close to in New York—at least not that I've met—and his family is on the other side of the Atlantic. I don't know them so I'm not sure how they'd react if I called."

"What about his ex-wife?"

"I don't think it's my place to decide how much to tell her. Graham would go ballistic if he found out. And if I call her she might not let Liam stay with Graham anymore. I don't think a custody battle would be good for anyone right now."

But I did feel bad that Liam was the only other person Graham saw regularly, so I sent him a text saying he could call me if he wanted to talk. Liam didn't answer—which didn't surprise me—but I felt a little better after opening that door.

When I told my sister what had happened, she offered to cash in some of her frequent flier miles and fly me out to Los Angeles for Memorial Day weekend, saying she was holding a reservation for a flight leaving in two days. I said I appreciated the offer but needed to think about it. I hadn't heard from Graham since I'd thrown him out of my apartment that morning, so as my anger subsided, I was getting more and more worried. I didn't want to leave town without knowing he hadn't OD'd.

That's the thing about heroin—what makes it different from other drugs: Every time you stick that needle in your vein, there's a chance that one hit could kill you.

THE NEXT AFTERNOON, I finally heard from Graham. He left me a long voicemail, but from the way he was talking, I couldn't tell if he'd meant to dial my number or if he'd bumped his phone and let me eavesdrop on his downward spiral.

"*Grammy, Grammy, Grammy—what the fuck are you going to do with yourself?*

"*My, my, my. So exhausted and tired.*"

It sounded like he opened the fridge.

"*No bread, noth-ing.*

"*Oh man, what the fuck am I going to do?*"

He made a couple of calls on his other line.

"*Hey Marcus. Graham here. Give me a call.*

"*Hi Caroline—It's Graham. I know I need to deal with my taxes. I had a glitch with my computer. My life is a disaster right now. Thank you for being patient.*"

He burped.

"*Excuse me. Excusez-moi.*"

There was a rustling, like he'd opened a bag, then he recited a list he was trying to make.

"*Patricia. Ellen. Angus. Javier.*

"*Fuck—where's my list?*

"*I've got to call HIP. Cancel my bank card.*

"*Fuck it—I'm getting a cat. I've always loved them.*"

In spite of my funk, that made me smile. I was more of a dog person, so I'd always protested whenever Graham talked about adopting a cat.

"*Fuck—I left Susan a message. Fuck, fuck, fuck.*"

After the voicemail ended, I must've replayed it half a dozen times. It was a relief to know that Graham wasn't stretched out cold with a needle in his arm, but the beep that cut off his message left me with a hollow sensation—like the emptiness he often described. Except what I felt was more like I couldn't stand to be home alone, feeling powerless, lost, and betrayed.

An hour later, Graham sent a text asking, "*I'm assuming that you and/or i are not going to our meeting with david tonite?*" I wrote back saying I wanted to go by myself—and that in the morning, I was flying out to L.A.

He texted back: *"Ask David if I can come and see him on my own."* That made my heart ache. It seemed like such a big step for Graham to admit that he needed help, but I wanted David to help me.

During most of that appointment, I just cried. I can't remember exactly what we talked about, other than some treatment options I could suggest to Graham, but I can still picture the look on David's face. It was sort of like waking up in a hospital bed and not having any sense of how badly you've been injured, except for the concern your doctor didn't try to hide.

While I was having dinner with a friend, Graham left me several messages. "I just want to hear your voice before you go," he pleaded. "Please call me back."

But when I did, late that night, neither of us knew what to say. I felt like he had split into two people—the man I loved, and the addict I hated—so I kept cycling between sadness and rage.

"I'm going to hang up now," Graham kept repeating, but then he didn't—and I couldn't. I listened to him sniffling, waiting for him to finally end the call.

Later, I sent him an email telling him some of the things I hadn't been able to say.

> *You can do this, Graham. I still believe in you and still believe you can be the brilliant person you have inside you. You're smart, generous, funny, loving, giving, supportive, wise, playful, devoted and at heart optimistic about life. Sometimes I think that's what brings you down—that you expect people to be as good and kind as you can be, and it's crushing when you feel let down. (That's one thing we have in common.)*
>
> *But you have to find healthier ways to deal with disappointment, or anxiety or pain, because there will always be some*

of that—you can't avoid it by isolating yourself. And if you keep everyone at bay, you miss out on all the love and support and wonderful things that happen when you connect with other people.

I still love you and I mean it when I say I'll do whatever I can to help.

I did mean that. Just because I didn't think I could be with him didn't mean I stopped loving him, and that realization was devastating to me. Because I didn't know how else to help Graham get clean.

Part Two

OURSELVES

"All the very best of us

string ourselves up for love."

—Matt Berninger, The National

CHAPTER SEVEN

May 2006
Los Angeles, California

On the flight to L.A., I woke up disoriented from a nightmare: I'd dreamed I was wandering around a crack house looking for Graham. Everyone told me it was futile—he was gone, I'd never find him—but I kept searching the rooms, scanning the faces of all the people I came across. I wasn't sure I'd recognize him if he looked anything like these slumped-over junkies.

But when I got to a room that was more open, like a warehouse, someone caught my eye: a skinny guy in a white T-shirt with a wool hat pulled down over his head. In the darkness, I could just make out that on the front of his shirt there was a screen-printed photo of Graham.

All the tension I'd been holding tight relaxed into relief. *He was alive. I'd found him. He hadn't OD'd.* But I was even more reassured by what that photo meant. The dream version of me decided that he'd printed up that T-shirt because he thought no one would recognize him if they came looking for him. He hadn't given up—he wanted help getting out of that place.

ARRIVING IN LOS Angeles felt like landing in an even more foreign world. After my sister picked me up from the airport, we drove to the house she was buying, passing taco joints and dry cleaners and gas stations and nail salons, all surrounded by billboards demanding attention. Whenever I visited, I found driving around L.A. overstimulating; I wasn't used to moving faster than a walking pace above ground.

My sister had given me the plane ticket partly because she was dealing with her own source of stress: This was her first home purchase, and she was nervous about the price. My role was to reassure her that she wasn't crazy to be buying in the middle of a real estate bubble; hers was to distract me from obsessing about Graham. We both kept up our end of the deal.

As she gave me the tour, I nodded in agreement with her plans for the kitchen, admired the bedrooms, and gushed about the spacious backyard. It had a pool and a hot tub, an outdoor fireplace and koi ponds, and it was landscaped with palm trees and bougainvillea in bloom. I was happy that she'd found a house she loved, after losing a couple of bidding wars, but the contrast between my life and hers was stark.

She's five years younger than me, but was doing better than me in many ways: earning a steady paycheck, dating a guy who wasn't a drug addict, and asking about the price of a gardener and someone to take care of her pool. Both a bargain, the real estate agent promised, making me cringe with his comment about all the immigrant labor around.

I stretched out in a lounge chair while he described the dermatology appointment he'd just come from, explaining how microdermabrasion treatments counteracted the damage from frowning in his sleep. My sister escaped to see how things were going with the inspector; I tuned out the skin care lecture and tried not to think about the things causing my wrinkles—not Graham or my mortgage or my own disturbing dreams.

The rest of the weekend was a blur of car rides and activities, busyness as an antidote for despair. We went to a birthday party, but I wasn't in the mood to mingle; we sat by a friend's pool, but I couldn't focus on the magazines I tried to read. I thought a drive up to Malibu might lift my spirits—seeing the ocean always did—but the happy beachgoers just made me more depressed. I checked my messages often, hoping for a text or email from Graham, but he had warned me that he wasn't going to write while I was away.

My last night in L.A., my sister invited a few people over for a Memorial Day barbecue. She made guacamole, her boyfriend grilled burgers, and I drank too many strong margaritas. Once the guests left and her boyfriend went inside to watch TV—no doubt tired of all the real estate and breakup talk—my sister asked the question that had been on my mind for days: "So what would you do if Graham actually got clean?"

It was dark out on the porch, which gave me some cover to compose my answer—one of those conversations where you feel like you're talking to the night air.

"Honestly, I don't know," I finally said. "He told me he's going to detox at home, on his own, because he doesn't want to wait to get into a program. But I've heard that before, so who knows if he'll really do it."

"Isn't that kind of risky?"

"That's what I'm worried about. He's had seizures before when he quit drinking, so he really should be monitored—or at least take something while he's tapering off. But Graham is so stubborn he's not going to listen to me. I sent him a *New Yorker* cartoon showing a guy with one arm hanging out of a really badly nailed-together coffin. The caption was a joke about the dead guy always insisting on doing everything himself."

"But if he did get clean," my sister persisted, "would you get back together with him?"

I hesitated, worried about how she'd react if I said "maybe" or "yes." I didn't know how she felt about Graham at that point—she hadn't given that away—but the stigma of heroin felt like something most people wouldn't ever get past.

"I don't know if I could trust him," I said. "That's almost a bigger issue than the relapse. Then again, I feel like he's made it impossible for me to fall in love with anyone else."

As soon as I said that, I expected her to tell me I was being overly dramatic, but she went for a gentler reply. "I think it's a little premature to write off the rest of the male population, Sus. Besides, maybe the next guy you're with will organize his silverware drawer."

That did make me smile. It had always bugged me that Graham kept his silverware all jumbled together—without separating the knives, forks, and spoons—and my sister fell closer to his end of the organizational spectrum.

"I'm not sure that's high on my list of necessary qualities anymore," I admitted.

"Well, at least you learned that."

THE NEXT MORNING, before I left for the airport, my mom sent an email suggesting I turn on the *Today* show at 8 A.M. "*They have a rebuttal of the Newsweek article of a few years ago re: women's chances of getting married after 40,*" she wrote. "*Very interesting to see the happily married women who didn't marry in their 20s.*"

I graduated from high school the year *Newsweek* declared that a single woman over forty was more likely to be killed by a terrorist than tie the knot. Now they were acknowledging what most people already knew: that their original article was totally wrong. But did my mom really think this was encouraging news to report, just after Graham and I had split up? I was only thirty-seven—I still had time left on the clock.

I'd like to say that I was amused by the poor timing of her message, or at least brushed it off as a well-meaning mother hoping her daughter didn't end up alone. But when she called before my flight, I snapped at her about it and she burst into tears, saying she felt like I'd shut her out.

She was right. Before I left for L.A., I had told my parents that Graham and I had broken up, but I didn't say why. Part of my reluctance had to do with my own difficulty talking about problems, but that wasn't the only reason I held back. Addiction felt like one of those taboo topics, like abortion or being gay in some families, that everyone knew happened, but most people preferred not to discuss. I wasn't an addict, but I felt a similar sense of shame—because Graham was using heroin, and because I still loved him in spite of his horrible habit.

The only conversation I had with my parents about the reason for our breakup was a couple of months later, when I was in Michigan and my dad asked if Graham had a problem with drugs. I was surprised that he'd picked up on that, but maybe it had been obvious when they met him in New York. Still, I thought it was strange that they hadn't asked me about it before. I couldn't outright lie, so I said yes and my dad said, "I thought so"—and that was the extent of our discussion. There were no follow-up questions about what I'd been through or how Graham was doing. I remember being upset—but also relieved—that they didn't ask more.

When I sent an email to my sister describing that conversation, I drew her into the circle of secrecy I helped impose. *"I didn't give details so if they press you please be discreet,"* I wrote. *"I really wish it hadn't come up."*

AS SOON AS I got back to New York I sent Graham a text asking, *"How are you doing? I'm worried about your DIY detox."*

"I'm ok," he answered.

"Do u want to talk?" I wrote back. *"Need anything?"*

"I'm just scared to hear your voice 'coz it's been the longest since we met and I'm missing you a lot. I'll try in a bit."

He didn't call, so I spent most of the night wondering why. The next day, he sent an email as if there were no problem at all: *"When do you think we'll be able to lay eyes on each other?"*

"I don't know," I replied, irritated that I'd lost sleep worrying

about him. "*But not until you've detox'd and aren't on a chemical roller coaster. . . .*"

I had no way of knowing if Graham actually was trying to detox, but on the flight back to New York, with thirty-five thousand feet of distance from my life, I'd decided to give him the benefit of the doubt. I was going to support him—not as his girlfriend, but as someone who loved him and couldn't stand to leave him (and Liam) to deal with this all on their own. Even though I hadn't known Liam that long, I felt guilty about leaving him in a tough situation, especially knowing how Liz's departure had affected him and his dad.

"Tu deviens responsable pour toujours de ce que tu as apprivoisé," Antoine de Saint-Exupéry wrote in *The Little Prince,* and I kept thinking about that line: *You become responsible, forever, for what you have tamed.* I didn't feel responsible for Graham in the sense that I thought I'd caused his relapse, but I did feel responsible for him just like the Little Prince was responsible for the flower he'd nurtured. Graham and I had taken care of each other, in a way neither of us had experienced with anyone else, and those feelings didn't disappear just because the pull of drugs was stronger.

So for the next few weeks, we settled into a state of relationship limbo, communicating mostly through email and text messages and the occasional call. That allowed me to keep my distance, but it also made everything we wrote more open to misinterpretation—and much more emotionally charged.

"*I know you think I'm not standing by you,*" I explained in one email. "*But that's not what this is about. We were in this destructive cycle that was horrible for both of us, and I could finally see that it wasn't going to change as long as you thought you could have me and not have to do the hard work of getting clean. You weren't really facing up to what was going on—or what it was doing to you—but anything I can do to help you, I will.*"

I told Graham I didn't want to give either of us false hope about the future, but it killed me to think that I might help him get through the hard part of quitting, and then watch him end up with somebody else.

"i love you as much as ever i miss you painfully and no one else will get the good me," he promised. *"i only hope you can trust and love me again and we can be happy together. i think we can— i think you do too. you sparked something in me that made me crazy in love with you. i hope and believe in our future."*

A few days later he admitted, *"the ambiguity of our friendship/ relationship is tough. i don't know if your over me and think that not saying it loud and clear is letting me down gently or whether we are still together in some capacity or whether if i prove myself we can move ahead. but i can't go from being your lover to just a best pal—i'm not that type. . . . sorry, babbling, tough day (if only you knew or could feel it)."*

Since I couldn't possibly know what he was going through, he tried to show me. That afternoon, he emailed a picture of himself wearing a black T-shirt with the word TRUST in big white letters across the front. Usually his self-portraits were lit to make him look sexy, but in this photo he just looked pale and ill. It made me think he really was trying to quit—which was probably the point—but it was still disturbing. I didn't want that image of Graham in my head.

When I wrote him back, I said I'd rather talk about our future later, and mentioned that I was planning on going to a Nar-Anon meeting that night. *"A bit nervous about it actually. The web site is kind of heavy on the god/higher power angle. Trying to be open-minded and just see if it's at all useful."*

Graham replied: *"Don't go. We need to talk more than you going to meetings."*

I immediately called him and began to unload. "It's creepy and fucked-up that you're discouraging me from reaching out for help dealing with all of this."

"When have I ever discouraged you from talking to anyone?" Graham interrupted. "I never told you not to call Ethan—I said I was glad you had someone else to talk to. I didn't tell you not to go see your sister. I never once asked you not to say anything to any of your friends. I'm sure they all think I'm a complete cunt now."

"You just sent me an email saying *'Don't go'* when I told you I was going to a Nar-Anon meeting!"

"I said I wanted to talk. Those groups are all about learning how to put up with whatever shit an addict dumps on you. They're going to try and convince you that you shouldn't leave me, and that's the last thing I want. I don't want you in my life because you feel guilty about walking away."

I was stunned. That wasn't at all what I was expecting him to say.

"I'm going to the meeting," I said, still pissed off. "I think it would be good for me to talk to other people who understand what I'm going through. And don't worry—I'm not doing anything because I feel guilty."

But that wasn't true; I felt guilty all the time. No matter what I did—stand by Graham, leave him, talk to him, cut him off—I felt like I was in a situation that didn't leave me any good choice.

WHEN I GOT to the meeting, at a church near Times Square, I had second thoughts as soon as I walked through the door. It was downstairs in a fluorescent-lit basement and there were just a few other people sitting around a big table. I was hoping to lurk in the back of a larger crowd.

I picked up some pamphlets before taking a seat, flipping through them while a few latecomers straggled in. The silence felt uncomfortable, like when you go to an event and the audience is sparse—you wonder if there's a reason more people didn't come.

The meeting opened with readings from one of the pamphlets I'd picked up. *"God grant me the serenity to accept the things I cannot change,"* everyone chanted. *"Courage to change the things I can, and the wisdom to know the difference."* I felt obligated to join in, but it reminded me of all the Sundays I spent in church with my parents, reciting prayers I didn't necessarily believe.

The Nar-Anon readings put me off for a similar reason: the unquestioning acceptance of platitudes and proverbs, the necessary faith in God or a higher power. Mostly, the idea of being powerless rubbed me the wrong way. During Mass growing up, I always refused to say, "Lord, I am not worthy . . ." so maybe that pride was still stiffening my spine. I knew I couldn't control Graham's addiction and that I wasn't responsible for his decisions, but I didn't believe that there was nothing I could do to help him get clean.

But once people started sharing their stories, it did make me feel less isolated to hear some of the same things I'd felt: *"I didn't even know what a crack pipe looked like. . . ."* (Me neither.) *"I wanted to believe he wasn't using. . . ."* (Of course.) *"He's so smart and knows what it's doing to him, so I don't understand why he can't quit. . . ."* (Exactly.) *"I feel this huge responsibility because no one else knows. . . ."*

At the same time, it was frustrating that the meeting didn't feel like an exchange. You weren't supposed to "cross-talk"—meaning, you couldn't offer somebody else advice. While I understood that in theory, in practice it felt like everyone just gave their own little speech. So when one woman described a brother who sounded a lot like Ethan (he didn't want to take time off to go to rehab), I wanted to tell her that I knew a guy who got clean without doing a twenty-eight-day program. But I thought that might sound too much like advice, so I waited to talk to her until after the meeting. She seemed grateful, but I would've preferred a support group with more give-and-take—ideally, led by a counselor who specialized in addiction.

I was also put off by Nar-Anon's outdated emphasis on *families*. As one brochure put it: "Nar-Anon is designed for us—the parent, spouse, child, brother, sister or friend of the 'user.' " There was no mention of "girlfriend" or "boyfriend" or "partner" in any of the pamphlets I read. The whole philosophy seemed to be about coping with someone you were tied to by blood or marriage, which didn't account for those of us who could more easily walk away. In that sense, Graham was right: One flyer said I shouldn't make any life-changing decisions until I'd gone to meetings regularly for three to six months. Presumably, that meant I shouldn't break up with him for at least ninety days.

In fact, half of the people at that meeting were in my situation—like one young woman who was about to get married and had just discovered that her fiancé was using cocaine. The invitations had been printed, she was getting fitted for her wedding dress, and she was too embarrassed to tell anyone else what was going on. I hope she got some comfort from sharing her secret with a room full of strangers, but I don't think we gave her much help with her choice. "I don't know what to do," she confessed. We all nodded sympathetically—and silently. *Where was she supposed to turn now?*

Still, some of the things people shared helped me get a clearer perspective on what I could realistically do for Graham, and see that I needed to establish better boundaries—so his needs didn't eclipse mine. When I finally did my own share, self-consciously raising my hand, I admitted this to the group: As much as Graham loved me, I couldn't ever compete with drugs, as long as they were part of his life.

"That's what's starting to dawn on me—he can't put me first," I wrote in my notebook later, sitting in a park until it was too dark to see. *"No matter how much he says he'd do anything for me, he really isn't capable of making what's best for me a priority. I have to do that."*

The next day, I sent Graham a long email, explaining what I had and hadn't gotten out of the meeting, and describing some of the other people I'd met.

He wrote back, *"i'll tell you my reservations later, but if its good for you then great. saying i miss you is the understatement of the year."*

Despite his reservations, Graham was still going to AA, emailing me about a meeting he'd been to at a church with no AC: *"Man what a humid day to be sat next to some fat sweaty recovering alky in a too small unventilated room in the church extension. With all of their codes for meetings—gay, straight, smoking, step, open, blah........they should have one saying 'ventilated.'"*

That was one of the things I missed about him—all his funny observations, and the way he wasn't afraid to say what he felt. Not just his emotions, but his unfiltered opinions, challenging conventions I was maybe too quick to accept. As much as Graham hoped some of my self-discipline might rub off on him, I envied his lack of inhibitions.

FOR MUCH OF the summer, Graham and I fumbled along as friends but still acted a lot like a couple: sharing the day's news, leaning on each other for moral support, and arguing over stupid misunderstandings. In some ways, I felt closer to him than I did when we were having sex. We saw each other occasionally, but mostly emailed or talked on the phone, which made it harder for me to tell if he was still using.

Graham was adamant that he'd quit heroin, but admitted that he took Suboxone, methadone, or Xanax once in a while—to help wean himself off dope, he told me. I was getting better at identifying the effects of different types of drugs: Crack made him fly off the handle, too much methadone made him drowsy. But we fought anytime I confronted him about whether he really was getting clean, and I had trouble figuring out when he was lying. Just because addicts lie doesn't mean they lie *all the time,* so I had to suspend my need to investigate everything he told me.

I was vague when Graham pressed me about our relationship status. *"i have no idea what your thinking, wanting, feeling,"* he wrote me, depressed that I was going to Michigan in July without him. *"i'm under the impression that we're probably broken up, but it's just getting drawn out like some slow death."*

That was fair enough—I hadn't ever said, point-blank, "It's over." Mostly because I was having a hard time letting go, but also because I didn't want to hurt him. Just when I thought he was doing okay, he'd call me up in a panic, saying he was feeling a craving and couldn't reach anyone else. "Could you just talk to me for a bit?" he'd ask. It was hard to pull away when he kept drawing me in, with loving emails or those desperate calls.

"The way I look at it is more like a separation," I wrote him back. *"Whether we can be together again depends on what happens with both of us—I do realize it's not just my decision.*

"I know you want a definitive resolution, but there's so much I don't know right now—who you are when you're not using, how motivated you are to make the changes that are going to increase your chances of staying clean, and which problems might still be there when you're not using.

"I really believe one-on-one counseling with someone who understands addiction is going to be key for you. Besides realizing I couldn't 'fix you' (to borrow a song lyric), I've also realized I couldn't fill the emptiness you feel sometimes—without having my needs completely consumed by yours. I think it's going to take therapy, not just AA, to help you address some of the underlying issues that make you turn to drugs for relief.

"I also have to sort out what I want now. I've spent so long setting aside what I wanted for various reasons—you, the book,

making money—it's almost become a habit not to step back and see the bigger picture. . . ."

As much as I wanted to support Graham with his recovery, I knew I needed to focus on my life. I was getting steady assignments, writing for magazines and *The New York Times,* but I'd already spent most of my book advance so I was worried about money—and I was still frustrated by the topics I was covering. During the day I'd interview people about the perks of business class travel, then after dinner I'd watch a documentary about addiction. The dissonance between my work life and my personal life was getting to be too much to manage: I finally realized that I needed help.

In late June, I decided to keep seeing David—on my own, without Graham. He didn't take insurance, but he gave me a break on his rate and my mom sent a check to help with the bill. I still hadn't told her much about what was going on with Graham, but it meant a lot to me that she was trying to be supportive. I think everyone who knew me could tell I was in over my head, but I don't think anyone knew how to help me.

When I told Graham I was seeing David, he said he'd found his own therapist: a woman named Debi who had an office downtown. Since he'd said he couldn't afford therapy, I was surprised that he'd changed his mind, but I took it as a positive sign. I was looking for any sign that he was willing to do whatever it took to get clean—and if he did, then the answer to my sister's question was yes, I probably would give him another chance.

"I can't let go completely of this desire to see what we'd be like together if we could ever put this behind us," I'd written in my notebook, during the flight back from Los Angeles in May.

At the time, I didn't really understand how much that longing kept me involved in Graham's life, but it had as tight a grip on me as drugs did on Graham.

CHAPTER EIGHT

August 2006
Tulsa, Oklahoma

In the cab from the airport to my hotel in downtown Tulsa—here on an assignment—I'm already on the lookout for places I might be able to cop. You can't come right out and ask a stranger, "Hey, where can I buy drugs?" but I've gotten pretty good at landing someplace I've never been and managing to score within a few hours.

Sometimes I'll tell the driver I'm a photographer from Scotland, working on a project about drugs. I'll be vague at first, asking about the city, which neighborhoods are safe and which aren't, then I'll pop the question: "Any idea where I can get a smoke?" You can tell by how the driver reacts if he's gonna play along, maybe even hook you up. One time a cabbie in Las Vegas took me straight to his own dealer—all I had to do was give him a few rocks.

This driver doesn't seem to care why I'm here so I look out the window, keeping an eye out for neighborhoods that look promising. Hookers, junkies, and crackheads are a dead giveaway, and it's easy to spot the corner boys—they're constantly in motion, checking everyone out. But if I don't see what I'm looking for on the way in from the airport, there's always the concierge. You have to be careful with hotel employees—they know who you are—so I'll usually say I'm scouting locations for a shoot and ask which parts of the city are a bit rough.

That's what I do as soon as I get to the hotel. The concierge seems eager to have someone to talk to, so he's telling me all about Tulsa's crystal meth problem and what a shame it is so many people have gotten hooked. Finally, I interrupt him and ask, "So are there any places around here I should avoid? My client is looking for an edgy setting, but I don't want to stumble into some drug den."

He pulls out a map and marks a few neighborhoods with a pen. I'm out the door before he can finish giving his advice.

As I walk closer to one of the areas he flagged—under the freeway, down by the train line—I spot a group of people hanging out where the street comes to a dead end, near a hole in a chain-link fence. Sweating and anxious, I stop for a second and look around. I'm never comfortable doing this in a place where I don't know who I can trust, but it's like I have a magnet inside me, pulling me through the curled-back edges of the cut metal.

"What's up?" asks a skinny white guy in his early twenties. He's scraping resin from a pipe—not trying to hide what he's doing, but his tone is a bit aggressive.

"Who's got?" I say, getting straight to the point.

He checks me out, but I'm dressed a bit scruffy so I fit in with the crowd by the fence—and I'm sure I've got that desperate look no undercover cop can convincingly pull off.

"See that dude over there?" he says, nodding at a guy sitting on an overturned bucket. "He's not gonna serve you but I can hook you up."

"Let me try it first," I tell him. "I don't want to waste my money on crap." Really, I don't want to give him a lot of cash and watch him run off, but it's always good to make sure you're not buying baking soda or some toxic cut.

"No problem. Gimme ten bucks and I'll get you a dime. But I get a blast for fixing you up."

I hand over nine dollars—paying full price makes you look easy—and watch the deal go down. The guy selling glances over at me, breaks a few rocks from an eight ball, and hands them to my new friend, who hurries back. "Me first," he says, sticking a rock in his stem and lighting up. I'm salivating just watching him, getting a bit pissed at how long he's holding on to the pipe.

"Alright, my turn," I say, grabbing it and adding another rock. The minute I inhale it hits me—my ears are ringing, my heart's racing, my whole body is tingling as waves of euphoria rush through me. The high is so intense I almost feel like I'm gonna throw up. It must show on my face 'cause when I open my eyes this kid is grinning at me like I've just had the best hit of my life.

"That's some real eighties shit," he says. "Bet you'll be back for more."

Forget coming back, I'm thinking, pulling small bills from my pockets and one of my socks. "Get me five for forty dollars—and I'll give you another rock for your pipe."

"Oh, he's a smart one," says a woman wearing a cheap sparkly dress. "Don't give it all away at once."

Once I have the crack and the pipe—which he'd totally scraped clean—the guy with the eight ball saunters up beside me. "I'm usually here or up by the Greyhound stop, near Fourth and Elgin," he says. "Always got that good shit."

"Thanks, but I'm only in town for a few days. This should get me through."

"Well, you know where I'm at."

On the way back to the hotel, I pass a park with these weird sculptures—twisting metal poles with plastic laundry baskets attached to the ends. I take a picture with my phone and send it to Susan. "Rubbish," is all I write.

THE NEXT MORNING, I take the elevator down to the hotel lobby to meet the writer. She's in from London doing a story about the death penalty—the magazine hired me to shoot the photos.

Looking at myself in the elevator mirror, I wish I'd gotten more sleep last night. My eyes are a bit bloodshot and my head feels thick and heavy.

Today we're going to meet a guy who helped get lethal injection passed when he was a young congressman, arguing that it was a more humane way to execute people than the electric chair. Now he's an Anglican priest in his sixties and a very vocal opponent of the death penalty. So am I—no matter how you do it, the whole concept seems totally barbaric.

Once we get to the church, he takes us to his quarters and tells us about his life. I shoot a few portraits of him in between the writer's questions. He's relaxed and doesn't mind being photographed, which is half the battle with people you've just met. Sometimes I only get five minutes with someone who's impatient about giving up any of their time.

"Can you go stand in that corner?" I ask, trying to catch his reflection in a mirror on the opposite wall. "That's great—just turn your body to the right and your head a little to the left. Okay, now look straight into the lens."

I shoot a couple of Polaroids, check the image, then replace the Polaroid cartridge with film. After taking some more pictures, I thank him and tell him I'm all set. I've done a lot of work for this magazine, so I know I've got what they want.

While he finishes getting ready for the service, the writer and I find a place to sit in a pew at the back of the church. It's one of those huge Gothic cathedrals with really high ceilings and lots of stained-glass windows. As the choir streams in—dressed in white robes, already singing—I take some photos of them lining up by the altar.

"My mum will be happy to hear that I went to church," I joke, picturing her heading off to church every Sunday in Scotland. But as soon as the service starts, I tune it out and let my mind wander.

It's strange to think that I'm in the same city where Larry Clark shot the photos in his book *Tulsa:* grainy black-and-white pictures of the people he did drugs with when he lived here in the 1960s. I used to spend hours looking at that book when I was at art school in London. All the photos were so different from the American kids I saw in movies growing up. But now that I've lived here for fourteen years, I've seen a lot of things that don't match that Hollywood image.

With the music lulling me to sleep, I have to fight hard to stay awake, so it's a relief when the service ends and the three of us head to a bar for lunch. I can't resist taking some pictures of the priest in his white collar with a pint in front of him, but I've got what I need so I leave them to finish their interview, detouring to the Greyhound station on the way back to the hotel. My stash from yesterday didn't last as long as I'd hoped.

As I'm walking, I'm looking for a mailbox so I can send a postcard to Susan. It's one of those old Kodak photo postcards, but instead of printing an image on one side I left it blank and wrote on the other side: "*Thinking, Smiling, Thinking, Laughing, Thinking . . .*"

I just want her to know I'm thinking about her, so I'm going to send her a postcard every day I'm in Tulsa. That's mostly how we've been communicating this summer: email, text messages, postcards, and photos. Last week she sent me a bunch of pictures from her trip to Fire Island. In one of them she's standing next to a street sign that says SUSAN—wearing the bikini I bought her in Hawaii. I usually like getting photos from her, but that one left me sort of gutted. It was like she was saying, "*I'm all yours if you just get your shit together.*"

I hate being in limbo like this, not knowing if we're together or apart. It's like we've broken up without really going our separate ways. Part of me wants to cut it off and stop putting us both through this pain, but then this little glimmer of hope always turns into a burning desire to see her—and when I do, I know I'm not gonna be the one to walk away. But maybe she'll finally decide to do it. Like my mum said when I told her we were taking a break: "Absence can make the heart grow fonder, but after a while it grows indifferent."

To be honest, I'm not really sure what Susan wants. All she's said is that she can't be in a relationship with me until I've gotten clean, but I wish she knew how fucking hard I'm trying. I quit dope a couple of months ago—on my own, no detox or rehab. It was brutal, white-knuckling it after Liam left for Scotland. That's why I went ballistic when Susan accused me of using when we went to see Joan Didion do a reading in Central Park. I really wasn't doing *any* heroin. I just took a little Xanax so I wouldn't get too anxious, but I hadn't been sleeping much so it really hit me. All I remember was feeling so tired I couldn't keep my eyes open. Then when Susan nudged me awake and asked what I'd taken—in that disappointed, accusing tone—I lost it. I knew I was being a cunt, but I couldn't stop myself. I stormed off and left her crying in the park. After going through the hell of kicking, it really pissed me off to have her doubt me.

I wish she could see that I'm doing my best, but I feel like I'm under a microscope and every little thing I do is examined and questioned. I know I'm not perfect—I'm just trying to get better, bit by bit, and when I slip it gets thrown in my face like I've made no attempt whatsoever to get clean. Every explanation is treated like a lie—even if it's the truth—or a feeble excuse that would be no big deal if someone else said it.

That's when I want to go back to the one thing I know will ease all the pain, and it is so fucking hard not to give in to that temptation. But I finally feel like I'm at the point where things are under control, especially now that I'm working again. I just need a little more time to kick this last habit—I couldn't do it all at once.

After I get back to the hotel, I watch TV, sort through my film, and smoke some crack. Not a lot—just enough to keep the craving at bay. My phone buzzes: It's a text from Susan.

"Found this online," it says. "What do you get when you cross ESP with PMS?"

Not waiting for me to guess the answer, she's written: "A bitch who knows everything."

That freaks me out. She has this way of popping up when I least want her on my mind.

I put the phone under the pillow and click the lighter a few times, waiting for that nice blue flame. The thing is, she doesn't know everything, and I feel bad about that. But I don't think she'd understand even if I did try to tell her.

ON MONDAY NIGHT, after hours of wandering around Tulsa's less scenic neighborhoods, I finally decide to call Susan.

"I was wondering what happened to you," she says. "I've sent you a couple of messages but I wasn't sure if you got them."

"I did, but I've been pretty busy since I got here. We went to church yesterday to meet with the priest—that was sort of weird, sitting there listening to his sermon—and today I've been running around getting ready for the shoot tomorrow. Did you get my postcards?"

"Postcards?" Susan laughs. "You know, technology has really progressed in the last decade. You can send messages instantly now."

"Listen, anyone can send an email or a text message. But who else is gonna send you a postcard from Tulsa?"

"That's true. What's it like?"

"Kind of boring. We're driving down to McAlester tomorrow so I'm trying to decide if I'm going to watch the execution. I can't take pictures inside the prison anyway, so I don't *have* to go, but I feel bad telling the writer I'm gonna skip it. I'm just not sure watching someone get killed would be good for my state of mind right now."

"Well, don't do it then. You know what you can handle. Just tell her you want to focus on getting some good pictures."

Susan always has a practical solution—I should listen to her more often.

"What else have you been up to?" she asks.

"Walking around town, taking some photos, just hanging out, really . . ." I feel a wave of guilt looking at the remnants of crack lying on the nightstand, but I push it away. It's always a relief when we can get through a conversation without talking about whether I've really quit or what I'm still using. Lately, I think Susan has been trying to be encouraging—without getting drawn into all the specifics.

"How are things with you?" I ask, hoping to head her off before she goes there. "I got the pictures you sent from Fire Island."

"I thought you'd like the one I took of the ferry, with the late afternoon light reflecting off the boat. It seemed like a very Graham MacIndoe photo."

"Not bad, but I think there are still a few things I can teach you. Maybe you can assist me sometime—I've got another job when I get back to New York."

"That's great," Susan says, sounding like my parents whenever I tell them I'm working. "What's the assignment?"

"A portrait of Andy Murray's coach for some tennis magazine. The editor used to live in Edinburgh so it must've been the Scottish connection that got me the job."

We talk for a while about Andy Murray—he grew up in a town near my parents—and Susan's record when she was captain of her high school tennis team. She tells me she hated all the pressure and wished she'd played doubles instead of singles. It makes me happy that we can still talk like this, but sometimes it feels like we're avoiding the real issue: whether our relationship has any kind of future. I'd like to think we can try again, but I don't know if she'll ever be able to trust me.

After we hang up, I rummage around in my bag and pull out another Kodak photo postcard to send her. On one side I write, *"Suzie, Thinking of you always. Love, Graham. Xxx."* On the other side I draw two hearts, with a line stretching between them in black pen.

WHEN THE WRITER and I pull up to the Oklahoma State Penitentiary the next day, there's a sign that makes me want to jump out of the car. "Drug detector canines are in use at this facility," it says. I'm wearing the same clothes I had on when I was smoking crack last night, so I'm panicking as we roll up to the checkpoint and hand over our IDs.

"Here for the execution?" the guard asks, checking a sheet of paper for our names. "You can park in front of the visitors' center on the left."

Walking toward the entrance, I'm on the lookout for dogs—*they'll sniff me out in a heartbeat,* I'm thinking. But once I realize that's probably for inmate visits, I relax a bit. The prison building is painted white, which gives it a less threatening feel. There's razor wire all around and giant floodlights next to the guard towers, but otherwise it's all sort of bland. I'm already wondering how I'm going to get any good photos out of this, especially since I'm not allowed to take pictures inside the prison.

Inside there's a media center set up, with plates of cookies and coffee on a foldout table. I read the fact sheet about the prisoner who's about to be executed, which describes his crime in horrific detail: A handyman shows up on the doorstep of a woman he's done work for and asks if he can borrow some money. She offers him ten dollars, he demands more and ends up stabbing her with a knife and a pair of scissors. The crime scene photos leave nothing to the imagination—her bloody body left for her husband to find. I don't believe in the death penalty, but it's hard to feel any compassion for someone who can do that to another human being.

Eventually two reporters from local newspapers turn up, then a spokesman comes in with a press release describing the prisoner's last meal: a pepperoni pizza with extra mushrooms and a large grape soda. Everyone is talking about the new fifteen-dollar limit on last meals and how people love talking about what they'd request. Listening to the prison guy describe the procedure for the execution—in a detached, businesslike manner—I'm glad I decided not to witness it. That's not something I want stamped on my memory forever.

The Xanax I took to level myself out this morning is wearing off, so I'm starting to feel a bit claustrophobic and jumpy. I need to get out and get some air. But once I step outside, it's warm and sticky—and so deadly quiet it's hard to believe I'm surrounded by hundreds of maximum-security prisoners. I wonder what's going on behind those walls, what all the inmates have done, and whether they know someone on death row is about to die.

I'm still keeping my eyes peeled for sniffer dogs as I pull out my camera and take a few photos—mostly of the guard towers, the high walls, and the building. Heading back toward the checkpoint, I'm trying to figure out what else I can photograph when the guard sticks his head out of his booth and tells me there are some protesters gathering just outside the main gate.

"There used to be a lot more of them but now it's only the hardcore ones that come," he says. "We don't mind as long as they stay off the main road—don't want anyone getting killed."

I expected the guards to be gruff and aggressive but so far they seem pretty friendly—then again, I'm not a prisoner.

As I pass through the gate I see a group of people gathered in a circle by the side of the road with their heads bowed. One of them is a priest and seems to be leading everyone in prayer. I take a few shots of the group—trying to get the prison in the background, with their rosaries hanging from their hands—then I notice a young guy wearing a vintage Clash T-shirt. He's got a video camera so I ask what he's filming.

"A project for school," he says, not taking his eye from the viewfinder. "I'm doing a media course and thought this could be a good story."

He lowers the camera and we talk for a bit about incarceration, the death penalty, and how many people are in prison because of drugs. "You wouldn't believe how many meth labs there are around here," he tells me. "*Hillbilly speed,* they call it."

A few other protesters have joined the group so I take some more pictures—crawling into the middle of the circle and lying on my back so I can shoot them silhouetted against the sky. I get some weird looks but I'm trying hard to pull some good images out of a tough situation and these finally feel like they'll work.

When I walk back through the prison gate, I notice a sign on a little building saying OKLAHOMA STATE PENITENTIARY HISTORICAL MUSEUM, which seems totally bizarre. It's closed, but I can see some of the exhibits through the windows. Along one wall there's a display of all the shanks confiscated from prisoners over the years, a collection of mug shots, and a door leading to "Old Sparky," the electric chair put into retirement when Oklahoma switched to lethal injection. I wonder who ever comes here— I doubt anyone visiting an inmate gives a shit about the history of the prison.

It's almost six o'clock by the time I wander back to the media center, trying to imagine what's going on in the execution chamber right now. It all seems so surreal—that as I'm standing here a bit bored, someone's life is about to end. The minutes pass. I wonder if he's dead yet. How long it took. What he said at the end.

I'm still standing in the parking lot when a prison van pulls up and everyone who witnessed the execution jumps out. An official heads down toward the protesters to tell them the prisoner was pronounced dead at 6:11 P.M. I see the writer—she looks a bit stunned. I'm sort of curious about what she's thinking, but I don't feel like asking her what it was like to watch.

The prison spokesman is talking with the two local reporters and a couple of other people I didn't notice before. "I can't believe he didn't apologize," one of them says. "He actually said his life had been a blast."

I'm half-listening to their conversation, anxious to get going, when I overhear something that stops me cold. It turns out that when the guy who was just executed committed the murder, he was high on crack. Hearing that word usually triggers a craving, but this time it has the opposite effect. Because some of what you hear about crack making people crazy is true. It hasn't ever affected me that way, but I've seen it—some people do really fucked-up shit because they're desperate for a hit.

CHAPTER NINE

December 2006
Upper West Side, Manhattan

By December, a year after I went over to Graham's house to get my picture taken, the ambiguity of our relationship came to a head. For most of the fall, I'd been focused on my own well-being and career, and Graham (I hoped) was busy working on his. We still talked often, and saw each other occasionally—usually in public, so we wouldn't be tempted to fall back into bed. But I was spending more weekends away from the city, taking the train out to Montauk or driving up to the Hudson Valley with friends. I missed being with Graham, but putting a little more distance between us made me feel like I could breathe again.

That's not to say we weren't close. If anything, I was leaning on him more than he was leaning on me. I'd been seeing David pretty regularly, learning how to open up more as we excavated my past. It wasn't easy for me, but I was beginning to feel things more deeply, and to express those emotions—tentatively, sometimes awkwardly—and the person I felt safest doing that with was Graham. He was a sensitive sounding board when all that mucking around in my mind got to be too intense.

Graham often mentioned his own therapist, Debi, who seemed to be helping him. He'd quote her advice about not letting frustration and anger ferment into negative thoughts, which led to irrational actions—even putting that advice into practice. He'd hang up if we were starting to get into a fight, telling me he wanted to cool down first so he didn't say something he might regret. And his emails were more lucid, with thoughtful observations about addiction. He really did seem to be on the right track. But when we

did get together—to look at art or have dinner—his mood sometimes shifted abruptly, and I couldn't tell if drugs were to blame.

He swore he'd been off heroin since his detox in June. "I'm not
using," he insisted whenever I asked. At that point, that was the
truth in Graham's head: "Using" meant heroin; crack or prescription drugs were different. It was almost like he'd bought into that
"at least I'm not a junkie" mentality. But at the time, I didn't know
for sure where he was on the recovery spectrum. He'd drop hints
occasionally, admitting he wasn't "one hundred percent," which
was the main reason I wasn't rushing into getting back together.

In some sense, we were in the same place as when we first
started dating—except there was no question that I still loved him.
I just didn't know if I could ever be with him again. That uncertainty was tearing him apart, so as the holidays rolled around, he
started pushing for some kind of resolution, emailing me the question I wasn't ready to address.

> *When you get back from thanksgiving can we sit down and
> talk about us? it's been a long time and much as i want to
> be with you, wake up with you, share my life with you i
> can't live indefinately in a sort of limbo just waiting. its not
> the torture it used to be - thank fuck! but i find it hard not
> to reach out and hold your hand or hug you or give you a
> kiss. so you see i'm still walking a tight rope in some
> respects - and i don't wanna fall.*

It was mid-December by the time we made plans to meet. But
when I emailed Graham on Friday asking when he wanted to get
together over the weekend, he didn't write back. At first I was
relieved—I didn't know what I was going to tell him. But by Saturday night, I was pissed. *How did he expect me to even consider
rekindling our relationship when he couldn't be bothered to answer my message?*

On Sunday morning I got a call from his ex-wife Anna, asking if I'd heard from Graham.

"Actually, we were supposed to see each other this weekend," I told her. "But I haven't heard from him so I'm not sure what's going on."

"He's been arrested," she said, without further preamble. "There was an explosion at his house that blew out some of the windows. Liam found out when he went over to see Graham."

I was stunned. "An explosion?"

"I don't think they know what caused it, but there was glass everywhere and now the police are searching the house."

"Is Graham okay?"

"It doesn't sound like anyone was hurt."

I was too shocked to ask anything else. After we hung up, I immediately hopped on the subway to Brooklyn. This I had to see for myself.

WHEN I GOT to Graham's house, it was officially a crime scene, with yellow police tape stretched across the front door, plywood covering the windows, and a plainclothes officer standing guard outside.

Just like the night I surprised Graham on New Year's Eve, I had to muster up the courage to open the gate and walk up the steps. Masquerading as a nosy neighbor, I asked the cop what was going on.

He was happy to share plenty of theories with me—and apparently, anyone else who asked: an explosive device, possibly a meth lab, something about a weapon.

A bomb? Crystal meth? A weapon? I knew Graham was hiding things from me, but none of that sounded at all like him.

"He's not a terrorist or a drug dealer," I wanted to say, but then I realized I should keep my mouth shut. I didn't want this guy asking if I knew the owner of the house, which might lead to other questions.

So instead of meeting Graham to talk about whether our relationship had a future, I met Anna at the Brooklyn courthouse to try to find out what had happened. We barely knew each other, but we were both relieved to be navigating this ordeal together.

It was a surreal introduction to the city's criminal justice system, which seemed designed to punish those of us deemed guilty by association—with someone who hadn't been convicted. The phone numbers we were given by the police rang without anyone picking up. At the courthouse downtown, the information window opened sporadically without revealing any answers. Every couple of hours, a clerk would tape a sheet of paper to the wall listing the defendants due to be arraigned in the next session. We'd all crowd around to search for a name, then sit back down on the hard wooden benches.

For a while, the cop-show quality of the experience distracted me from the emotional impact of the day's events. But as the afternoon faded into evening and Anna left to get dinner for Liam, there was no escape from the questions ricocheting around my head. *Was this all some post 9/11 overreaction, exacerbated by Graham's foreign accent and anti-authoritarian temper? Or was he guilty of crimes I couldn't even imagine?*

The waiting, the not knowing, was excruciating, finally propelling me to approach the information window again—to take action.

"Your first time here?" asked the male clerk who had taken over window duty. The question bordered on flirtatious, so I seized the opportunity to get some answers.

"It is," I said, playing the girl in over her head. "This is all kind of overwhelming so I'm hoping you can help me—I'm trying to find out what happened to my friend."

It turned out Graham had been arrested on a drug possession

charge, a misdemeanor. But there was a problem with the paper-work, the clerk told me—a sketchy search warrant, I guessed. He said he doubted that Graham's case would be heard that night.

"Is there any information about an explosion?" I asked. "Or a weapons charge?"

The clerk typed, then paused, then typed some more, staring at a monitor that looked like it was decades old. Trying to look grate-ful, I leaned in, hoping to see what was written on his screen.

"I'm afraid that's all I can tell you," he said, abruptly clicking something that made the text on his computer disappear. I thanked him and returned to my seat.

It was almost midnight when I left the courthouse, but before going home I stopped by Graham's house and used my key to let myself in. The cop and the yellow police tape were gone, but it still looked like a crime scene. I was stunned by the violence of the mess.

Whatever the police were searching for, they were way more thorough than I'd ever been—pouring boxes of cereal and cans of coffee on the floor, ripping open couch cushions, emptying draw-ers, pulling books from the shelves, all left in piles that suggested an angry trajectory.

I didn't turn on any lights, but the streetlamps lit random ob-jects in the shadows. In the bedroom downstairs, I picked up a box from a pregnancy test we'd once bought, an unused wand still intact. That's where I'd stashed the crack pipe I found the night of my book party, hiding the box in a wicker hamper. The pipe was gone. *Had the cops found it?* I panicked as I realized I never threw it away.

That was followed by relief that the pregnancy scare was a false alarm. I couldn't imagine having a child with someone who was locked up in jail, but I felt bad for Anna—and Liam. I hoped he hadn't come inside and seen any of this.

Down the hall in Graham's office, I couldn't find his laptop, my mind racing through all the emails we'd sent mentioning drugs. *Could they be used as evidence? Would I have to testify about what I knew?* Then again, I didn't know anything that might explain what led to this destruction.

Stepping through the chaos, I noticed there were photos scattered on the floor, as if a pile had been picked up from the desk, thumbed through, and tossed aside. They were pictures from our trip to Hawaii, but now the happy caption I'd imagined had changed.

Seeing my face trampled on the floor felt like a personal violation—a hot flash of lightning cutting through the brewing storm of my outrage. The cops had made a wreck of the most intimate parts of our lives, but Graham had exposed us to this. This was where his drug habit led.

THE NEXT DAY, I went by myself to the arraignment, sliding across a bench in the courtroom where a bailiff directed me. I hadn't eaten or slept much, so I leaned my head on my hand for support, looking up when the door at the back of the room opened and a line of defendants shuffled in.

I saw Graham before he noticed me, a jolt of recognition that made my heart race as I visually patted him down, searching for clues. He was wearing jeans, sneakers, and a navy hooded sweatshirt—typical attire on the streets of New York, but in a courtroom, his outfit said "hoodlum." At first I was relieved that he seemed okay, not visibly hurt or dope sick, which I took as a sign that maybe he hadn't been using.

But once he looked my way, we had a charged silent exchange, communicating all the emotions of the moment through an intense long-distance stare. He seemed surprised to see me, but not necessarily glad I was there, gratitude and shame trading places on his face as he reached up to brush a finger under his eye, then fix his hair.

The message I sent was a calculated combination of worry, disappointment, and anger—communicated through the slump of my body, the hardened line of my lips, and the watery blink of my gaze. As much as I told myself I'd gone to the arraignment because I needed to find out what had happened, I was mostly there because I wanted him to see how I felt. He once told me he was always taking pictures in his head—that he didn't need a camera—so this was one image I wanted him to have.

It still wasn't clear if Graham was guilty of any crime, and the brief proceedings didn't produce any answers. When his case was called, a heavy, court-appointed lawyer shuffled up to represent him, a cliché with his stack of folders and harried manner. But no one from the police department or the DA's office was there to present any evidence, so the judge adjourned the hearing, setting bail at $1,500.

The mention of bail took me by surprise, since that wasn't the reason I'd gone to the arraignment. I had no idea how to bail someone out of jail. I also wasn't sure I wanted to do Graham that favor.

IT WAS A week before Christmas, and for the next twenty-four hours, I felt like I was living inside my own Dickensian tale, escorted by ghosts from the future, present, and past. But mostly it was the ghost from the future that held my hand, showing me a life I didn't want to have.

After a crash course in posting bail, via Google and calls to lawyers and the New York City Department of Correction, I learned that a bondsman wouldn't handle a measly $1,500 bail. I'd have to pay it in person—and because the fax machine at the

Manhattan Detention Complex wasn't working, I'd have to go to Rikers Island, where Graham had been transferred.

This information was communicated to me by an unhelpful clerk—as if the connection between a broken fax machine and my bail money made perfect sense.

I was tempted to let Graham stew in a cell until his next hearing, and didn't especially want to drain my bank account on his behalf. But Anna had called his parents in Scotland, and they'd promised to wire the money, so I said I'd handle the payment. They couldn't stand the thought of their son spending Christmas in jail—and as mad as I was, neither could I.

Still, I was nervous about going out to Rikers Island carrying $1,500 in cash. On the subway, I kept reaching into my bag to feel the thick envelope of bills, sure I was telegraphing "mug me" to anyone who looked my way. When I got out of the subway in Queens, I had to ask a traffic cop where to catch the bus to Rikers Island, mortified to admit where I was headed. But once I boarded the nearly empty bus, I relaxed a little—I wasn't likely to get robbed on a shuttle to jail.

Although I'd set off with scenes from Hollywood prison movies looping in my head, Rikers Island was much less imposing than I expected. Since it's next to LaGuardia Airport, there are no high-rises or towers; only the razor wire on the chain-link fence around the buildings seemed sinister. I had to leave my cellphone and iPod in a locker outside, but even the security screening compared favorably with most airports: There was no line, I didn't have to give up my water bottle, and no one yelled at me.

It wasn't until a guard gave me a form to fill out that the grim reality of the situation set in.

"This will take two to three hours," he said.

I told him I wasn't planning on waiting for the inmate I was springing.

"It takes that long to process the bail," he explained. "You have to stay."

Suddenly, I felt like I was in jail.

The guard directed me to a line of people in the next room, who were waiting to be helped by three clerks sitting behind thick windows. It felt like the post office, except you couldn't leave in a huff over the glacial pace of service. I decided that the sharpest employee was a large woman with a sign posted on her window saying, "Attitudes adjusted while you wait." I got a break: When her window cleared, it was my turn.

I handed her my form, half-expecting to be complimented for remembering all the codes I'd collected over the previous few days: an arrest number, a New York State ID number, a docket number, a "book and case" number, a charge number, even a number indicating which jail Graham was in.

But she just gave it a cursory glance and told me I could take a seat. Flirting clearly wasn't going to get me anywhere with her.

Eyeing the crowd in a row of molded plastic chairs facing the clerks' windows—mostly women bailing out wayward men— I wandered to another part of the room, but a different guard intercepted me and told me I had to sit with everyone else. It seemed bossy at first, but since we were in the same place where they process inmates being released, I figured the point was to herd us together so they could keep an eye on things.

The room had the bright fluorescent lighting that makes you long for a dimmer, two machines dispensing sodas and snacks, and a pay phone that was monopolized by a woman speaking a language someone guessed was Chinese—as in, "That Chinese lady been on the phone *forever*."

In the chair next to me, a girl who seemed about twenty was eating chicken and rice out of a Styrofoam container. It smelled awful, and she kept complaining that it tasted terrible, so I wished she'd just throw it away. But she was also the main diversion in our corridor of captivity—directing inattentive people in line to the next open window, bemoaning the long wait, at one point jumping up to explain why a skinny guy with jeans hanging off his hips was declining the MetroCard inmates are given when they're released.

"He don't want no MetroCard because he got a *ride*!" she shouted at a male clerk who was having communication difficulties. Frankly, the possibility of getting picked up at Rikers Island hadn't occurred to me, either, but I was relieved that Graham would have a way to get home without me waiting.

It was too dark to see anything out of the window at one end of the room, but I pictured Graham somewhere on the island, sitting on a bunk bed, staring blankly ahead, with nothing to do except contemplate how his life had gone off the rails. That image made my heart ache, then clench—I was feeling claustrophobic myself. I turned away from the window, pushed those thoughts out of my head. I wanted to be angry, not sympathetic.

My talkative neighbor had fallen into a conversation with a young dark-haired woman who had been stuck in this room all day, waiting for bail paperwork in transit from Manhattan. At first, I just listened in: how the chatty girl's last boyfriend had been at Rikers for a year, how she used to come see him every week, how she had to wait several hours for a one-hour visit, how the screening process for inmate visits was much more of an ordeal.

"Your body gets used to it," she said, explaining how she adjusted to the routine—the subway and bus rides, the searches, the long waits. Despite her complaints, she understood something about the bureaucracy that hadn't dawned on me yet.

"They got to make it a *process*," she said, drawing out the last word. "They got to teach you a lesson so you rain down hell on the guy that brought you here."

It was an interesting theory, though clearly it hadn't turned out to be enough of a deterrent in her case, since here she was posting bail for a new man. But she swore she wasn't going to go through that visiting nightmare again. The other young woman just nodded her head, surprisingly calm given how long she'd been waiting.

After a couple of hours, just as our confinement began to feel unbearable, the sharp clerk told the chatty girl her paperwork would be ready soon. We all got excited because it meant things were actually happening, that we weren't waiting in vain. Feeling optimistic, I went to the window to see if my paperwork was coming along, too, but it was clear from the clerk's question—"What's the inmate's name?"—that it hadn't been on the tip of her tongue lately.

"The thing is, I have to pick up my son," I blurted out, instantly regretting the lie but forging ahead. "You said it was going to take three hours, and it's already been more than two, so if it's going to take a lot longer, I don't know what I'm going to do. . . ."

She eyed me warily but picked up the phone, calling someone I pictured at a metal desk piled high with papers. "I know you're busy," she said, using the syrupy voice people resort to when they need a favor, "but could you check on the status of some paperwork for me?"

While she was on hold, I stood there burning with shame, desperate to get back to my chair. Finally, someone came back on the line with an answer.

"They're really backed up," the clerk told me, hanging up. "But they're working on it."

I thanked her and slunk back to my seat, horrified that I had invented an imaginary child to elicit sympathy. I didn't believe in recovery theories about hitting bottom being a catalyst for change—you could always sink lower, it seemed—but this whole experience was a new nadir for me.

Not long after I sat down, the clerk called the chatty girl's name. While she was at the window, I started talking to the other young woman, who was posting bail for her ex-boyfriend—as a favor to his parents, who lived in another state. After sharing her tale, she asked me the question that had been on my mind, too: "What are you doing here?"

I told her an abridged half-truth—that a friend had been arrested on a drug possession charge, and that his parents also lived far away.

"You're a good friend to come all the way out here," she said, obliquely suggesting I find some new friends. That might've been presumptuous in another context, but at the moment it struck me as wise—even caring.

When the clerk finally called my name, I felt bad that she didn't have news for my serene seatmate, but I grabbed my bag and hustled up to the window. First, I had to confirm that the tiny black-and-white copy of a photo she showed me was Graham—a grainy image that triggered a sharp pang of pain.

"Is this him?" the clerk asked, her long fingernail tapping the picture.

No, I wanted to say, that isn't him. This isn't me, this isn't my life, that scowling guy isn't the man I ached for back in Christmas past. Numbly, I nodded instead.

Then she carefully placed sheets of carbon paper between the pages of a bail receipt and handed me the thick form to sign. "Press hard," she said. "You're making five copies."

I pointed out that Graham's name was spelled wrong, but she said it didn't matter. I wasn't going to delay the proceedings by protesting, so I signed and handed over the stack of fifty-dollar bills I'd withdrawn from the bank that morning. It seemed like days ago in a place very far away. The clerk counted the money using one of those machines that spins the bills, then put the cash in a big Ziploc bag with a copy of the bail receipt.

"This will take another fifteen minutes," she said, offering no explanation for why I had to wait.

In fact, I had no idea what transpired behind the bank of windows while I was there, what paperwork was shuffled, faxed, or delivered by hand. But the whole process did take nearly three hours, and as I said goodbye to the dark-haired woman, I wondered how long she'd have to wait. I gave her my copy of *The New York Times* and wrote my name and phone number on the front page, well aware that we'd never speak again. Before long, the clerk called my name.

"You're free to go," she said. I couldn't remember the last time I had so viscerally experienced what that means.

As I waited for the bus to take me away from Rikers Island, shivering by the parking lot but unwilling to spend any more time inside, I thought bailing Graham out of jail would be the last thing I'd do for him—that it would release me to walk away for good. But bailing out has different meanings, and it turns out leaping overboard wasn't the one that came naturally to me.

When you're in a rowboat that's taking on water, bailing out can mean scooping up the water and dumping it over the side, over and over again. As long as you keep at it, you can keep the boat from sinking—save everyone, save yourself. And for a while, it works. You feel like you could keep up this rhythm forever: scraping a plastic cup along the bottom of the boat, lifting it up, pouring out the water. But it's exhausting. Your arms begin to throb with pain; everywhere else goes numb. Finally, as the water rises and the boat really starts to sink, you realize the only option left is the other kind of bailing out—to jump.

It's not about saving yourself, because once you take that leap, you'll still be out there in the unknown, drifting away from the boat that's disappearing as you helplessly watch it go down. You'll still need someone to come along and save you, or hope you somehow make it to shore.

When Graham called that night to thank me, as he waited for the same bus hours later, I was too angry to talk, too fed up for apologies, too tired for all his dubious explanations. And yet for a while I listened, scared of what would happen to us both if I hung up, abandoned ship, let go.

CHAPTER TEN

December 2006
Boerum Hill, Brooklyn

I'm downstairs hanging out with a couple of pals when out of nowhere there's a loud BOOM right above our heads. I hear the sharp shatter of broken glass hitting the street and small rocks rattling inside the walls—then it's dead quiet.

"What the fuck was that?" Tye says, jumping up and looking out the window. "There's glass everywhere, man! That sounded like a fucking bomb!" He backs away from the window and stares at the ceiling like it's going to fall in on us. Izzy is too caught up in her high to realize what's going on.

I run up the stairs and the first thing I see are the two front windows completely blown out, shards of glass everywhere and papers strewn all over the floor. It looks like a mini tornado spun through my living room, did a few laps, and escaped by bursting through the windows. There's no fire, no smoke, no clue as to what really happened.

I can hear sirens in the distance and see neighbors opening their doors. Tye comes up behind me, takes one look at the mess, and says, "I can't be dealing with this shit. Call me later—I'm outta here."

Rushing back downstairs, I shout at Izzy to gather up any drugs and get the fuck out before the police show up. She's moving painfully slow, so I grab her stuff, shove it in her bag, and hustle her out the door below the stoop. She hesitates, like she doesn't know where to go.

"Move, Izzy!" I yell, following her out to the front yard. "The cops are going to be here any second."

People are gathering in the street, staring at the broken window frames and the glass covering the sidewalk. I take a quick look at the damage and head back inside before any of them can ask what's going on.

Within minutes, a bunch of uniformed cops are streaming into the house, followed by firefighters weighed down with equipment. They immediately start bombarding me with questions: "What caused the explosion? Where were you? Is anyone else in the building? Was anyone injured?"

I tell them I have no idea what happened—maybe it was a gas leak—but it doesn't seem to be sinking in because they keep asking me the same things over and over.

As the minutes pass, I get more and more anxious, wondering if there are any drugs left in the house. The way these cops are nosing into everything seems overly aggressive—turning over couch cushions, looking behind furniture, opening cabinets. I'm just about to say something when one of the firefighters announces, "This is what caused it—an air canister for a BB gun." He's holding up a ruptured gray cylinder, torn metal sticking out from one side. "It was behind the radiator. Must've blown when the heat came on."

How did that get in here? I'm thinking—then the answer hits me. Now I know I'm fucked.

As I walk toward him to get a better look, I catch the scene outside the house. It's like something out of *NYPD Blue*—police cars, an ambulance, people gawking, yellow tape being tied to the fence. One cop is shouting at everyone to move back. A nervous panic washes through me. I wish I'd bounced with Tye and come back later acting shocked, but it's too late for that. Before I can get close to the fireman holding the air canister, a couple of cops intercept me. "Where the fuck's the gun?" one barks.

"I've not got a gun," I say—which is true, since it doesn't belong to me. I'm still hoping I can make up some excuse that will get them all to leave.

"You look fucked up—are you on drugs? Are there any drugs in the house? If you don't tell us and we find them, the charges are gonna be a lot worse."

"You know we've got your junkie friend outside," the other one chips in. "One of your neighbors ID'd her and said she left the house after the explosion."

"I don't know who you're talking about," I say. "I'm the only one here."

"Don't give us that shit," says a female cop joining the circle. "She already told us she was with you."

Suddenly, questions are coming at me from all directions: "Who was the guy running from the house? . . . Does he have the gun? . . . Are you holding for him? . . . Is he your dealer?"

My head is spinning. I just want to crawl into bed and make it all go away. They're half-pushing me back downstairs with threats of arrest for withholding evidence. I'm hoping they're bullshitting about Izzy—and that she took the last of the crack with her.

Downstairs, two cops are rummaging through the desk in my room, pulling stuff out of drawers, checking pens and lighters, and dumping everything on the floor.

"Tell us where the gun and the drugs are or we'll tear this fucking place apart," says the guy who seems to be in charge. I feel sick—I don't know what to do. They don't have a warrant so I'm not sure if they can really search my house. But that doesn't seem to matter—they're already rifling through everything and seem intent on keeping at it.

I swallow hard and brace myself, knowing this may be a bad move. "Okay, listen. There is a BB gun in the house, but it's not mine and it's really just a toy. It only fires pellets." I don't tell him it belongs to my son.

I caught Liam playing with it a few weeks ago—he told me he'd gotten it from a kid at school. So I took it off him and hid it in a closet under some towels. It never occurred to me that there was an air canister that went with it. *Why the fuck did he hide that behind the radiator?*

Before I can get mad, one of the other cops turns around with something he's found in a box on my desk. "Look what we've got here," he says. He's holding up a broken piece of crack pipe for everyone to see—a blue rubber glove covering his hand.

Instantly, I'm up against the wall being cuffed.

"You can make things easier and tell us where the gun is, or you can leave it up to us. Either way we're going to find it—and the drugs."

"Alright, give me a second," I say, trying not to sound as scared as I really am. "It's in the hall closet, on the bottom shelf, under the towels. It's just a toy and there aren't any pellets. It's not mine," I add, already knowing they won't believe that.

Two cops are holding me roughly by the arms, the cuffs digging into my wrists as they drag me into the hall. I watch as another one opens the closet door, throws a bunch of towels and toiletries aside, and pulls out the gun. A satisfied grin spreads across his face as he drops it into an evidence bag.

"Take him to the precinct," he says. "And let's find whatever else he's hiding."

"I told you—that's all there is."

As they push me toward the downstairs door, I hear the sound of furniture being shoved around upstairs, feet stomping, and dishes clattering in the kitchen. The last thing I see when I pass by my room is a cop pulling my collection of photography books off the shelves.

It's a bright Saturday morning and my eyes hurt from the light. I'm totally disoriented as I take it all in: the yellow tape, the fire trucks, the broken glass, the neighbors' stares. Once I'm in the back of the squad car, I turn my head and see Izzy sitting in another car looking vacantly ahead. I can't believe she came back— *Why the fuck did she do that? What has she said?*

Two cops jump in the car, turn on the siren, and speed off to the precinct with the light flashing. As they're talking into their radios, I'm trying to grasp what the fuck just happened. One minute I'm hanging out with my pals—listening to music, talking shit—the next thing I know I'm about to get thrown in jail.

I feel sick when I think of Liam seeing this—the house torn apart and me nowhere to be found. He's meant to be coming 'round later, before he heads off for Christmas with his mum. I'd promised him we'd do something fun this weekend, but now he's gonna be faced with whatever mess the cops leave behind. I wish I could call him and warn him not to come. His mum is gonna go ballistic when she finds out.

Then it dawns on me that I'm supposed to meet Susan tomorrow—I've really fucked that up now. I want to bang my head against the divider or pound my fist on the seat, but I'm cuffed so I just clench my fists hard, my nails digging into my palms. It doesn't do any good. I've got no way to block all of this out.

THE FIRST THING I see when we pull up to the station is a huge sign saying: WELCOME TO THE 84TH PRECINCT. *Yeah, right,* I'm thinking, as I'm yanked out of the car by my arm. Inside, we pass people filling out accident reports and reporting thefts. One woman looks up at me warily as I'm buzzed into the secure part of the precinct and hauled up in front of a big desk.

The arresting officer pulls out his pad and reads his notes to the captain on duty. Another cop writes something down in an ancient-looking ledger. I feel so small in front of them I think the desk must be designed to give them a sense of power. I feel even more worthless as I'm led off to the holding cells.

Each cell is about eight by ten feet with bars on the front, an open toilet, and a couple of hard wooden benches. The few people in them are either sleeping or sitting quietly—except for one kid whose hair is half-braided and half-Afro, as if he got arrested in the middle of getting his hair done. He's pacing back and forth rapping to himself, every so often mimicking the sound of gunfire: "blat-blat-blat." I'm locked in a cell with a guy who's curled up and snoring contentedly, like he's home in his own bed.

I pace for a while, trying to get my head around the last hour and how the fuck to deal with it. Putting everything out of my mind is practically impossible, seeing as how the arresting officer keeps coming in and asking me questions. There's a weird smell I can't place—not from the toilets, and not bleach—so that's bugging me when the kid with the half Afro shouts, "Yo, man, what they get you for?"

"Possession," I mumble, not really wanting to get into a cell-to-cell conversation.

"Oh yeah, can't put that rock down once you start, right? I ain't never touched it but that shit's like the devil."

I don't answer. This guy could be a snitch.

Before long, the arresting officer comes in and takes me to a processing room to get fingerprinted. He makes me press hard into the ink pad, then even harder into the little boxes on the card, rolling my fingers from left to right. Even though he's wearing rubber gloves, it's strangely personal to have my fingers manipulated—especially by another man.

"Do you know what I'm being charged with?" I ask.

"We're working that out now," he says, directing me to stand against a wall. "Look straight into the camera."

It's weird being photographed—I'm usually the one doing the picture taking. I wonder if my mug shot will end up online where anybody can see it. He asks me a bunch of questions—address, birth date, Social Security number, ethnicity—all the time writing stuff down or entering it into a computer. He's systematic but slow, so the booking process is starting to feel endless.

"Do you think I'll get out tonight?" I ask.

"That's up to the judge," he says coldly.

He pulls out the bag of property taken from my pockets, counts the coins, rifles through some scraps of paper, and gives me a receipt for my paltry possessions. I wasn't allowed to grab anything except my ID when they arrested me. After photocopying my green card, he hands it back and says, "Hang on to this—you'll need it later."

Back in the cell, I curl up on a bench and rub ink from my fingers with the cuff of my hoodie, trying not to think about Liam. I know he's gonna be crushed—I'd promised him I was getting my shit together. He must've known I wasn't totally clean, but things were definitely getting better. I was going to his soccer games, we'd been hanging out more lately. We were supposed to go pick out his Christmas present this weekend, but there's no chance of that now. I just hope he doesn't find out about the gun.

And then there's Susan—she'll be pissed when I don't call and she can't reach me. But she's used to me being scatterbrained, so maybe if I get out tonight I can make up some excuse for why I disappeared. I'm trying to think of a believable story but I've been up for days and my mind is foggy. I close my eyes, finally giving in to exhaustion.

A while later, the sound of heavy keys jangling against metal bars wakes me. A young, fresh-faced cop is leading my cellmate out and shouting at me to get moving.

"What's going on?" I ask.

"You're going to court," he says, holding a pair of cuffs in his hand.

"Can you not put them on so tight? My wrists are really sore."

"It's not the cuffs, it's moving around too much that makes them tighten. Try and keep still."

I want to say: *Then don't tug my arm every time you move me.*

We shuffle through the precinct to a rear exit where there's a van waiting to take us to central booking, somewhere in the bowels of the Brooklyn courthouse downtown. Once we get there, we move from one dingy cell to another before getting squeezed into a holding pen that's totally overcrowded. There's no space to sit, so I stand there trying not to look freaked out. I'm the only white guy except for a short bald man wearing a tank top. They're all talking nonstop—about judges, bail, and their chances of getting released tonight.

"You're better off here on a weekend than a weekday," the guy next to me says, addressing no one in particular. "They make it quicker so they can all go home early."

"That's bullshit," cuts in a fat dude hogging half of a narrow bench. "They're pissed they have to work Saturday night so they come down real hard."

I've got a million questions, but I don't say anything. Better just to keep my head down.

Every so often, one or two people get pulled out to meet with a lawyer or see the judge. The lucky ones don't come back—they've gotten bailed out or released. The ones that do are mad, cursing about having to spend Christmas at Rikers.

"Yo this motherfucker is outta line. He set bail at a grand. I can't get that kind of paper."

"Shit—a grand? I gotta come up with five stacks. Cash only, no bond."

Fuck, five thousand dollars? I doubt I could pull that together.

My name finally gets called for a meeting with a public defender, who talks fast through the divider between us—he'll be my lawyer, he's not sure what evidence there is against me but he'll try to get me a low bail. It sounds like a speech he's given a million times.

"But I've not done anything," I tell him. "The explosion was an accident."

"We'll know more when we see what the DA has," he says, a bit gruffly. I'm wondering if I should hire my own lawyer, but I'm still hoping the case will just get dismissed.

Based on the number of people coming back to the cell, it seems like the later it gets the less chance you have of getting released. So by the time I'm led into the courtroom, I'm totally in a panic. The public defender doesn't say anything to me, just nods and approaches the bench. I watch the judge rifle through some papers, then talk to my lawyer and another guy who must be from the DA's office. They're all handing documents back and forth and asking each other questions.

I'm wondering if I'll get a chance to explain what happened, when my lawyer comes over and asks, "Why didn't you tell me you were arrested in September?"

I stiffen. "Why does that matter?"

"Because you had an adjournment in contemplation of dismissal—that means you were supposed to stay out of trouble for six months."

I got busted right after I got back from Tulsa. Just my luck I went out to buy on a night the streets were crawling with undercover cops.

"The judge released me straight from court, so I didn't think it was a big deal," I tell him. "And I did stay out of trouble. The explosion wasn't my fault."

"No trouble means no contact with the police," he says, turning and walking back to the bench.

The judge says something about problems with the criminal complaint and missing information, so he delays my arraignment until Monday. In the meantime, he's remanding me to Rikers.

Rikers Island—the thought stuns me.

"Can't I get bail?" I ask.

"Not until you're arraigned," my lawyer says. "You'll probably get it Monday. Just make sure you've got someone in court with the cash."

Who the fuck is going to bail me out? I can't remember anyone's phone number—except for a couple of dealers and Liam's mum, but I'm way too scared to call her. I try to think of Susan's number but all I can come up with is the first six digits.

Then it's back to the holding cell with everyone else heading to Rikers. The court officers take us out one by one and cuff us, lead us single file through a labyrinth of corridors, and buzz us through a heavy door leading to a barbed-wire enclosure where a bus is waiting.

That's when it really sinks in. I've heard a lot of stories about Rikers from guys I've hung out with in the projects, so I know I can handle myself—I'm not some sheltered white guy. But it's hard not to feel nervous as I climb onto the bus. People look out for me in the projects, so no one messes with me there. In Rikers I'm not gonna know anybody, and that makes me feel totally fucking alone.

INTAKE AT RIKERS is like everything in this outdated system—it takes forever. More fingerprints, more photos, more questions, and then the final humiliation: the strip search. There's about twenty of us, all shapes and sizes, standing there totally naked. We hand our clothes to a bunch of guards who search the pockets for contraband. I look straight ahead, trying not to make eye contact.

We turn and squat and lift our balls to show we have nothing hidden before we're allowed to get dressed. No one's talking—all the banter has stopped—so there's just the sound of rubber soles squeaking and jeans getting zipped. I'm shocked that this could actually be legal. I haven't even been charged yet, never mind convicted.

Then it's back to being moved from cell to cell. There seems to be no rhyme or reason for the constant shuffle—and no sense of urgency.

"Bullpen therapy," one guy calls it. "They do this just to fuck with you."

"They spin it out for the overtime, man," says a wrinkly guy with gray hair. He looks about seventy—too old to be in jail.

"Yeah, they got it all computerized in some joints I been in—bar codes and all that technical shit. But we're on the island. Nobody gives a fuck about anyone in here."

I'm desperate for a piss but there's only one nasty toilet in the corner of the cell and it's already practically overflowing. Every time someone goes to use it a collective groan goes around, along with threats of "Don't shake up that shit" and "Hold that slam dunk." But that doesn't stop people from pissing and even one guy taking a dump—right there in front of everyone.

I hunker down in my corner, waiting to see what happens next.

Every so often someone gets pulled out and handed bedding, a small worn towel, a green plastic cup, and a toothbrush, then is led off by a guard. We're all tired and cranky—all I want is somewhere I can lay my head down. It's hours before my name is called and I finally get out of this cell.

A couple of guards lead about eight of us through long, empty corridors, stopping at every door and gate we come to as men get dropped off at different dorms. There are only two of us left by the time we climb the last set of stairs, pass through another locked door, and enter a scene that totally blows my mind. I thought it would be quiet and orderly but what's in front of me is a fucking free-for-all. About fifty guys are milling around, playing cards, watching TV, and arguing. Some are listening to radios, others are stripped to the waist working out. I don't see a white face anywhere.

The corrections officer points me to a bed opposite a couple of phones where inmates are lined up waiting. Nearby, two other COs are in a booth overlooking the dorm, but they seem totally detached from what's going on. I put my stuff on the thin plastic-covered mattress and look for a pillow (there isn't one), then sit on the edge of the bed, trying to take in everything around me. The energy doesn't look like it's gonna die down anytime soon.

I don't bother undressing or making the bed. I just pull the rough gray blanket over my head and spend a miserable night tossing and turning, thoughts ricocheting around in my head. Worrying about Liam. Wondering if my parents know. Hoping Susan doesn't find out. Anxious about my house. Eventually I doze off to the sound of men grunting and snoring.

When I wake up the next morning, it's still dark outside and the dorm is deadly quiet. I don't see anyone else up, except for a guy in the bathroom doing pull-ups using the bar between stalls. Slowly, rhythmically grunting every time he gets to the top. I want to piss and clean my teeth but tales of jailhouse bathrooms make me a bit nervous. *Fuck it—I can't hold it.* I walk over to the open toilets, piss quickly, then turn and face the row of sinks.

I try to look at myself in the mirror but the metal plate has been worn down with so many years of scouring that all I see is a distorted reflection. Even though I don't have any toothpaste, I turn on the tap and clean my teeth with the cheap plastic toothbrush— the bristles make my gums bleed. Then I head back to my bed, watching the sky change from dark to light as the dorm comes to life.

I'm not sure what time it is when breakfast is brought to us on carts rolled into the dayroom. Trays are clattering, and the guys serving are shouting, "Chow time!" I look around at the men still curled up in bed, dead to the world. *How the fuck can they sleep through this?*

There aren't any tables left, so I take my tray back to my bed. Out of nowhere a young white guy pops up in front of me—I didn't notice him last night. He's talking fast and his eyes dart past me, never quite catching mine.

"What are you in for?" he asks.

"Nothing that'll stick," I tell him. "I should get out tomorrow."

"Good luck with that," he says, laughing. "I've been in for seven months going back and forth to court. Five minutes in front of the judge, then sent back here to wait. Can't get money for bail so I'm stuck."

The thought of not getting bail makes me shudder. Since he asked me, I feel okay asking him why he's here.

"Conspiracy charge," he says. "I was just selling a few oxys on the side, but my connect was getting them from some bogus pain doctor and I got caught up in his bullshit. See that dude with the neck tattoo? He's been fighting his case for two years—that's how fucked-up this place is."

The shock must show on my face because he says, "You'll be okay. Sounds like you ain't in deep shit. Anyway, I'll catch you later."

As soon as he's gone, an empty feeling seeps through me—the comedown I've been fighting crushing me again. Ever since I got arrested, waves of depression have been crashing over me as the cravings come and go. I just want something to take my mind off everything that's happened in the last twenty-four hours, but I've got no way to distract myself. There's nothing to do except watch the rabble around me.

My bed is right across from the toilets, so all day people stream past me, pissing and shitting in earshot. The smell wafting out of there is disgusting. The stalls don't have doors and the showers are open, so as much as I'd love to rinse off I'm not ready to tackle that—and I'd just have to put on the same clothes I've been wearing.

I'm trying to will the day away, but the endless fights about the phone and the mindless conversations are driving me crazy. I just want to scream "Shut the fuck up!" but I don't think that would go down too well. Lunch finally arrives—bologna sandwiches— and then five hours later, dinner: potatoes that look like wallpaper paste, a few soggy vegetables, and a rubbery piece of meat coated in breadcrumbs.

Other people are wolfing their food down like they haven't eaten in a week, but I just sit on my bed picking at the vegetables before taking my tray back to the dayroom. "Not good enough for you?" the server says, grinning. "You'll get used to it."

After dinner I try to watch TV, but I can't get close enough to hear anything and I'm too agitated to sit still. I don't know how people survive in this place—even a week would drive me insane. I pace back and forth the length of the dorm, avoiding a couple of guys swaggering around, rapping along with whatever's playing on their prison-issue radios. I'm hoping I can wear myself down before lights-out.

As I walk back to my bed, I see a few guys huddled by the showers—I swear I smell crack, a whiff of burnt foil filling my nostrils. *How the fuck did they get that in here?* Just the thought of a hit sets me off. My mind goes into overdrive, the smell triggering every receptor in my brain. I want to see if it's for real but I'm too scared to walk over and check it out. I just sit on my bed, letting the cravings surge through me. At least I'm not dope sick. It's the only positive thing I can grasp on to right now.

ON MONDAY MORNING I'm woken up at 5 A.M. for the long journey back to the Brooklyn courthouse. It can't be more than ten miles away, but it takes hours to process us all out. Everyone piling onto the bus is wearing street clothes, since most of us haven't even been charged yet. Once we get there, we're crammed into a cell for another excruciating wait to see a judge.

When the court officer finally calls my name, I'm cuffed and led from the holding pen into the courtroom, in a line with half a dozen other defendants. A crowd of mostly black and brown faces is staring at us, but one of the lone white faces jumps out: It's Susan, sitting at the end of a wooden bench. She looks exhausted, the dark rings under her eyes accentuated by bad lighting.

Part of me is angry that she's here—this is the last place I want her to see me—but I'm relieved that at least someone showed up. The way she's looking at me kills me, as if I've turned out to be the biggest disappointment of her life. Even if she had been willing to give me another chance, clearly that's not gonna happen now. Blinking hard, I look down at my feet. I can't fucking start crying in court.

Once my case is called, I try to focus on all the back-and-forth between the judge and my lawyer—a different guy than the one I met Saturday night. They're rattling off arrest charges, discussing evidence, and talking about legal codes I don't understand. It all makes this whole situation sound way worse than it really is.

I'm still trying to figure out what's what when the judge impatiently bangs his hammer. He sets bail at $1,500 and schedules another hearing for Friday morning—four days from now. My lawyer quickly explains that I'm heading back to Rikers and suggests I find someone to bail me out.

I try to catch another glimpse of Susan, but before I get a chance I'm hustled out the door and back to the holding pen. I'm wondering if she'll post bail or if this was her way of having one last look at me. I can't believe this is how it's gonna end, after months of trying so fucking hard to get her back. I want to run back into the courtroom and explain everything to her—that the gun wasn't mine, that the explosion wasn't my fault, that it'll all get sorted out—but I know she'll never believe that I wasn't using. I'm sure that's all she really cares about, besides the fact that I'm now in jail.

By the time we get back to Rikers, we've missed dinner so all we get is a cold sandwich while we go through intake. It's another tedious process, another long night trying to fall asleep with a million depressing thoughts bouncing around my head.

Early the next morning, I get woken up by the sound of planes taking off from LaGuardia Airport. It makes me wonder when Susan is leaving to go see her family for Christmas. I really hope she has the heart to post bail before she goes. I was hoping the judge would just release me, but I might have to call Anna and ask her if she'll do it. I'm dreading that conversation, but I don't know how much longer I can put it off.

The day drags. Every minute seems to last an hour, the boredom broken only by inedible meals. Just as I'm bracing myself for another sleepless night, a CO comes in and starts calling out names, followed by "Bailout!" A buzz of anticipation ripples around the dorm. I'm hoping but not really expecting to hear my name, so when he shouts, "Ma-see-an-doe!" at first I'm not sure I heard right.

I grab my stuff and rush up to the CO, who checks our IDs and says he'll be back in a bit. But it's after eight by the time a prison bus picks us up, trundling between buildings to collect other inmates. Eventually we get dropped off near a parking lot, where a city bus will take us to Queens Plaza. We've each been given a single-ride MetroCard to get home, but someone says the next bus isn't leaving for half an hour.

I don't have a coat and it's freezing out, so I go inside the visitors' waiting area next to the parking lot. Grabbing one of the newspapers lying around, I practically shit myself: Susan's name and phone number are scribbled in pen on the front page. I know she bailed me out—that was on one of the forms I had to sign—but I didn't think you had to come out to Rikers to do that. It looks like her handwriting, but why would she have written her number on *The New York Times* and left it here? It's too fucking bizarre.

With her number in front of me, I pluck up the courage to call her from the pay phone—collect, so maybe that's why she doesn't pick up. I pace around for a bit, wondering if I should ask to borrow somebody's cell. There's a girl by the door who's giving her boyfriend a hard time about getting busted. She's got a phone in her hand so I decide to give it a shot.

"Could I use your phone for a second?" She looks at me warily so I add, "I just wanna let my girlfriend know I'm out."

"Make it quick. It's a prepay and I ain't got many minutes left."

"I won't be long," I promise. "She's not too happy with me right now."

"Neither is my girl," the guy says.

"You got that right," she tells him, swiping him on the head before giving him a kiss.

The phone rings for a while before Susan answers—her voice is wary when she says hello.

"It's Graham," I tell her. "I'm still at Rikers but I borrowed someone's phone so I can only talk for a minute. I just wanted to say thank you. I can call you when I get back to my house—it shouldn't be too late."

"Don't bother," she says.

I figured she might be angry, but I didn't expect that icy response. It just confirms all my worst fears as she launches into the longest rant I've ever heard from her.

"It took me an hour and a half to get home from Rikers. One bus and two subways, after hours of waiting around. And I had to withdraw fifteen hundred dollars from my bank account—which

I'd better get back soon because I have to pay my mortgage. So obviously I'm pissed off and tired, and by the time you get home it's going to be late and I'm really not in the mood to hear whatever excuse you're going to come up with to try to hide the fact that you were doing drugs and some girl you were partying with spent the night, which I know because she got arrested with you—"

"You mean Izzy?" I interrupt. "I'm not sleeping with her, if that's what you're suggesting. She came over with Tye—they're friends of mine, I've told you about him. And it wasn't a party, we were just hanging out. I wasn't using. I know the cops are saying they found stuff, but they trump up all these charges and half the time they don't stick. Like the gun they're saying I had—it was a BB gun. That's what caused the explosion, did you know that?"

Susan just listens, not really saying much. I can tell she's done with my excuses, done with me.

The girl whose phone I borrowed is looking at me impatiently, waving her hand for me to give it back. I hold up my index finger, trying to stall her.

"I have to go," I tell Susan. "Can I call you tomorrow? When are you leaving for Michigan?"

She doesn't answer, so I tell her I'm sorry and thank her again. I wait as long as I can before hanging up, hoping she'll say something, but the only thing I hear is silence.

WHEN I GET back to Brooklyn I hardly recognize my house. The broken windows have been boarded up and the yard is littered with bits of trash and glass—it looks like an abandoned building. I find the key hidden under my stoop, unlock the door, and fumble along the wall for the light. Nothing could have prepared me for what I see when I switch it on.

The place has been totally ransacked. Not just the mess from the explosion, more like looters came through with bats and knives. Every drawer has been emptied out, pictures pulled from the walls, furniture overturned, and the whole living room is covered with tiny white balls.

At first I can't figure out where they came from, but then I see that Liam's beanbags have been cut open. As I try to take it all in, I spot the broken frame from a Gilles Peress photograph that used to hang above the couch, which is now on its side halfway across the room. When I pick up the photo—one he took of a child running with a flag in Bosnia—I feel sick. The glass is broken and the picture looks like someone put a foot through it. Gilles gave it to me years ago when I helped him install an exhibition of his work.

I head downstairs, stepping over piles of towels and laundry in the hallway. Even Liam's room has been torn apart, his bed tipped over, his clothes and schoolbooks tossed around, pictures of him playing soccer pulled off the wall. *Did he come by and see this? What must he have thought when he opened the door?* I pick up a photo I took of him and put it back on the dresser.

My room is even more of a wreck—prints and negatives and camera lenses scattered all over. I look around for my laptop, but I can't find it anywhere, then I panic remembering the money I left in the desk and the watch my dad gave me—also gone. Every so often I see reminders of Susan: photos and cards and the little tripod she sent me, which I wasn't supposed to open until Christmas.

My head is spinning. I'm so fucking angry I want to put my fist through the wall. I can't believe they're allowed to do this, like I'm some drug kingpin they've been planning to raid for months.

I can't stay here—it's too depressing—so I find my phone and call a guy I know from the projects.

"It's Graham, I just got out," I tell him, knowing he must've heard what happened. "My house is a fucking disaster. Those assholes totally trashed the place. Can I come over? I really don't want to be here if they come back."

———

BY THE TIME I stumble home the next morning, I'm feeling more like I can deal with things—figure out how to replace the windows, put my house back together, call Liam's mum. I'm dreading that conversation, but I need to talk to her before this all gets blown out of proportion.

When I eventually get her on the phone she doesn't say much, except that I should call my parents since they know I was arrested. I ask if I can talk to Liam but she says she thinks it would be better if I wait until after the holidays. There's no point arguing with her—Liam is sixteen, so I'm sure he'll do whatever he wants. But she flat-out tells me she doesn't want him staying with me as long as there's all this chaos in my life. She didn't know I was using drugs, so now that she does, I don't know what to tell her. First Susan, now Liam—I feel like I've lost both of them. I'm upstairs with the windows boarded up, looking at the wreckage around me, and I don't know what the fuck to do next.

I put off calling my parents, hoping I can come up with a way to make this situation seem less bad, but an hour later my phone rings. The caller ID flashes MUM & DAD.

I'm tempted to let it go to voicemail but I pick up, picturing my dad on the crappy old phone in their hall.

"Graham, is that you?" he asks. The connection to Scotland crackles.

"Yeah, it's me."

"Are you alright? Your mother and I have been worried sick."

"Anna said there was an explosion," my mum says—she must be on the phone in the living room. "What happened? Was Liam there? Were there drugs in the house?"

The barrage of questions annoys me. The last thing I need right now is to get put on the spot.

"I'm fine," I say, trying to think of a plausible story. "It's not that bad, really."

"Not that bad?" my dad says. "You were locked up in jail—how much worse can it get?"

I tell them it's all a mistake, that I was having a party and a broken radiator exploded. Some friends had drugs at the party and the cops overreacted, but my lawyer told me the charges would end up getting dismissed. I don't know if they believe me, but I'm telling them what I think they want to hear.

"What's this about a gun?" my dad asks.

"Remember when I told you I found that old gun in somebody's trash down the street? The cops must've come across it when they were searching the house. It was in pieces, there weren't even any bullets."

I promise I'll call them in a few days and tell them not to worry, everything's fine. But after I hang up, I feel like shit about lying. I just don't know how to be honest about what's really going on.

I pull the crumpled paperwork I was given out of my pocket and try to work out all the arrest charges listed: criminal possession of a weapon, reckless endangerment, criminal possession of a controlled substance, criminal use of drug paraphernalia. The form says I was just arraigned on the drug possession charge, but I can't tell if the cops actually found anything besides the pipe. They sure fucking tried hard enough.

Later in the afternoon, I send an email to Susan, thanking her for bailing me out and promising I'll get the money to her ASAP. I don't want her to worry, so I let her know the arrest really isn't a big deal.

My lawyer said he's going to get it dismissed as no drugs were found and the gun was a BB gun with plastic caps. He

also said i should sue as they had no warrent and searched
for 2 days and i have several things missing and broken.

I don't hear back from her until after midnight. She sends a long email describing what happened when she went to the courthouse the first time, what the charges are against me, and where I'm supposed to go for my next hearing. It's all very businesslike— the only bit that's slightly personal is at the end.

I did get the sense that things weren't necessarily handled
the way they should've been (re: the search warrant, how
the charge kept changing), but I can also imagine that the
situation was complicated by the fact that there had been
an explosion and it probably wasn't clear at first what
caused it.

After rereading her email, hoping I missed some sign that she might be able to forgive me, I click the button to close it. I didn't miss anything. It's clearly over between us.

CHAPTER ELEVEN

January 2007
Upper West Side, Manhattan

As the ball dropped in Times Square and 2007 arrived, I wrote in my notebook, "*I keep thinking about all the lies.*"

"You're going to go back over everything that happened," Graham had warned me. "All the things I said, all the things I did—and you're going to doubt me."

He was right. And it wasn't because of the explosion, which wasn't really his fault, or the fact that he was still smoking crack, which wasn't really a surprise. It was because I called the therapist he had supposedly been seeing and found out she didn't have a Scottish patient with a drug problem.

"I know you can't talk about clients because of patient confidentiality," I explained when I called her. "But if you're *not* seeing a Scottish photographer who came to you because of a drug problem, you could tell me that, right?"

She paused before answering, pondering the ethical loophole I'd drawn.

"Because he's been arrested," I added, eliding my own dubious motive for calling. "I just bailed him out of jail. So if you do have a patient who fits that description he really needs help now."

"I'm sorry," she said. "It's possible I had a consultation with someone like the person you're describing, but I probably would've referred him to another therapist. Addiction isn't really my specialty."

That revelation blew me apart. All summer and fall, Graham had talked about how much "Debi" was helping him—negative behaviors he was addressing, questions she had asked, how she'd "laid on a plate" the root causes of many of his problems. One night in November, he walked off in the middle of a fight, telling me he really needed to talk to her.

"She said I should call if I was having an emotional reaction that was overwhelming," Graham explained, leaving me standing outside a Chinese restaurant on St. Marks Place. "I'll be back in ten minutes. I just want to find somewhere quiet so I can hear her."

I had my doubts at the time—how many therapists interrupted their dinner to take a call from a distraught client? But I didn't doubt Debi existed; I just didn't believe he was going to call her. *Tompkins Square Park was two blocks away.*

That memory made me furious. I'd spent thousands of dollars on therapy, plumbed the dark corners of my own psyche, pored through all the journals I'd kept since third grade. Meanwhile, Graham was feeding me lines he'd probably read in a self-help book he picked up for a dollar at a stoop sale. Even worse: *I believed he was seeing a therapist because his behavior did actually change.*

But once my anger faded—and with Graham it usually burned out quickly, like crumpled paper—I thought about how desperate and alone he must've been feeling to conjure up a shrink who gave him advice. And if he knew he needed help (it turned out he did have one appointment), why didn't he try harder to find someone?

Maybe if he had called another therapist, if he hadn't been so stubborn, if he'd had insurance and counseling was covered, there wouldn't have been a crack pipe in the house when the windows blew out. And we might've had a chance to get back together, but that possibility was gone now. When he got arrested, Graham crossed a line and I wasn't going to follow him where he was headed.

I sent him an email just after the New Year, our non-anniversary weighing on my mind. I kept picturing him in his dark house with the windows boarded up, the cold wind sneaking in, the ghost of my surprise visit a year earlier slithering around the couch, the bed, the stairs, and the floor. I wondered if he'd swept up the tiny white pellets that looked like snow.

"I really think it would help you a lot to find someone to talk to—a real Debi," I wrote. *"I know you're scared to do that, and worried that it won't help. All I can say is that I was way more resistant than you were when we first started seeing David, and when I finally started being open with him, it changed my life."*

Graham wrote back: *"i don't know what happened to get me here. your right—i need to stop doing things myself. i'm scared to go to someone and fail."*

When I read that last sentence, I cried. It was one of those moments that made me think Graham was still reachable—that if someone could just get through to him, maybe he could be pulled back from the brink. But those tears were tainted with guilt and the bitter taste of failure: I already knew that that "someone" wasn't going to be me. And by that point, so did he.

JUST AS GRAHAM was distancing himself—no more phone calls, only a few emails—my own life yanked my attention away. Over Christmas, my doctor had called to tell me the results of a biopsy I'd gotten before I left for Michigan: The spot on my forehead was skin cancer.

It wasn't a devastating diagnosis, just a small basal cell carcinoma; my mom had already had the same surgery twice. But the black crisscrossed stitches left me looking like Frankenstein, and the Tylenol with codeine I was taking barely made a dent in the pain. I wasn't supposed to drink, exercise, or do yoga—all of my avenues for escape—and I didn't want to go out because of the scar on my face.

So I didn't have much time to feel sorry for Graham; I was too busy feeling sorry for me.

During my days on the couch, I reread Daniel Gilbert's book *Stumbling on Happiness,* which Graham had found in a giveaway box on his street. I'd read it first and hadn't ever given it back, a deliberate omission in our post-breakup exchange of T-shirts, photos, and CDs.

"I keep thinking of the happiness book," I wrote in my notebook that miserable January. *"How we can't predict what will make us happy because we can't account for a future we can't predict. I suppose at the end of 2005 I wouldn't have glimpsed even a tiny bit of what happened last year."*

With my lucky number 7 tattooed on Graham's arm and Gilbert's advice buzzing in my ear, I tried to convince myself that 2007 might turn out to be better than I expected—and in many ways, it actually did. *"Negative events do affect us, but they generally don't affect us as much or for as long as we expect them to,"* Gilbert wrote. I just had to get through a rough patch first.

Other than David, there wasn't a consistent person I turned to as my relationship with Graham went through another ending; I relied on different people for different reasons at different times. Friends tried to be supportive, but I felt like I was living the parable of the blind men holding different parts of an elephant, each person's perspective influenced by whether they were touching the trunk, tusk, or tail. I think we all tend to view addiction through the lens of our own experience with this affliction. In some sense, we're all a bit blind.

Still, I was surprised by how judgmental some people were about Graham. Sure, he made bad choices and had to deal with the consequences, but wasn't it a bit hypocritical not to look in the mirror and acknowledge one's own struggle with vice? Listening to drinkers who doled out advice well into their third cocktail, smokers who bristled at any comparison between drugs and nicotine, pill poppers who relied on a doctor friend's prescription pad, and drunk drivers who didn't consider their own behavior criminal, I was struck by the empathy gap.

Graham was right about one thing: In the cultural perception of addiction, heroin addicts were definitely at the bottom of the barrel. And he sank even lower after he was arrested and went to jail.

But for every harsh judgment someone let slip, another friend propped me up with sensitive, caring advice. Ethan always seemed to have my best interest at heart—even if it stung when he finally said, "I'd cut bait." Although, years later he'd tell me that his views on addiction had gotten more "nuanced" after his own relapse, which made me wonder if his opinion about Graham's situation had also changed.

The best advice I got came from a colleague I didn't know very well—or at least, not well enough to know that she once had a boyfriend who had a drug problem. When she told me about her ex, I instantly recognized the relationship she described, the intensity of his affection eventually trumped by the upheaval of his constant drama.

The way she put it seemed so simple: "I realized I had to choose his life or mine."

I understood that decision—it was exactly how I felt after I bailed Graham out of Rikers. But there was one question that still troubled me, more as a moral dilemma most of us don't want to face: What happens to these addicts after the sober, sane people in their lives leave them?

We all know the answer: Many of them don't get better. We lock them up, or they overdose and die.

ON FEBRUARY 13, a year after Graham and I were strolling on the beach in Hawaii, I sent him a message saying I'd see him at his hearing the next day.

He wrote back: *"Your better off not coming tomorrow 'coz my lawyer said it's just getting postponed again probably. last time i was there all of 6 mins. i'd rather see you under better circumstances - especially seeing as we don't see each other anymore and haven't even spoke in ages - you understand?"*

I reminded him that it was actually my responsibility to make sure he showed up for these hearings, since I was the one who had paid his bail. The receipt I'd signed at Rikers made that quite clear: *"I undertake that the defendant will appear in this action whenever required and will at all times render himself/herself amenable to the orders and processes of the court."* It also warned: *"The bail will be forfeited if the defendant does not comply."*

Even though it wasn't my money at stake—Graham had already paid me back—I wanted to follow through on that commitment. More importantly, I felt a responsibility for him beyond the love some people feel for an ex. I was the last functioning adult Graham had been close to when he got arrested; there was no one else who could make sure he didn't go completely off the rails. Graham was already teetering on the edge.

After the explosion, a local paper had described him as a "suspected drug dealer" living in an "alleged crackhouse" in brownstone Brooklyn—based on speculation and anonymous leaks by the police. I knew Graham was devastated by that article, so I went to his hearing partly to let him know I didn't believe it. But if there was any evidence to back up either of those claims, I certainly wanted to hear it.

He was supposed to be at the courthouse by 9:30 A.M., shuffling through security with the mass of people filing through the metal detectors—mostly African American and Hispanic men. But Graham wasn't there when I got to the courtroom upstairs, and he didn't pick up when I called him. I debated walking over to his house, which was only six blocks away.

I knew Graham had hired a lawyer, so I tried to guess who that might be among the attorneys sitting on the front bench—the only suits in a crowd of winter coats, heavy work boots, and jeans. "Take your hat off in the back!" one of the uniformed court officers yelled. "Sir! No talking in the courtroom!" (Also not allowed: sagging pants, tank tops, or do-rags.)

After 10 A.M., probably the fifteenth time I turned to look as the door opened, Graham finally walked in, wearing a down jacket and pants I'd never seen. The new clothes were jarring, marking the three months since our paths had crossed: long enough that his wardrobe—and the season—had changed.

"I told you not to come," he said, sliding into the aisle seat on the bench beside me.

"And I told you I was going to come anyway," I whispered, hoping Graham would mimic my lowered voice.

"Where's my lawyer?" he asked, still at full volume.

"Quiet down!" the court officer shouted.

Graham looked around. "He isn't here. I'm gonna go call him." Grabbing his messenger bag, he went out to the hall.

From that brief interaction, I couldn't tell if Graham was using; even I was on edge with the court officer constantly shouting. That tension was magnified by seeing Graham for the first time in months. But I didn't get a chance to talk to him—when he came back in, a tall man I assumed was his lawyer was by his side.

One of the benefits of being able to afford a private lawyer is that your case is usually called earlier in the session, so you don't waste as much time waiting around. That was the main activity in the room full of what seemed like an excess of court personnel: everyone waiting for someone to find a piece of paper, or the right folder, or the answer to a question the judge had asked. It was nothing like the fast-paced courtroom dramas I'd seen on TV.

Once Graham's case was called, he stood next to his lawyer with his hands clasped behind his back, facing the judge's bench—

IN GOD WE TRUST on the wall in front of him, flanked by two flags. It was all over in minutes, and I couldn't hear most of what anyone said.

"The DA's office hasn't filed any evidence," Graham's lawyer explained, once the three of us reconvened in the hall. "They've got another month to do that—ninety days after the arraignment. If they don't do anything by then, the case will get dismissed."

"Does that mean they don't have any evidence?" I asked.

"Hard to say," he answered. "Sometimes these things take a while."

I wanted something more: answers about the legality of the search, proof that the police had or hadn't found drugs, some facts that would clarify what had actually happened. But the lawyer rushed off so I asked Graham if he wanted to go get a cup of coffee. I knew it was my only chance to pin him down.

He hesitated, probably weighing up whether I was going to grill him—or calculating how soon he was going to need a hit. The more time I spent with him, the more I was sure crack was still part of the equation he was trying to manage, and now maybe heroin again. I could finally see how exhausting that must be.

"I'm not going to yell at you," I promised. "I came all the way down here to make sure you're getting good legal advice, so at least you can talk to me for a few minutes."

Graham looked at me like he doubted my motive, but I knew he couldn't say no when I was standing right there in front of him. "Alright," he said. "But I can't stay too long. I've got a lot I need to do today."

After we sat down at an old diner near the courthouse—a relic on a street sprouting expensive boutiques—I steered the conversation toward safer topics at first: how the window repair was going (the neighbors were complaining about his new "nonhistoric" windows), whether he'd finished his website redesign (almost done), how Liam was doing (fine, although Graham hadn't seen him as much lately, with exams coming up). We both avoided the real reason Graham was seeing less of his son.

Graham asked me about the scar on my forehead, which had faded to a jagged red mark by then. "I've decided it makes me look like Harry Potter," I said, showing off one of the benefits of nine months of therapy (optimism!). "My doctor said it'll barely be noticeable once it heals."

"I think you should find a new doctor," Graham told me. "Why did he make such a long cut for something the size of a pencil eraser—was he charging by the inch?"

That was one of the things I missed about Graham: He wasn't afraid to tell me things he thought I needed to hear. Uncharacteristically, I hadn't really researched the doctor who did the surgery—a mistake I wouldn't make when I needed it again.

The diner was starting to fill up with the lunchtime rush of office workers, and I could tell Graham was getting antsy to get on with his own pressing errand. But there was one more topic I wanted to bring up before he slipped away.

"Listen," I said. "I'm not here to judge you or lecture you about drugs, but I'm worried that you might not be in a frame of mind to deal with this case. You don't make the best decisions when you're using, and I don't want to see you end up in a situation that spins out of control."

"You heard what my lawyer said," Graham snapped. "The case is just gonna get dismissed."

"*If* the DA doesn't file any evidence. But you know how the legal system works: It's not whether you're guilty or innocent, it's whether you have money for a really good lawyer."

"I have a good lawyer. I'm paying him a fucking fortune to show up in court for ten minutes every six weeks."

"I know. That's why I want to make sure he's doing his job,

and I don't know if he understands how this case could affect your immigration status. When I get home, I'm going to email you an article I read that said any conviction involving drugs could get you deported."

"I'm a legal permanent resident. They're not gonna kick me out of the country because of a misdemeanor."

"Just promise me you'll read it, and talk it over with your lawyer?"

"Alright, but I think you're being a bit paranoid about this."

That was the reaction I expected, but at least I'd delivered the message I thought Graham needed to hear. After he paid the bill, he walked me to the subway and gave me a hug before I descended underground—to the same platform where he kissed me the day he took my picture. Neither of us mentioned that it was Valentine's Day.

"I'll call you," Graham said, which was what he always said whenever we parted. And I always believed him, like Charlie Brown running to kick the football Lucy always yanked away.

Later that afternoon, I sent him the article, highlighting this sentence: *"A non-citizen who has entered the country legally but who has a conviction under 'any law relating to a controlled substance' is subject to deportation."*

In case he didn't read the whole article, I explained, *"Even seemingly minor charges that wouldn't be a big deal for a U.S. citizen are treated very differently if you're not a citizen, even if you have a green card—and most people don't know that. This country isn't particularly friendly toward immigrants these days."*

At that point, I didn't think it was something Graham needed to be too concerned about, since it did seem like his case would get dismissed. I shared it more as a warning—another motivation for quitting. I'm not sure I would've admitted my own reason for worrying: that he might get sent far away from me. Seeing him had churned up emotions I hadn't expected to feel, like a fever returning with a new round of chills.

"*I'm glad I went today,*" I wrote. "*It was good to see you.*"

"*Likewise,*" Graham answered. "*Reminded me that i like you............a lot!*"

He didn't acknowledge the article I'd sent, which I was pretty sure he didn't bother to read.

The next day, Graham rode his bike uptown and left a bouquet of flowers outside my building, propped in a corner next to an envelope with my name. Inside was a card he'd made, using a photograph he'd taken of a door painted with a red heart. "*Happy V Day on the 15th,*" Graham wrote in the card. "*A picture says a thousand words! And my lips are sealed right now.*"

Over the next few days, I probably spent a thousand minutes trying to figure out what he meant. That he wasn't telling me everything? That he couldn't, because of his court case?

"*Right now*" suggested that at some point, he would.

THREE WEEKS AFTER Graham's hearing, I met with a real estate agent to discuss listing my apartment.

By early April, it was officially for sale.

Within days after the first open house, we had a deal.

Even in the frenzy of New York's heated-up real estate market, it was a fast pace for a transaction involving a mortgage—not to mention the approval of a co-op board. It was a record pace for a major decision for me.

I'd been thinking about selling my apartment on and off for years, as prices doubled, then tripled, and the residents in my building went from artists and writers—often, living alone—to married bankers and lawyers who needed two salaries just to make ends meet. Since my income wasn't rising along with all of my bills, I finally decided it was time to cash in.

Having money may not have bought me happiness—as Daniel Gilbert warned it wouldn't—but it certainly eliminated a lot of my stress.

My main source of anxiety was finding another place to live. Since I had to sign a lease before I got the check from my sale, I didn't have many options; my income was too low to get approved for a rental involving a broker. So when a friend passed along a tip about a sublet in Brooklyn, I was intrigued: It had a roof deck, a fireplace, lots of light, and a washer and dryer (a rarity in New York City), but it was ten blocks from Graham's house. I wanted to move to Brooklyn, but not necessarily so close to him that we'd bump into each other on the street.

By spring, we had settled into a new phase of our relationship: not trying to be friends, but not entirely cutting the cord. There's no doubt Graham still had a mysterious pull over me, a mix of what-might-have-been regret and a lingering worry about his case. I saw my role as sort of a guardian angel—I even sent him a photo of another snow angel I made, with a caption to that effect. But most of our communications were digital: I'd email and ask how he was doing; he'd text me a photo once in a while. The only times we saw each other were at the courthouse in Brooklyn. I knew when Graham had a hearing because I'd signed up for email alerts from New York's "WebCrims" database, which made it easy to track his case online.

I went to look at the sublet the same day as Graham's fourth— but by no means final—hearing. The police had filed a ballistics report about the BB gun a couple of days before the deadline was up, which meant the case hadn't gotten dismissed. But Graham's lawyer said that there had been some "procedural errors"—by the police or the DA's office, it wasn't clear—so he was still optimistic about a dismissal. (In fact, the case would drag on for another year and a half.)

Since I wasn't sure I could make it to the hearing, I didn't tell Graham I might stop by. The courthouse wasn't far from the sublet I looked at—and really liked—so I detoured there afterward, catching Graham just as he was hopping on his bike. He said nothing new had happened, just another adjournment. When I told him I was considering an apartment in the neighborhood, he didn't seem to mind.

"It was nice to see you today—a surprise too," he wrote me later. *"Took me about half an hour to get rid of the lump in my throat after we parted! i won't go on.....love g."*

A few days later, I sent him an email saying I'd signed the lease. He wrote back: *"I can see your smile from here, which in turn has made me happy 'coz of your happiness. As i said if you need any help just ask - i'm right here."*

I'm not sure I would've described myself as happy, but I was definitely excited about moving on. For months David and I had been discussing my anxiety about change—where it came from, and what I could do to get "unstuck." Selling my apartment was a big step out of that semiparalyzed state.

"It's like you're not safe enough in the world to let go of anything you have," David once commented. It was a fair assessment of how I felt at that point, but it didn't track with how I'd lived much of my life: leaving Michigan to go to Stanford, spending my junior year in Italy, moving to Argentina without speaking any Spanish. Up until my thirties, I took a lot of leaps off into the unknown.

By mid-2007, I think my insecurity was partly influenced by how much everything was changing, and how precarious everyone I knew was feeling, in their homes, their relationships, or their jobs. It was like we were all playing a game of musical chairs, scrambling to find a seat every time the music stopped—and within a few months, it would screech to a grinding halt. Selling my apartment gave me a financial cushion to ride out the recession, but it also left me feeling somewhat adrift.

Without the security of home ownership, a staff job, a spouse, or any kids, I was untethered from the things that usually anchor people down. On the one hand, that could be viewed as liberating: *"If it's any comfort,"* one friend wrote me, *"know that most women our age are at heart jealous of your freedom—or maybe that's just me."*

Surrounded by moving boxes and trying to get an air conditioner, cable, and a phone line installed, I saw it from a different perspective: I wondered why I was doing this all alone.

FORTUNATELY, THE TRANSITION to Brooklyn was easier than I expected, and the nightmare of moving didn't last as long as I'd feared (Daniel Gilbert was right!). But my new apartment was a lot smaller than the one I had sold, shrinking my home office, so I decided to join a workspace for writers—which had the added benefit of getting me out of the house. I made some new friends there, gossiping in the kitchen and playing on the softball team, and started swimming again, at the local YMCA.

I loved my new neighborhood. I finally felt like I lived somewhere I wanted to be. Every time I went away that summer, I was happy to come back home. I'd sit on the roof deck and watch the birds circling overhead, or water the flowers I'd planted—repotting the ones the squirrels dug up—and generally felt pretty good about my life.

As it turned out, I never ran into Graham. Not when I was buying paint at the hardware store, picking up groceries, or having dinner at one of the many new restaurants on Smith Street. We actually didn't have any contact from May until August, after an email spat that started with Graham telling me to stay out of his business and ended with me firing back, *"You don't have to worry about me showing any interest in your life—time to let go."*

Even before that fight, our communications had been tapering off. After the first few hearings, I'd stopped going to court, because the proceedings felt like a charade. The judge would just adjourn the case and Graham was ROR'd—released on his own recognizance—even though it was obvious he didn't recognize the trouble he was in. So when I got an alert later that summer saying Graham's case was going to trial, I broke the silence, sending him an email asking what was going on.

"I'd rather you didn't come to court," Graham wrote back. *"It's not a place I feel comfy at the best of times never mind with you there—please."*

I understood why he didn't want me to see him in that setting, branded as a criminal, still with no proof of his guilt. But I went anyway. When I'd asked David if he thought I should go, he told me I should act more on impulse—or just act, without deliberating so much. "Not having an experience is what's dangerous for you," he said, which was true. Sometimes seeing Graham kept me from dwelling on him, either idealizing how things were when we were together or worrying about how he was doing. It was a reality check I needed once in a while.

And despite his protests, Graham always appreciated my concern. He was like a teenager who slams his bedroom door but really does want someone to knock and ask what's wrong. The difference was, Graham never had a problem talking. Sitting on a bench outside the courtroom, we filled each other in on our lives: Graham said he'd had a few jobs but no big commercial shoots, so he was constantly stressed about money; I told him about my apartment, articles I'd been working on, and a recent trip to the West Coast. It was always strange to see him and have these semi-normal conversations, then all these intense feelings would rise up and wash over me later, as if my emotions were set to a half-hour delay.

As it turned out, his case didn't go to trial, but I was still glad I went—and so was he. His attorney seemed useless, which I told Graham before we parted, sending him an email later to drive home that point.

> *I really didn't get the impression your lawyer is bringing his*
> *A game to your case. From what I've seen, he doesn't seem*
> *to be all that aggressive about your defense. Shouldn't he*
> *have noticed that the paperwork regarding the search*
> *warrant was missing? And would he have asked about that*
> *if I hadn't asked him? I found it alarming that he didn't*
> *seem all that prepared—or knowledgeable about the*
> *immigration issues involved.*
>
> *You need an attorney who's really going to go to bat for*
> *you, and who knows the implications if you get convicted*
> *or agree to some kind of plea. Setting aside all the*
> *emotional baggage we have together, I'm offering to help*
> *you because I don't want to see you get sent back to jail or*
> *deported.*

Graham wrote back: "*Your right and I do want you to help. I'll call you in a day or so.*"

This time, I wasn't surprised that he didn't call.

Then out of the blue, Graham would text or email me—messages that made me feel like I was doing the right thing by keeping our line of communication open. They were also a sign that he was still capable of caring about me.

> *Just emailing to make sure your ok (I'm sure you are) and*
> *to let you know I am okay also. I was going to call you on*

one of those fine days last week to ask if you want to do
something but got cold feet.

I actually was okay—writing about more interesting topics and traveling more for fun and for work. But Graham was clearly picking up speed in his tumble downhill. By the end of 2007, he'd been arrested a few more times for drug possession, and his financial situation was just as bleak.

In December, when he was trying to refinance his mortgage, he called me in a panic about the terms of the loan. He didn't have enough cash to pay the closing costs, so I offered to lend him money to complete the deal. I asked him to drop off one of his vintage photographs as collateral, worth far more than the check I was giving him. Instead he brought a heavy portfolio with his whole collection—dozens of black-and-white prints by photographers like Bruce Davidson, Abelardo Morell, and Weegee—either overcompensating to prove I could trust him, or to make sure he didn't sell them and blow the money on drugs.

I couldn't be sure he really was refinancing, but I trusted him enough to take that risk. Graham had paid me back quickly when I bailed him out, and I really didn't want to see him lose his house. Outside New York City, the real estate market was already tanking, and the economic downturn was clearly headed our way.

"*Closed okay but it was very stressfull—my interest rate was* 9.99%," Graham wrote me. "*I just had to go with it and hope that remortgaging in 3 months with my credit up and with stated income will bring it in at under 7%. Thanx for the money, it means a lot.*"

He deposited what he owed me directly into my checking account, but he didn't come by to pick up his photos. I was getting used to this cycle, so I tried to put Graham out of my mind—until Heath Ledger's death a month later. He used to live down the street from Graham, but any news about an overdose was always disturbing for me. As the media churned through the usual angles—who knew, how could this have happened, why didn't he ask anyone for help—I went to the courthouse one more time, hoping the headlines had also scared Graham.

In some sense, it was easier that he didn't try to hide the fact that he was using—and using a lot, I guessed. But it was a shock when I saw him, literally wasting away. His clothes were filthy, his hands were shaking, and sweat was dripping down the side of his face.

Graham blew up when I said I was thinking of calling his parents.

"You're not my girlfriend, you're not my wife, it's none of your fucking business!" he shouted.

"If you had a girlfriend or a wife, I wouldn't be here," I said—testy, but not raising my voice. "You obviously can't handle this yourself."

The truth is, if I'd had a boyfriend or a husband I probably wouldn't have been there, either, but I hadn't been in another relationship since Graham and I broke up. That's not to say that I hadn't met anyone I was interested in; I just couldn't get past the crucial liftoff stage. David wanted to "problematize" my inability to find a new partner, but I'm not sure he fully appreciated what it was like for a single woman approaching forty, especially in New York City. I knew plenty of women who were frustrated by the pool of available men—who seemed to have their pick of eligible women.

When a friend offered to set me up on a blind date, she warned me that the guy had "recently been through a terrible breakup" and wasn't at all what she thought of as my type. I politely passed on that opportunity, envisioning an awkward night trying not to look at my watch.

Someone I'd met at a party canceled three times before we finally went out for a drink, both of us realizing it hadn't been worth all that effort. There just wasn't any spark between us—and he was eight years younger than me.

And a guy who'd been emailing me several times a day and calling for hour-long talks told me he liked our "deep connection" but wasn't interested in anything more: *"i certainly have only wanted to have a friendship with you, and from my perspective i never did anything to suggest otherwise. yes, of course i called you a lot and we had long conversations and sent each other a lot of e-mails . . . did i cross some line in male/female relations? maybe so. but how can i know unless you let me know?"*

Guilty as charged. I should've addressed our ambiguous status sooner, but in my defense, I wasn't sure I wanted to get involved with him. I think we both used our friendship as a replacement for exes we weren't totally over—although he did admit to a pattern of leaning on women he didn't want to date: *"this has happened with at least four female friends, so i'm certainly open to the possibility of my own implication."*

Eventually we settled into a less frenetic friendship, and he was actually a valuable confidant on the thorny topic of my ongoing involvement in Graham's life. When he told me it seemed like I was still in love with Graham, I disputed that theory, insisting that *loving* someone and being *in love* weren't the same. I knew some people saw that as a dubious distinction, but I didn't. Graham as I knew him didn't exist anymore. As addiction overtook him, like vines you stop cutting back or trying to control, it was getting harder and harder to remember who he used to be.

But I'd still catch glimpses of him every once in a while, which was what was so frustrating for me. Graham wasn't completely dysfunctional, he wasn't totally gone—there was a part of him that was still somewhere in there. That's who I kept trying to reach, through the thorny vines that kept piercing me.

After Graham's outburst in January, I sent him the names of a few drug treatment programs a friend recommended. He wrote

back to thank me, then a couple of weeks later sent a message saying, *"just to let you know i'm okay."* I didn't answer, and I didn't
follow through on my threat to call his parents, which probably
wouldn't have made much of a difference. Even if I had known
who else to call, or had tried to organize some kind of intervention, I'm not sure who would've shown up. By that point, Graham
had succeeded at pushing everyone away—even me.

As 2008 UNFOLDED, a sadness settled over me as I succumbed
to the fear about the future gripping most of the world. When I
confessed that anxiety in an email to my friend Alex, another
writer I'd recently met, she weighed in with her usual Zen-like
counsel.

  *"Among your greatest strengths, in my opinion, is your ability
to sympathize and empathize with others,"* she wrote. *"My advice
is to accept the sadness, but take your energy away from dwelling
on it and put it to productive use instead."*

  I tried. Mostly it was the shrinking media landscape that was
precipitating a crisis of confidence. With fewer outlets to write for,
it was getting tougher to get pitches accepted, and I started to
wonder if I was going to have to abandon the freelance life. I
bristled whenever anyone suggested I consider a career change,
and spent a lot of my sessions with David discussing healthy ways
to handle rejection.

  By summer, I learned that my thyroid hormone levels had
plummeted, which partly explained why my energy level and
mood had also gone downhill. Once I was on medication, things
perked up pretty quickly—just in time for my sister's wedding in
July. She got married at our parents' house in Michigan, in a beautiful ceremony overlooking the lake. I was the maid of honor, and
probably didn't fulfill my duties with bridal-magazine enthusiasm,
but it seemed like everyone had a good time.

In October my parents came to New York to celebrate my dad's seventieth birthday. I took them out for dinner, splurging on reservations at the River Café in Brooklyn, one of those restaurants where the setting almost eclipses the meal. As we enjoyed our dinner on a floating barge with a view of Manhattan—*"a truly special nite that I will never forget,"* my dad emailed me later— a message I'd gotten from Graham that morning niggled at the back of my mind. He wanted to pick up his portfolio of photos and wondered when he could come by.

I hadn't written him back, partly because my parents were in town, but I was also trying to put off whatever emotional disturbance I knew Graham would leave in his wake.

A week later, he wrote me again. Since David was drilling into me the downside of avoidance, I figured I should get it over with, but I wasn't prepared for what I saw when Graham stumbled in. He looked worse than I'd ever seen him, and shared news that blew me apart.

"I've got a new girlfriend," he announced, without any preamble—or awareness of my stunned response.

He sat down in my leather chair, scratching his head and rubbing his eyes, as if he was about to nod out. I numbly asked questions, trying to fill in the blanks.

"What's her name?"

"Tracy."

"How long have you been together?"

"A few months—she lives with me."

"When did she move in?"

"Just after we met—she needed a place to stay."

"What's she like?"

"She's alright."

"Just alright?"

"She's got some problems. I'm trying to help her get clean."

As each detail tumbled out, I felt another twist of the knife. It's not that I hadn't considered the possibility that Graham might meet someone else; I just thought it wouldn't happen unless he got clean. And since he wasn't exactly on a path to recovery, I wasn't prepared for how much his moving on would hurt me.

It didn't seem like much of a romance, but for me Graham's indifference was almost worse. If he'd given up on love, he'd given up on turning his life around—especially now that he was involved with another addict. Graham was heading for an ending I couldn't bear to see.

When I asked him about Liam, he couldn't remember where his son was in college; he just squinted his eyes, shook his head, and blinked. Liam was the person Graham loved most in the world, so for a second I thought he looked as pained as I felt—but maybe that's just what I needed to believe.

Seeing him in that state tore me apart, and that wound would take a long time to heal. But as it turned out, those photos weren't the last link between us, and that encounter wasn't as final as I thought it would be.

CHAPTER TWELVE

May 2010
Wyckoff Housing Projects, Brooklyn

When I wake up, I don't clean my teeth or make myself a cup of coffee. I don't look at a clock or worry about being late for work. I just roll off the inflatable bed I've been crashing on at my friend Joe's place and grab the pipe wrapped in a sock in my sneaker. It's been eight hours since my last hit so I feel like shit—I need to clear my head.

I don't have any crack but there's enough residue left for a decent hit. With a thin piece of metal, I carefully scrape the res down the sides of the glass. Once it gathers on the screen—a bit of copper kitchen scrubber—I push the charred nub to the other side of the pipe, grab my lighter, and flick it with my thumb. It doesn't light. I flick it again and notice the gas is almost out. On the third try it catches so I move the low blue flame to the end of the stem, sucking in the warm smoke.

Holding my breath, I wait a few seconds for the payoff—a rush of euphoria so exhilarating it demands every cell in your body pay attention. My ears start to ring, the craving disappears, everything is fucking brilliant. I've got about ten minutes before the comedown, enough time to find my dope and get straight.

It takes me a minute to remember where I hid a couple of baggies before I fell asleep, paranoid another junkie will steal my drugs. I've got so many hiding places—between the pages of a book, inside the fuse box, under the sink—I can't always keep track of them, but today I'm spared that frantic search. Reaching behind the radiator cover, I pull out what's left of a bundle, unfolding a small glassine baggie stamped "Get Fucked Up." I've been collecting these baggies for years, all marked with different dealers' brands, like "Ace Of Spades" or "Crooklyn." Sometimes I photograph them, but lately I've been more caught up in taking pictures of myself. After setting the self-timer on a digital camera to take a photo every ten seconds, I prop it on a shelf, then carry on with my routine.

I open the baggie and tap the powder into a spoon, then find a packet of distilled water and tear it open with my teeth, dribbling the water onto the dope. This time the lighter catches right away. Holding the flame under the spoon, I'm practically salivating with anticipation as the dope dissolves and the water heats up and bubbles. I add a bit of cotton to the spoon to filter out whatever the heroin is cut with—quinine, crushed-up painkillers, sometimes shit that can fuck you up if you're not careful.

With a new needle from the exchange around the corner, I insert the point into the cotton, then pull in the liquid—slowly, trying to savor the moment. Flicking the syringe to get rid of any air bubbles, I set about finding a vein. Mine are large and still easy to stick—no need to tie off. I just cross my right leg over my left upper arm to make the vein pop. Avoiding the skin bruised by track marks, I jab the needle, pull back, plunge.

Within seconds, any regrets about being an addict are gone— the pain I'm in, the pain I've caused, all those feelings swept away by the warm bliss of the heroin rush. As the dope moves through my system, a sense of calm overtakes everything else. I love it and I hate it, but it's utterly efficient at making everything seem just fine. It's not strong enough to make me nod out, but it gets me level. Now I can face the day.

I deflate the bed and shove it back in the closet, put the kettle on to make myself a cup of tea. Joe's apartment is on one of the top floors of the projects, and some days I'll spend hours looking out the window—south to the Verrazano-Narrows Bridge, west to the Statue of Liberty, down to the streets below. People call it getting "stuck," when you just can't move, having too many thoughts or none at all.

That's sort of where my head is at right now: either a torrent of worries, anxieties, and fears, or nothing, just completely numb. Not capable of thinking beyond the moment. Maybe that's fear, too. Fear of how much my life has spun out of control.

SO THE DAY I'm arrested—May 7, 2010—is typical in the sense that my life has narrowed to the same routine: get up, get straight, get to a point where I don't have to think too much. But I'm still dimly aware of how fucked up it is that all this has started to feel normal. Like it doesn't faze me when my friend Kia calls and asks if she can bring a trick over to Joe's place.

"Just for five or ten minutes," she promises. "That's all it takes when I'm on a roll."

I've known Kia for years and most of the time she's looked out for me—made sure I didn't get dope sick, let me stay with her when the cops were looking for me at my house. But now she's homeless because her boyfriend OD'd and she got kicked out of their apartment, so she's crashing on friends' couches and floors.

Most people would dismiss her as a crackhead, oblivious to all the shit she's lived through—with no welfare, no housing, no food stamps, and no options. But I've gotten to know her as someone who manages to stay upbeat despite the crap cards she's been dealt, which is one of the reasons we get along.

"As long as you're quick," I tell her. "Joe's going to be back soon and you know he'll go ballistic if you're here with a date."

I moved in with Joe after I sold my house last year, but it's not my apartment and he doesn't like it if anyone comes over while he's out. He's older than me, and fiercely protective, so his place was sort of a refuge after everything I'd lost.

"I'm on my way," Kia says. "He's not gonna catch me. I promise I'll bounce the minute I'm done."

Fifteen minutes later, she shows up with a middle-aged white guy who looks freaked out that he's in the projects. Kia introduces him to me as if we just met in a bar. I shake his hand and they disappear into the bedroom—probably not what he pictured when he arranged this sexual encounter. There's a disheveled bed with clothes scattered around the linoleum floor, a TV hooked up to someone else's cable, and a dresser with broken drawers.

It must be my day to help women looking for a favor because while I'm waiting for Kia to finish, my ex-girlfriend Tracy calls. At first I don't pick up, but after she calls three more times I answer, already knowing what she wants.

"Please, Graham. I'm really dope sick. I just need a couple of bags to get straight—I'll meet you anywhere."

My relationship with Tracy had been brutal. Whenever she lost it, she was confrontational and volatile, so I'm trying to keep away from her, but she's painfully persistent. It's easier to say yes than put up with her calling every two minutes—or worse, coming over here and banging on the door.

"Alright, but you've got to stop calling me," I tell her, already pissed off. "This is the last time I'm helping you out. Meet me at Starbucks in half an hour—and don't look obvious."

As soon as the trick leaves, Kia spends all the money she just made on crack, easy to score from the kids who sell drugs in the stairwells and halls. We both take a couple of hits before she walks out with me, hassling me for agreeing to meet Tracy.

"The more you do for her, the more she's going to keep coming back," Kia says, shaking her head. "She's like a bad habit—without the high."

"Listen, if I don't do this she's just gonna show up here, making a fucking scene. Then someone is going to call the cops to get rid of her, and I really don't need that right now."

Kia just rolls her eyes. "I wish someone would call the cops on her and get that bitch locked up."

She isn't the only person who can't stand Tracy, which is partly why I don't want her coming over here. Tracy's belligerent attitude doesn't go down well with dealers, and I don't want to be searching for a new connect 'cause she's gotten me caught up in her drama. It was enough of a nightmare getting her out of my house when I was trying to sell it—she kept threatening to call the cops on me, and actually did a few times.

After unlocking my bike from the scaffolding outside the building, Kia and I walk the block between the Wyckoff and Gowanus projects. I've been arrested near here and stopped and searched too many times, but that doesn't concern me. It's the quickest route to where I want to go.

I stop at a deli to buy a new lighter while Kia waits outside with my bike. As I'm paying, she ducks her head in to tell me not to come out, there are undercover cops around. I've missed a few court dates for a previous charge, so I've been dodging the warrant squad for months.

I buy a cup of coffee and drink it too quickly, then get restless lingering in the store. The guy behind the counter is eyeing me suspiciously. Through the window, I can't see Kia or anyone else outside so I decide, *Fuck it—I'll be fine.*

As soon as I step out and grab my bike, I can see Kia across the street, mouthing something to me. I can't make out what she's saying, but there's a guy walking toward me, fast. I can tell he's an undercover cop—too clean, too healthy, too determined for this part of Brooklyn. Just as he approaches, an unmarked car pulls up and a few more undercovers jump out.

They flash their badges, surrounding me with a flurry of questions: "Where are you going? . . . Where have you been? . . . Where did you get that bike?"

Everything is happening fast, but I'm trying to stay calm. If I act like this is all some kind of mistake they might just tell me to move along. Then one of them looks at my sneakers and sees a small spot of blood.

"Why is there blood on your sneakers?" he asks. I don't answer right away so he repeats his question a couple more times.

I'm starting to panic, the crack in my system is making me paranoid, and now they're all fixated on my feet. *This is crazy,* I'm thinking. *Don't these assholes have anything better to do?* But I can hardly tell them that the blood came from shooting up that morning.

I blurt out something about cutting myself shaving. Instantly, all the cops look up and scour my face. One of them grabs my chin, moving in for a closer look.

"I don't see any cuts," he says. At this point, I know I'm fucked.

Kia is still on the other side of the street, shouting something I can't understand. One of the cops notices when I look her way.

"How do you know her?" he asks.

"She's a friend of mine."

"A friend?" he scoffs. "You know she's a prostitute, don't you?"

I'm not sure what he expects me to say, but there's no point arguing with him so I let it go.

They ask to see ID, which I don't have on me. I know they're going to take me to the precinct to run my name, but I'm still trying to think of a way out.

That hope dies when they start searching me and find a crack pipe hidden in my sock. I'm standing in the street, arms out, legs spread, and a crowd is starting to gather. The cops call in my details and find out the warrant squad has been after me for months.

"What else have you got on you?" one of them asks. "Any weapons? Anything that can stick me? Any drugs?"

I shake my head, picturing the dope stuffed in my underwear as I'm getting patted down. They don't find it—the glassine envelopes are thin and easy to hide. Then I'm shoved against the car and the cuffs are on me—too tight, as always. Someone reads me my rights and tells me they're taking me in.

I've been through this routine too many times, so I already know what's ahead: the precinct, central booking, court, then released on bail if I get lucky. But this time I know that's a long shot. Now that I've got a warrant for missed court dates, I'm pretty sure I'm headed for Rikers.

As it all starts to sink in, I fixate on Tracy—I wouldn't have left the apartment if she hadn't called. Kia was right, I should have just told her to fuck off.

I wish I could go back to Joe's place and get high, safe in my own little world. Instead, I'm gonna go through the system dope sick, and there's nothing I can do to avoid what I know is coming.

AT THE 76TH Precinct, my name and arrest info are entered into a big worn-out logbook—slowly, by hand—and I'm taken to the back room and locked up in a cell. It's a relief to get the cuffs off, but what comes next is worse: the humiliation of getting strip-searched by two grown men wearing rubber gloves.

I know they'll probably find the two bags of heroin hidden in my underwear, but I'm hoping I can sneak at least one out and use it to delay the withdrawal. No such luck. Strip, squat, cough. While I'm standing there naked, the cops are going through my clothes and out fall the two dime bags of dope.

"I thought you said you didn't have any drugs on you?" one of them says, waving the baggies. "You know this is going to be another charge."

"I forgot about that," I mumble, not even trying to be convincing.

I've been in this situation when a cop with heart will know you're gonna get sick and slip you a bag, but not these guys.

They're threatening to give me a cavity search. I don't really care—I'm already starting to feel like shit and it's only going to get worse. After they give me my clothes back (minus my shoelaces and belt), I lie down on a bench in the cell and fall asleep.

With no watch and no clock, I only have a vague sense of time, but as the day wears on the cells start to fill up. Some of the young guys are treating it like a joke, rapping and fronting and hollering at people in other cells. They've been picked up in some stop-and-frisk—they know they'll be back on the street by morning. But the noise is grating on me, and the waste of everyone's time is depressing.

At this point, everything is annoying: people shouting, keys jangling, doors banging. Even when I manage to nod off, I'm woken up for the slow-moving machinery of the booking process. Posing for yet another mug shot, getting more fingerprints taken—now with a digital scanner that freezes constantly. And every time there's a shift change, answering the same questions over and over. "What's your name? What were you arrested for?" *As if they don't already know.*

I have to sign a voucher listing all the property I had on me when I was picked up: 1 Mac laptop, 1 gray bike, 2 cameras, 4 pairs of sunglasses, 2 watches, 1 cellphone, 2 batteries, 1 iPod, 7 rolls of film, and 8 keys on a ring. It looks like I've just robbed a pawnshop, but I couldn't leave anything that might be traded for drugs at Joe's place so I dragged it all around in my backpack whenever I left the apartment. The form says it's being held for "safekeeping," but I'm not sure it's any safer with the police than it is in the projects.

Another voucher lists a "black switch blade knife" that's checked off as arrest evidence. It's a small penknife on a key ring that I bought in a shoe store—hardly a weapon. But there's no point arguing. If it shows up as a charge it'll probably get dropped.

One of the cops asks for the password for my computer. At first

I refuse to give it to him, but he says if I don't they'll assume it's stolen property. I reluctantly tell him—to prove that it's mine.

"You're not from here, are you?" he asks.

"I've lived in Brooklyn for almost twenty years."

"But you're not American, are you?"

"I'm Scottish—but I've got a green card."

I wonder if he thinks I'm here illegally but he doesn't say anything. He just hands me a copy of the property voucher and locks me back up in a cell.

BY THE TIME we get lined up for transfer to central booking the next morning, I'm dope sick—not really bad, but getting there. The precinct is in the middle of a residential neighborhood, so it's humiliating to be escorted to a police van in handcuffs as parents are taking their kids to school. I used to be one of those parents, walking with Liam. He's away at college, so we haven't talked in a while. I mostly check his Facebook page to see what he's up to, but it's too painful to think about him right now. I look at the floor, and that fucking spot of blood on my sneaker, wishing I'd never left Joe's.

Once we get to the jail opposite the courthouse in downtown Brooklyn, it takes ages to see a judge. For some reason, they cram us all into a few holding cells—elbows touching, legs cramped—when there are plenty of empty cells all around. Some people know each other, but most don't. I notice a Puerto Rican guy I've met a few times. He tells me he's in for crack possession, I tell him I got busted for dope. Everyone seems to be in for something related to drugs.

I can tell I'm not the only one going through withdrawal: Occasionally we catch each other's eyes—we know. There's no hiding the red-rimmed eyes, constant sniffle, and agitation caused by your body starting to panic, wondering why its regular dose of heroin was cut off. I wish I could just fall asleep and escape what's happening, but there's not enough room to lie down.

I don't really have a grasp on time over the next few hours, but at some point I get transferred from the holding pen to the court-house through a tunnel that connects the buildings underground. There's another set of cells, another group of mostly black and brown faces, and more waiting with nothing to do to pass the time.

Finally, a court-appointed lawyer comes to meet with me, a trim, gray-haired guy in his fifties. He explains my charges and tells me it doesn't look good: heroin possession, drug parapherna-lia (the crack pipe), plus the warrants. He seems like a nice guy—genuinely concerned about me, which isn't always the case with these lawyers. I'm not used to this kind of compassion, so for a moment it makes me feel hopeful.

"Can you get me out of this?" I ask.

He laughs, but it's not malicious.

"I can't work miracles," he tells me.

"What about bail? I can get the money." I've burned through a lot of the money I got from selling my house—mostly settling debts and paying back dealers—but I've still got some left in the bank.

"You've been dodging a few warrants, so the judge isn't going to give you bail."

"There's got to be something you can do. How about a pro-gram? Or drug court?"

He looks at me like he wishes he could help, but we both know I've run out of options. Other judges have given me a chance to get treatment, but I skipped the drug tests, blew off the counseling sessions, made excuses for why I didn't show up. I always thought I could get clean on my own—when I was ready, not when I was forced.

"I'm afraid you're going to have to do some time," he says. "But I'll try to keep it as short as possible."

I knew that was likely, but hearing it out loud hits me hard. My gut is churning, I'm light-headed. I feel like I'm gonna throw up.

"Are you okay?" he asks.

I want to tell him how not okay I am, how scared I am of the withdrawal that's coming—and how I'm gonna deal with being locked up. But he looks worried and I don't want to dump my problems on him, so I just nod.

A few minutes later, I'm led into the courtroom for my arraignment, my hands cuffed behind my back. The judge hardly looks at me as he reads my charges, then shoots down any deal my lawyer tries to offer. It's all over in a few minutes. Guilty, no bail—straight to Rikers. He orders me back to court in a few days for sentencing.

I'm dazed looking around the courtroom, wondering if Susan has somehow gotten wind of this and turned up. But why would she? The last time I saw her was when I was selling my house, and then I cut her off—like everybody else. I'm sure they've all given up on me by now.

Then it's back through the tunnel, back to the holding cell, and another eternity of waiting as other people are called into court. Some of them come back angry—they're going to Rikers. Others don't reappear—they've gotten released or bailed out. At least the cell is less crowded, but it's filthy. The toilet stinks and there are half-eaten peanut butter and jelly sandwiches scattered all over the floor.

I wish I could eat something to fill up the emptiness I'm feeling, but even thinking about food makes me nauseous. It's been a day and a half since I last used, so I'm agitated and restless. I can't concentrate. My thoughts are going off on tangents—imagining an escape, wondering what Liam is doing, half-listening to the conversations around me. The chemicals in my brain are going haywire, trying to figure out how to function without drugs.

After the last person has seen the judge, we get cuffed to each other in pairs and file onto buses for the trip from the courthouse to Rikers. These Department of Correction buses always go fast—like they've got the right of way on the Brooklyn–Queens Expressway—so we're sliding around and bumping into each other every time the bus changes lanes. I'm trying hard not to tug on the guy next to me, whose bicep is about the size of my leg.

I don't bother looking out the window—it's too depressing to pass by familiar streets and not know when I'll be free to walk down them. I just close my eyes and put my head on the back of the seat in front of me, cradling it in my one free arm.

As we cross over the bridge between Queens and Rikers Island, it's dark out and the bus is quiet, the incessant talking reduced to the odd comment or murmur. I've been here for short spells and got along fine, but this time everything feels much more ominous.

I'm thinking about the movie *Papillon* with Steve McQueen and Dustin Hoffman, who plot to escape a French penal colony, but when they get the chance Hoffman won't go. Then I remember an old guy from the projects telling me that the first time he went to Rikers it was by ferry—the prisoners were chained to the benches. My mind is pinballing, barely landing on a single thought, but mostly I'm worried about how dope sick I'm getting.

When people ask what it's like to go through heroin withdrawal, I tell them to imagine the worst flu they've ever had, add a bad case of food poisoning, mix in a deep depression, and top it off with a good kicking. Now multiply everything by ten. That's close to what it feels like, and I'm about halfway there right now. I'm aching all over, my eyes are tearing, my nose is running, and I keep breaking out in cold sweats. I'm so sick I just want to pass out.

After we file off the bus, we get uncuffed and line up to be re-photographed, re-fingerprinted, and jammed into cells. There's hardly room to stand at some points, but I manage to curl up on the dirty concrete floor. Names are called, people get moved, I'm dimly aware of what's going on. It must be obvious that I'm in withdrawal because I get pulled out of the cell by a couple of guards.

"Do you need methadone?" one of them asks.

"Maybe just a hit to take the edge off," I tell him. In five minutes, I'm thinking, I could feel almost normal.

"We don't give hits," he says. "If you take it, you're on the program. Probably mandated once you get out."

I've used methadone occasionally when I couldn't get dope, but I don't think it's a great long-term solution. I've seen what it does to people, replacing one drug with another, still stuck in addiction. So as sick as I am, as much as I don't want to feel this pain, I tell them I don't want it—even adding, "I'm good."

They look at me, shrug, and put me back in a cell.

I don't know how long it's been since my last hit, but I can't keep the sickness at bay. Once I throw up, everyone curses at me and yells for the guard. I'm starting to shake, my stomach is cramping, I'm just hoping I don't shit myself. Someone calls me an asshole for not taking the meth, but no one makes any move to help me.

I'm facedown in the bullpen next to my vomit, surrounded by guys who hate me, and I don't really blame them. I know I'm a fucking mess, but there's nothing I can do about it. Eventually the guards come and put me in a cell by myself, where I finally pass out.

———

THE NEXT FEW days are a blur of withdrawal. At some point, I get moved to a dorm where inmates are detained while they're waiting for their cases to get resolved. The most excruciating pain and nausea have slowly subsided, but the depression and anxiety are constant. My joints ache, I'm either too hot or too cold—it's like I've been transplanted into someone else's body and it keeps trying to reject me. I break into sweats for no reason, only to start shivering the minute I peel off some clothes. If I lie down, I want to stand up. If I try to walk, I have to sit. I'm dehydrated and hungry but I can hardly keep anything down.

About a week after my arrest, I get woken up at the crack of dawn, along with all the other inmates who are due back in court. Once we line up for the bus ride to downtown Brooklyn, I'm handcuffed to a guy who makes it clear he doesn't want to be anywhere near me.

"Why am I cuffed to this skanky cracker?" he complains.

That doesn't do a lot for my self-esteem, but I'm sure he's right—I'm wearing the same clothes I had on when I got arrested, which are grimy and smelly by now.

When they open the gate to take us to the bus, it's a beautiful spring morning. We only walk about twenty yards, but the air feels good and there are seagulls flying around. This time I look out the window as we slip and slide all the way back to court.

My lawyer comes to speak with me before I see the judge. He mentions something about my immigration status. I tell him I'm a permanent resident—I've got a green card. He says it could still be an issue, which reminds me of all the times Susan brought this up. The other day, I signed a form saying I didn't want to talk to anyone from immigration. I was three days into detoxing—I hardly knew what was going on—but it did seem weird that they knew I was at Rikers.

I wonder if I should try to get in touch with Susan later, when my head is straight. But sitting in a holding pen, sick and depressed, I can't imagine how the fuck I'd explain everything that happened since I last saw her. After all the times she tried to help me, it got to the point where I couldn't face her. I was too ashamed to let her see what I'd become. Now I've sunk even lower, but I'm so exhausted by the withdrawal I can barely comprehend the fact that I'm about to be sentenced. I just lean my head against the metal bars and close my eyes.

Once I'm called into the courtroom, it doesn't take long for the judge to decide my fate.

"Six months for each charge," he says.

I have three charges, so that's eighteen months—way more than I expected. I look at my lawyer in a panic.

"To run concurrent," the judge adds.

It takes me a minute to realize he means six months total—not eighteen. I close my eyes, thankful for this small break.

My lawyer tells me he thinks it went well—it could've been much worse. With time off for good behavior, I'll probably only do four months.

May, June, July, August, I'm thinking. *Out in September—just in time for Liam's birthday.*

"Can you do me a favor?" I ask him. "Could you call my ex-wife and tell her what happened?"

"Sure," he says. "What's her number?"

As he writes down Anna's info, I can picture her reaction to the shit I'm dumping on her. I wonder how she'll explain this to Liam—or the rest of my family, if she decides to tell them. But mostly I'm just glad I don't have to make any of those calls myself.

CHAPTER THIRTEEN

June 2010
Cobble Hill, Brooklyn

In June 2010, I sent Graham an email message with the subject line: *Are you alive?*

"*That's all I want to know,*" I wrote. "*Well, actually that isn't all I want to know, but that would give me some peace of mind. Your phone isn't accepting messages so even if you're not going to call me how about just a reply with some sign of life?*"

Years earlier, this type of appeal would usually prompt some response from Graham—a photograph with his blurry reflection in a window, a misspelled text I'd scrutinize to gauge if he sent it when he was high. But this time, weeks passed without an answer. The message on his phone said his number was no longer in service. His website was down, his portfolio of photos replaced by a cryptic error message.

He was on my mind because a friend had called to tell me about someone she knew who had died of a heroin overdose. With this seed planted, then watered over the course of many more conversations about her friend, I started to wonder if Graham had met a similar end.

News about someone's death generally arrives on its own schedule, whether it's long dreaded or a complete surprise, but I put off contacting anyone who might know what had happened to Graham because I thought I could control grief's timing.

At first I was too overwhelmed with deadlines to face the prospect of mourning—or at least, that's what I told myself. Then I had a trip planned to visit my family in Michigan, which I didn't want to spend crying about Graham. But after I got back to Brooklyn I thought I was mentally prepared for the overdose I assumed had finally happened. I sent a delicately worded text to Anna, figuring she could at least tell me if Graham was alive.

She didn't reply.

For weeks I debated whether this meant Graham was dead and she couldn't face spreading that news, or she didn't know where he was and wasn't in the mood to type up a response. She and I hadn't had any contact since I bailed Graham out of Rikers years earlier, but I began to worry that she might blame me for something I had—or hadn't—done.

"There's no way to know why she's not answering," my friend Alex told me. "Maybe this means you're not ready to find out."

More than anyone else in my life, Alex didn't judge me for continuing to worry about Graham; she never told me I should just let it go. She bought me drinks, listened to stories about an ex she had never met, and offered guidance instead of the opinions most of us can't resist doling out.

Her advice boiled down to a consistent theme: that we all have to learn how to live with uncertainty, because some things are simply out of our control. It wasn't a particularly novel lesson, but for anyone dealing with an addict, it's a difficult one to learn. Even if you accept that there's little you can do to influence the course of someone's addiction—and I still struggled with that—it's tough to strike a balance between detaching with love and giving up. I'm not sure I ever got it right.

BUT AFTER GRAHAM told me that Tracy had moved in with him, in late 2008, I really did try to put our relationship behind me. With the economy tanking and a midlife crisis looming, I had plenty of other things on my mind.

I turned forty a few months later—throwing a big party to celebrate the occasion, not trying to hide from it. But it did feel like I'd missed out on the milestones most women hit by that point: engagements, weddings, and babies. Almost everyone I knew was married and at least thinking about kids; in April, my sister told me that she was pregnant. I was genuinely happy for her—I never begrudged any of my friends their growing families, partly because I had mixed feelings about juggling that work-life balance. But I was still hoping to find someone who made me feel the way Graham did, and I was still trying to switch gears with my writing.

I was pitching plenty of ideas, including a story about bailing Graham out of Rikers, but I was getting back lots of "not quite right for us" rejections—or worse, just silence. In some sense, that was more frustrating than not having a partner. I didn't feel like I had much control over what was going on with my career, but I actually felt okay about my personal life.

After three years of therapy, I had decided to stop seeing David, sending him an email explaining why: *"Therapy has been enormously helpful to me, in many, many ways, but something about constantly questioning and analyzing everything in my life was getting me down. I need some space to see what's working, and what's not, so I can get a clearer sense of what I still want to address or change."*

I told him that all that self-analysis was starting to feel paralyzing; I was getting tired of second-guessing myself. If I sent another email to someone who hadn't answered my first message, was I accommodating their nonresponsiveness, or was I being proactive by refusing to wait and wonder? Should I date a guy who I didn't think was right for me, or was ruling him out too soon being overly picky? I felt like I'd lost my internal compass—I wanted to trust my instincts again.

When David wrote back, I was relieved that he seemed to support my decision: *"I do understand what you are saying, and I believe that the times when one steps away from therapy are very often times of real growth and change and consolidation, all of which I think will be the case for you."*

It was. I felt like I had accomplished a lot since I started seeing him, but in the end, I think quitting therapy was my biggest triumph. I was done dwelling on the past—I had made peace with those hurts. I wanted to look forward, not back in time.

But even though I had finally distanced myself from Graham, I hadn't completely eradicated him from my life. Just when I thought I'd never hear from him again, he'd pop up in my inbox, drawing me back in—like in May 2009, when he sent an email saying his original case had finally been settled, so he wondered if I'd gotten the bail refund yet.

I had. I just hadn't given it to Graham, mostly because I assumed he'd blow it on drugs. But he'd already paid me back, so technically I owed him that money, and it sounded like he was totally broke. Tracy had turned out to be a nightmare, but she refused to move out and the bank was threatening to foreclose on his house.

Graham wasn't exactly asking for my help—it was a sort of roundabout appeal—but it was close enough that I picked up the phone. Maybe I couldn't help him break free of addiction, but I'd just sold my own apartment, I'd written articles about real estate, I'd grown up with parents who discussed housing prices at dinner. *This was one thing I knew how to do.*

I used the bail check as leverage to get Graham to meet me, hoping to convince him to call a broker and put his house up for sale. He still had a lot of equity he could walk away with if he found a buyer before the bankers swooped in. It galled me to think that some shady lender might end up with all that money.

We met at a local bar one afternoon—not an ideal location, but all the cafés nearby were always crowded with people bent over laptops, and I wanted to be able to sit and talk. When Graham walked in, he looked better than the last time I'd seen him, but he was limping and had a big bruise on his neck.

"I got in a bike accident," he told me, pulling the collar of his jacket up higher. I didn't know whether to believe him, but it didn't really matter. I was there to talk about real estate, not whether he'd gotten into a fight.

For a while, we caught up and laughed and he seemed almost like himself again; those familiar feelings were starting to stir. I didn't want to ruin our reunion by bringing up an unpleasant topic, but I finished my beer and finally blurted it out: "So what's going on with your house?"

"Those fuckers totally screwed me when I refinanced," Graham said, staring at the seltzer glass he was gripping. "My monthly payment ended up doubling, then a big job I was supposed to get fell through, so I was living off savings and when that ran out I got behind on my mortgage. I've been trying to sell some photos, but I'm so deeply in debt I don't think there's any way I can scrape together enough cash to get the bank off my ass."

Since I had loaned him the money to refinance—when I knew he was using—hearing that made me cringe. *Maybe I should've insisted on seeing the terms.*

"I know you love that house," I said, nudging Graham's chin so he'd look at me. "But maybe a change of scenery would actually be good. If you sell now, you'll have some money left to get back on your feet. Rent an apartment for a while, get into a program—or at least find a therapist and really try to quit."

I thought Graham might bristle at that reference to rehab, but he didn't even flinch. "I don't think a shrink can help me at this point," he said, sort of wistfully. It made me livid to see him so resigned.

"Well, then do it for Liam. Don't you think you owe it to him to try to keep some of that money? I mean, even if you just put a sign out front saying *'for sale: best offer,'* you'd be better off than doing nothing. Just take whatever price you can get. This is one thing you can't afford to fuck up."

Now I was the one getting worked up, but I couldn't tell if I was getting through to Graham. When we said goodbye, I gave him a long hug, trying not to cry as I watched him limp away. But I felt a little more hopeful after he sent me an email the next day.

> *thanks for your advice and your right—it would be idiotic*
> *not to sell. it all sort of snowballed so quickley and i tried*
> *to pretend it wasn't happening and then fear and panic*
> *made me hide from/avoid the obvious and here i am broke,*
> *scared, frustrated, and somewhat angry (at me). i've even*
> *felt like just packing up, cutting my losses and going back*
> *to london. start again! thank you for your advice and con-*
> *cern it's very much needed and appreciated—it really means*
> *a lot to me. i didn't get to the mortgage people today i was*
> *to busy in the city trying to sell photos (nothing concrete*
> *yet) i'll deal with them tomorrow. somethings got to give*
> *soon and i hope its not me! seriously though i'll give you a*
> *call if i need words of advice or otherwise (is that ok?)*
>
> *thanks susan,*
> *love graham. x*

I told him I was happy to help him, but he found an agent himself and had it on the market within a few weeks. The day of the open house, I offered to meet him and go for a walk—something a friend had done for me when I sold. I didn't even like my apartment and it was an emotional process, so I figured Graham would have a much harder time moving on.

When I walked through his front door—already open for buyers—all these memories assaulted me, like they'd been waiting for me to come back this whole time. Wandering from room to room, they popped up like haunted house goblins: the day Graham took my picture, my book party, the police search. I wondered where we'd be if Graham had actually gotten clean. *Maybe living here together.* That thought made my heart ache, surrounded by couples making renovation plans. I found Graham in the basement, in the room he'd built for his photography gear. "Let's get out of here," I said.

We rode our bikes out to a pier in Red Hook, sitting on a bench facing the Statue of Liberty. Graham was so out of it I'm not sure much about that day even registered with him. Mostly, he ranted about Tracy, and how she'd ruined his life.

A couple of weeks later, he forwarded a message from his real estate agent, listing all the offers he'd received. At the top Graham wrote, *"almost sold . . ."*

I emailed him back advice about finding a good real estate lawyer, telling him to make sure the contract didn't have any loopholes that might let the buyer back out. *"For all of your talents, reading through fine print isn't at the top of the list, so I strongly suggest you have someone else look at anything before you sign!!"*

All Graham wrote back was "cheers!" That was the last time I heard from him for the next eight months.

When he shut me out, I felt like Charlie Brown all over again, tricked after trusting Lucy. But I'd let myself get drawn into Graham's drama, knowing where it would probably lead—just like when I googled his name a month later, I knew I might be upset by whatever I found. I just didn't expect to stumble on hundreds of self-portraits he'd taken: extremely graphic photos of Graham smoking crack and shooting up. I slowly clicked through every single image, sure he couldn't have meant to post them online.

After closing my laptop, I wrote in my notebook about how looking at those pictures affected me.

I didn't think anything could cut through me like this. It's taken me right back—that sick, hollowed-out feeling of seeing something you wish you didn't know about. Except that in some way, this is exactly what I'd been curious to see. All those close-ups of the needle going into a vein, his expression during and after, the preparations, the rooms and bathrooms and stairwells I never saw. This is like watching a movie of what happened behind doors I imagined but couldn't follow him through—all the dates starting in 2006 right up through recent months.

Here I thought I'd accepted what he was doing, that I was past being shocked. I'm not. These pictures show someone so far gone it's hard to imagine him ever giving it up. This is the world that existed apart from me—the life I didn't want to see as much as I constantly searched for evidence that it existed. Every photo is tinged with despair. Hopelessness. Waste. Maybe the point is, "So you wanted to see? Here it all is." And then we're supposed to feel sick over our voyeurism, because maybe we didn't need to see that after all.

A few days later, I got a bad case of shingles. At first I didn't know what was causing the tingling on the left side of my back and chest, then I broke out in a rash that hurt so badly I couldn't bear to have a shirt touch my skin. When I saw my doctor, she told me that shingles was sometimes brought on by stress, so I wondered if that was my body's way of dealing with seeing Graham's pictures. It was as if all that emotion worked its way along my nerves and erupted, screaming out in excruciating pain.

At the time, I had a yoga teacher who always asked what people in the class wanted to get out of their practice. If someone said, "I want to get rid of the ache in my back," she'd ask, "What do you want to replace it with?" As my shingles pain faded, I realized that I wanted to replace it with acceptance. Graham was gone.

Addiction had consumed him just like Alzheimer's gradually takes over a once-vibrant mind. It was only a matter of time before there was nothing recognizable left.

I didn't know Graham's deal had gone through until later that fall, when I was having lunch with my friend Scott—who had lost touch with Graham shortly after that summer in Montauk. When Scott asked if I'd heard from Graham, I just said that the last time I saw him he wasn't doing too well, and that he had just put his house on the market.

Scott and his wife were in the midst of their own real estate search, so he opened an app on his phone, typed in Graham's address, and showed me the results: Graham's brownstone had sold. *Good for him,* I thought. *Somehow he managed to pull that off.*

Hearing that news was unsettling—it meant that I might not ever see Graham again. I couldn't go by his house if I wanted to find him. But I didn't email him, and I didn't call.

The rest of 2009 went by in the usual holiday blur. I spent Thanksgiving with my cousins, my sister had her baby, I flew to Michigan to see my parents for Christmas. As the recession deepened, layoffs and foreclosures dominated the news, and then in January, a massive earthquake struck Haiti. Compared to most people around the world, I felt lucky: I had money in the bank and a roof over my head. What other people were going through put any of my problems in perspective.

AT ONE POINT when I was trying to decide if I should have any contact with Graham, David had warned me, "Most people have a hard time following through when they say they won't do something ever again." He was right about that—but he was also right when he said that I should act more on impulse.

So when Graham's birthday popped up on my calendar, in March 2010, I dashed off an email saying: *"Just wanted to wish you a happy birthday. Wherever you are and whatever path you're on, I hope fabulous by 50 is still on the horizon."*

I was shocked when Graham wrote back, just two hours later.

thanks. i've sort of been out the loop for a bit! had no computer, didn't check emails for weeks, was living out a suitcase, went a few places, gained some money, lost some money, procrastinated, saw a few films i'd been meaning to see, read a bit, slept a bit, thought a bit. and came to the conclusion that no matter how much you read or how many people you talk/listen to there are some things in life you'll never ever fucking understand!
apart from that i'm okay. you?
i'll call you - really.

That cryptic summary piqued my curiosity. Graham actually did sound okay, but he didn't say where he was—and he didn't ever call. After that, he disappeared: no more emails, no more text messages, not even a photo.

Three months after that, I sent Anna the text message she didn't answer. Then two months later, I found her email address and tried again.

Sorry to put you in the position of (potentially) being the bearer of bad news, but do you know where Graham is and if he's OK? The last time I heard from him was around his birthday. I know he sold the house, and he seemed alright then, but now his phones are out of service and his Web site is down, so I've been wondering if something happened. I understand if you don't want to share any details—maybe you don't know either—but rather than assume the worst I thought I'd ask.

Once again a few days passed without a response. I polled friends (again) about how they would interpret her silence. They told me (again) to just let it go.

Finally, on August 23, an email from Anna arrived.

I hope all's well with you. Unfortunately graham is in jail. He was arrested for drug possession a few months ago. As bad as the scenario sounds, he seems to be doing ok and I think (and hope) it has been a real wake up call for him. He has detoxed and sounds like he is clean. I have spoken to him a couple of times, the last a couple of weeks ago. He sounds in good spirits under the circumstances and he is working in the kitchen there and really seems to want to change his ways.

I've been paying his storage, so he can keep all his things, but haven't paid his phone, hence why it's been disconnected.

He's due for release soon, sometime at the end of this month and there is a chance he could be deported although he's convinced this is highly unlikely.

I did get your text message a while ago and I'm sorry I didn't answer sooner, as I didn't know if I should pass on the info. When I spoke to Graham I did tell him you had got in touch and he said it was ok to tell you. And then I took vacation time and didn't get around to getting in touch with you. I think I've gotten to the stage where I sometimes shut down from it all, as it can be so worrying and I think I get tired of dealing with him. I've told his brother and sister, but they asked that I didn't tell his parents.

Once I hear any more from him, as to his future where-
abouts I can let you know.

In quick succession, I cycled though a series of emotions: relief
(*he's not dead*), annoyance (*why didn't Rikers inmates show up in*
the "WebCrims" database I'd checked?), and dread (*he's going to*
get deported).

Not that it was any of my business, but I was irritated that
Graham hadn't called me, that Anna hadn't gotten back to me
sooner, and that he'd never become a citizen—because of apathy
and Scottish pride. It wasn't "highly unlikely" that he could get
deported; it was much closer to certain.

If Graham didn't already have a good lawyer, it was probably
too late for me to help him. But knowing what was likely to happen to him if he got picked up by immigration, I felt like I had to
try.

CHAPTER FOURTEEN

June 2010
Rikers Island, Queens

A few weeks into my sentence, I'm still reeling from where I've landed, but I've finally come to terms with the daily routine. I've been moved from C-95, for detainees with drug problems, to the 6 building, for sentenced inmates. Almost everyone is doing less than a year for stupid shit, but there are definitely some guys in here who deserve to be off the streets.

At first I was so traumatized bouncing around the system I thought I was going to have a breakdown. I wasn't scared, just totally alone and depressed and beaten down by the constant humiliations. Like the day after I got sentenced, a bunch of us were strip-searched and lined up naked in a dingy room full of T-shirts, uniforms, underwear, and socks. The CO asked my size, reached over to a shelf, and handed me a pile of clothes.

I quickly pulled on the boxers and unfolded the ugly green jumpsuit—which looked like it would've fit Magic Johnson. When I told the guard it was way too big for me, he said, "You wear what you get."

That's when it hit me: *I'm not a detainee anymore, I'm a fucking prisoner.*

There was a three-hundred-pound guy next to me who'd gotten a uniform that was about four sizes too small, so without saying a word we swapped. That's how it is in here—you figure out how to get by, adapting almost by instinct.

I've been off drugs for almost a month now, so the dope sickness has faded, but it's been replaced by a persistent, gnawing depression and these crushing waves of regret. At least with the physical effects of withdrawal you know they'll eventually end—the mental agony feels like it could go on forever. That just adds to the painful monotony of each day, which follows the same mind-numbing routine.

5:00 A.M. *Breakfast*

I have no idea why we get woken up so fucking early for breakfast, but if you skip it, lunch isn't until noon and since dinner is at five o'clock, that's a long time to go without eating. But after a while I don't bother getting up. It's not worth it for some shit coffee, a piece of tasteless fruit, a mini cereal box, and a few slices of bland bread. "Sleep late, lose weight," everyone says—and that's no joke. I already feel bloated, eating way more than I did when I was using.

7:30 A.M. *Shave—if you're lucky*

A CO steps into the dorm and says "razors" so quietly sometimes no one hears her—usually it's the female guards who like to fuck with us. But if it's actually audible, everyone who wants to shave has to line up, exchange their IDs for a cheap single-blade razor, and try to shave using a mirror that's been scoured so much you can hardly see your reflection. Not that I really care how I look—I know it can't be good.

8:00 A.M. *Coffee*

Once I've got some money on my commissary account, I can make instant coffee—52 cents for a small pouch of coffee, 10 cents for a tiny creamer, and 5 cents for a packet of sugar. It's not great, but it's better than the insipid crap they serve in the mess hall. Sometimes the only newspaper I can find is a day-old *El Diario*, which I can't read since it's in Spanish, but I look at the pictures and try to figure out the story. This is always the worst time of the day for me, realizing I still have fifteen hours to get through until lights-out.

10:00 A.M. *Yard time*

Before we can go out to the yard—a patch of dried-up grass—we get searched multiple times: standing against the wall with our arms and legs spread, then passing through a metal detector, then another pat-down with guards constantly shouting, "Shut the fuck up or you're going back to the dorm!" All just to walk in circles around a dusty track or wait for a turn to lift a set of rusty barbells. Sometimes I lie on the grass watching planes take off from LaGuardia Airport—so close I can almost make out the faces in the windows.

12:00 P.M. *Lunch*

After we line up and shuffle to the mess hall, we each get handed a plastic tray through a slot in the wall, with a meal that barely passes for food—salad you wouldn't feed to a pet rabbit, a taco shell dripping with mushy meat, and a bruised banana or mealy apple. Sitting at the table assigned to our dorm, everyone crams it down and trades whatever they don't want while the guards pace back and forth. We don't get much time before we're ordered to clear up, passing our trays through another slot on the way out.

2:00 P.M. *Quiet time*

Every afternoon the dayroom shuts for an hour or so, which means no TV, no playing cards, and no phone calls. The COs call it "quiet time," like we're all in kindergarten. We can read, write, nap, or talk *quietly,* but there's no milling around. I don't mind—it gives me a chance to read. You can have books sent to you, or occasionally the "library" opens, which is really a bunch of tables with donated books in the old gym. It was weird coming across all these writers I've photographed, like Dave Eggers and Jonathan Franzen, but in here meeting James Patterson or John Grisham would be a lot more impressive—their books are always in demand.

3:30 P.M. *Another count*

By midafternoon we're next to our beds for the third count of the day. If the CO marching up and down the dorm doesn't come up with the right number, he has to start all over and do it again. Sometimes the numbers don't add up and there's a shutdown of the entire jail. It's one of those things you get used to, the annoyance of stopping whatever you're doing while a guard mutters numbers and we all wait—five times a day.

5:00 P.M. *Dinner*

Another trip to the mess hall, but at least it means we're getting closer to the end of the day. My request for a vegetarian meal hasn't been approved, so I keep trading my meat for whatever vegetables other guys don't want. It's never enough, so I end up eating too much bread to fill myself up. We all have to bring our green plastic cups to every meal—if yours gets stolen or lost it can be a nightmare trying to get a new one. That's one of the many ways this place makes you feel like a child.

6:30 P.M. *Evening mayhem*

As the day progresses, boredom turns into frustration and then anger as the noise level gets louder. I can't believe how much everyone around me seems to be alright with this shit—laughing and joking while I'm practically tearing my hair out. I wish I had someone to talk to, but I guess I look pretty rough from kicking dope so people seem to be avoiding me. Mostly I just pace back and forth or sit on my bed staring at everyone else, hating myself for letting this happen.

11:00 P.M. Last count, lights-out

The last of the day's many counts, but at least it brings an end to the mindless conversations around me. Once the lights go out, it usually takes me a long time to fall asleep, so I lie there looking around at all these grown men curled up in single beds, trying not to think about how I ended up here. I remember years ago telling myself, *I'm not going to lose Susan, I'm not going to fuck up my photography career, I'm not going to lose my house, I'm not going to get locked up.* But all those things happened and now here I am.

If this is what I have to get through for the next hundred-plus days, I can't imagine how the fuck I'm gonna make it.

THINGS START TO look up when I bump into an old friend, Marco, in the yard. He's a wiry Hispanic guy who grew up in Brooklyn—we used to buy from the same dealers and hang out in the same spots in the hood. As we wander around talking about who else we've seen on the island and what news we've heard from the outside, he mentions he's got a job in the kitchen. I beg him to hook me up.

"You've got to get me in there. I've been working in the mental health dorm occasionally, but it's really boring and I'm only on call. I need a job that'll take my mind off this shithole."

"I can try," Marco says. "But my boss is tough—and you'll have to tell him you're doing a bullet."

"What the fuck's a bullet?"

"A year, dumb-ass. If you're only doing a short bid they don't want to hire you. It's too much of a hassle to train you."

It takes three days before Marco manages to sneak me into the kitchen during lunch. His boss is a quiet guy with a pained expression on his face—as if he's the one dealing with being locked up. The so-called interview is easy: Marco's bragging about what a great worker I am and how I went to college. I get the job, starting a couple of days later when another guy goes home.

I thought working in the kitchen would involve more real cooking, but in reality it's mostly dishing up things that have been prepared somewhere else. It's still busier than I expected, with guys wheeling racks of food around and trolleys coming and going and the constant clatter of metal pans being dropped. My two shifts consist of loading hundreds of dirty trays into slots in a conveyor belt that feeds into a huge dishwasher that belches steam and sprays hot water the whole time. It's exhausting, and I'm only making about twenty dollars working seven days a week—a long way from getting paid thousands of dollars a day to shoot big advertising campaigns, with catered meals.

But working two shifts a day eats up a lot of time, and it helps me make friends in the dorm. All the kitchen workers sneak food out, jamming a piece of chicken or some fruit into a rubber glove, stuffing it down their pants, and tying the fingers around the waistband of their boxers. I usually share whatever I bring back, so before long I'm mixing with the other guys in my dorm, even playing in some of the card games at night. The first time I was asked to play on one of the card teams, I finally felt like I'd been accepted—which was a weird feeling, realizing I was starting to get comfortable in jail.

Marco and I only work together during the lunch shift, and for those few hours we manage to take ourselves out of Rikers. He grew up surrounded by drugs and criminality, cycling in and out of jail ever since he was sixteen, but he's a different person when he's not getting high, telling me how much he misses his kid and how badly he wants to change. We talk constantly as we work, taking turns lifting and loading the trays—making plans for getting out, starting over, staying clean.

"If you fucking relapse when you get out of here, I'm going to kick your ass," he says, punching my arm so hard I drop a tray into the dish machine, causing it to jam and shudder to a halt. When I look at Marco, I know he's talking about himself as much as me.

"Trust me," I tell him, yanking the tray out and restarting the machine. "I'm done with all that—it brought me nothing but misery."

But the truth is, I'm pretty fucking worried about how I'm going to keep away from everyone who's gonna be all over me once I'm out. At least Marco has a halfway house set up—I've got no place to live except in the projects, surrounded by people desperate to get me back on the pipe.

Usually I don't think too much about what I'm gonna do, but now it's on my mind as I walk back to the dorm—down the long corridor, through the heavy doors, and up the stairs. Thinking of all the people I used to know, friends who aren't junkies or crackheads, I can't imagine how they'd react if I suddenly popped up saying I needed a place to stay. I haven't seen or even talked to most of them in years.

The only person I've talked to is Anna. I called her a few weeks ago, after finally plucking up the courage. Considering how I expected her to react, she's been pretty good about all this—paying the fees for my storage unit, putting money on my commissary account, and letting my brother and sister know what happened. But she hasn't told Liam yet, so it kills me to think he has no idea where I am or why I haven't been around. I'm desperate to talk to him, but Anna wants me to wait until she speaks to him first.

It makes me sick picturing him hearing that I'm in jail. I can't imagine how he's gonna feel about me—I just wish I could tell him myself. I wrote Anna a couple of long letters, trying to explain how I ended up here, my whole trajectory even going way back to our divorce, when Liam was young. That's one of the hardest things about being in here, just dealing with how far I let myself fall. I'd become all the worst things anyone ever said or thought about me.

Once you've detoxed and can think straight, you've got to face up to all the shit you did and all the people you've hurt, with no way to escape the guilt and shame. Mostly I try to keep busy so I don't dwell on it too much—which is why I'm taking every shift I can get in the kitchen. But it still rears up at me every so often, the things I saw and the people I was around and the life I basically accepted. You can't ever erase any of that.

"ANOTHER DAY, ANOTHER tray," one of the COs tells me as I walk into the kitchen for the lunch shift. She's taken to calling me "Lucky Charm"—like the cereal—because she thinks I'm Irish.

"Why don't you tell her you're Scottish?" asks my friend Jimmy, an Irish American guy who's just about the only person I've met in here who isn't a drug dealer, junkie, or wannabe gangster.

"It's better than Braveheart," I tell him. "That's what everyone was calling me when I first got here. I hated that film."

Jimmy laughs and makes one of his many *Seinfeld* references before heading off to his job with the cleanup crew. It was such a relief to meet him when I got moved to 5 upper, the kitchen workers' dorm. He got busted out on Long Island for driving with a suspended license—the judge gave him a year, all over some unpaid traffic tickets—but he and some other guys ended up getting transferred to Rikers because of overcrowding in the local jail. Some of them seem freaked out to be here, but not Jimmy. He doesn't let things get to him—unlike me.

"You're quiet, but you sure don't take shit," he told me, right after I moved in and had to stand up to this asshole who wanted one of my apples. I told the guy to fuck off and he got up in my face about it, but eventually he backed down. I knew he wasn't going to risk losing his good time by getting in a fight with me—and if I gave him an apple, he would've been back the next day wanting my phone calls or my sneakers, and they cost me ten honey buns.

One of the kids who works in intake had stolen them and I was the highest bidder—the Jackie Chan slippers they give you were killing my feet. Sometimes I feel bad picturing some poor guy getting released and finding out his sneakers are missing, but that's how things work in this place. If a dirty cop doesn't pocket your cash when he busts you, chances are you'll lose a watch or a ring or something else while you're going through the system.

But Jimmy doesn't let any of this stuff faze him—I think people respect him for that. He doesn't give a fuck about where anyone's been or what they've done, just as long as they don't bother him. Ever since meeting him, time has gone faster and there have even been moments I've almost forgotten I'm in jail. I actually look forward to coming back to the dorm and chilling out after a hard day's work.

Tonight after my dinner shift, I take a shower, put on a fresh T-shirt and pants, wash my other set in the sink, and head to the dayroom with Jimmy. Even when he's talking to me or playing cards, he's got one eye on whatever's going on in the rest of the dorm.

"Looks like the evening show has started," he says, nodding toward the guys working out down by "the projects"—what everyone calls the area by the bathroom. Jimmy got my bed moved to the "Upper East Side"—the corner farthest from the toilets, with the only fan. The strip running through the dorm is "Broadway," and the section next to the CO's bubble is "Police Plaza." There are always guys with their shirts off doing press-ups by the bathroom, trying to impress the trannies—but pretending they're not.

"Did you see the one that got brought in today?" I ask him. "I swear he looks so much like a woman I did a double take in the bathroom."

"Big lips, purple hair?" Jimmy says, sitting down at one of the tables and dealing a hand of rummy. "Yeah, I saw her. We've sure had a weird mix pass through this dorm lately."

It's true—gangbangers, trannies, skinheads, suburbanites, old farts, young punks, and guys from just about every corner of the globe. But the person everyone's talking about is the jail's new celebrity, Lil Wayne. He's up in protective custody—kept away from anyone who might want to hurt him. Rumor has it he's been buying up everybody's phone time and rapping to some producer, making beats for a Rikers album. I don't buy it, but every time I've delivered meals to his dorm he's been on the phone.

As Jimmy lays down another run—he almost always beats me—we talk about his kids and how his ex-wife is dealing with him being locked up. When he asks me about Liam, I tell him how much it hurts that I let him slip out of my life, and how worried I am that he won't be able to forgive me. There were times I saw him when I was really fucked up, but he always treated me like I was his dad—he didn't ever act out or confront me. That's what's on my mind all the time lately: how much I must've hurt him and how I'm gonna deal with that when I see him.

"You've got to keep yourself clean if you want to have a relationship with your son," Jimmy says. "If you relapse, it's not gonna happen."

"I know," I tell him. Jimmy doesn't let me get away with feeling sorry for myself. That's how he is—no bullshit, no whining. Man up and move on.

Just as I'm dealing another hand—after finally winning for a change—a young Jamaican guy comes up and asks, "Yo, Jim, can

I get one of your calls? It's my mom's birthday and I already used my phone time talking to my girl."

"Sure," he says. "Let me finish this game and I'll set you up."

We each get a couple of phone calls a day, but Jimmy rarely uses his so he's always trading them or giving them away. That's one of the reasons everybody likes him—the Mexicans make food for him, he's always getting asked to be on somebody's card team, even the big gangsters come to him for advice. The other night, one of the older Crips was almost in tears, upset about all the young gangbangers running around with their bullshit and swagger, disrespecting people.

That's the crazy thing about Rikers—some people act like it's cool to be here, bragging about whatever they did on the outside. It's like a finishing school for criminals. If you got busted for dealing, you're guaranteed to meet a better connect. If you're in for shoplifting, you'll learn how to beat the store detectors. If you boosted cars, someone will teach you how not to get caught. Everybody comes out of here even more embedded in a life of crime—and it doesn't seem like there's any attempt to give people better options.

JUST BEFORE AFTERNOON count on the Fourth of July, two mess hall guys wheel a cart into the dorm and start handing out small tubs of ice cream with a Stars and Stripes flag on the lid. We all hurry to line up like they're giving out hundred-dollar bills. Everything you take for granted on the outside has a whole different value in here, so pretty soon people are trading their ice cream for phone calls or envelopes or stamps. I give mine to a kid I know who's just come in, only to see him trade it for a stamp. I don't mind—I'll get more in the kitchen later—but I tell him he should've gotten a stamp *and* an envelope. It won't take him long to figure out what things are worth.

Since our dorm is on the far west side of the island, we can see the sky above Manhattan, so everyone is talking about watching the fireworks once the sun goes down. Last year I watched them from the roof of the projects, high on dope—so broke I was getting drugs on credit, promising dealers I'd pay them back once my house sold. But it took forever to close, so it got pretty scary with dealers threatening me, adding interest to the money I already owed. Everybody was coming after me—drug dealers, banks, credit card companies, fucking Time Warner—and by that point I'd pushed away anybody who could've helped me. The last person who even tried was Susan. Apparently she emailed Anna a few weeks ago, asking where I was.

I told Anna it was okay to let her know I'm at Rikers, but I'm surprised Susan still cares about me. The last time we saw each other was just after I'd gone out to Coney Island Hospital to detox—one of many attempts to get clean—and when I got home, there was a foreclosure notice stapled to my door. It seemed like it was a done deal, but Susan convinced me I should try to sell, so I pulled it together enough to clean the place up, plant some flowers in the yard, and throw a coat of paint on the walls. I remember she came over the day of the open house, but it took a while to actually sell, so I was really drowning in debt by the end of last year. After everything she'd done to help me, I couldn't ask her to lend me money, and I didn't want her to know how bad off I was. Seeing her was always a painful reminder that I'd lost her—I didn't want to put myself through that again. Then once the closing finally happened, all my promises to myself that I'd get clean went out the window. The worst thing in the world for a junkie or a crackhead is having money.

I'd thought about going back to London or Scotland, but I'd lost my passport and my green card, and trying to replace them felt too risky. I still had open warrants, so I doubt I could've gotten out of the country anyway. I was basically trapped at Joe's place, with no one to turn to and nowhere else I could go. I thought that was just the way it was going to be, and I was going to see it through until I ran out of money. Then I got arrested and dumped here, and now I've got to figure out what I'm gonna do once I get released.

Jimmy and I have been talking about getting an apartment together, maybe somewhere in a different part of Brooklyn. He knows people who can help us find a place—it's tough if you've got a criminal record—and I've got money for the deposit, so hopefully it'll work out. He wants me to go into business with him, scrapping cars, since I'll have my driver's license and he won't get his back for a while. I told him I'd think about it—I doubt I'll get work as a photographer. But I can't wait to be able to take pictures again.

I'd love to be able to photograph what it's like in here. Not just the shitty parts about being locked up, but there are times when you can still appreciate the way flashes of lightning illuminate the dorm or the sun comes through the slats of the windows. Like tonight—the sunset is casting these bands of orange and yellow light across the walls and the shadows of people passing by make it look almost like a painting. There's a breeze coming in, so the dorm has cooled down and everyone is in a pretty upbeat mood waiting for the sky to get dark. Once the fireworks start, even though they're way off in the distance, we all crowd into the corner where you can see them, the occasional burst of color leaving long trails in the sky. It almost feels like we're out there enjoying it with everyone else, except we're not having barbecues or drinking beer or lying on blankets in the grass, so pretty soon the reality of where we are kicks back in. As people drift off after the fireworks end, you can tell the mood has changed. It's quieter than usual when the CO shouts, "Lights out—it's bedtime. No talking!"

———

THE FIRST TIME I get a call for a visit I'm at work in the kitchen. "MacIndoe!" the CO yells. "You've got a visitor. Find someone to cover for you and get back to your dorm."

They never tell you who the visitor is, but there's only one person it could be: Tracy. She's been writing to me and told me she was going to visit sometime, but I thought maybe she'd changed her mind. I don't particularly want anyone to see me in jail—and I'm *really* not sure how I feel about seeing her.

After I got arrested, I blamed Tracy for a lot of the shit that had happened to me, especially since I was on my way to meet her when I got stopped by the cops. I was glad that she was finally out of my life, so when I got her first letter, I was angry at her for tracking me down. But she kept writing to me and I hadn't been in touch with anyone except Anna and the odd phone call with Joe, so I was feeling pretty isolated at that point. Eventually I wrote her back, she sent me her number, and then I called her. And that's how Tracy got back into my life—after me vowing I'd never see her again.

Once I get to the dorm, I'm escorted with about eight other guys to the visiting area, where dozens of inmates are waiting in a long corridor, a few complaining about being there for hours. A guard hands me a basket and tells me to change out of my uniform into a gray jumpsuit and a pair of plastic flip-flops, then tells me to take a seat and wait for my name to be called.

Some people sit there silently, clearly bored, others are going on and on about who their visitor is, the talk rising and falling with the noise from an old telly mounted on the wall. As names are called, prisoners come back and change into their uniforms— a few waiting to pick up packages left by their families, which have to go through a separate search. I sit there so long I'm starting to think Tracy must've left when a CO finally calls my name and number.

He leads me into another area where I get strip-searched in

front of other inmates. An overweight guard orders: "Lift your balls . . . turn around . . . squat . . . pull your ass apart . . . spread your toes . . . open your mouth . . . stick out your tongue. . . ." As I'm going through all these humiliating motions, all I can think is: *What the fuck do they think I'm going to smuggle OUT of jail?*

After I get dressed, I'm led into the visiting area—a big open room with a play space for kids and a bunch of tables. I spot Tracy, give her a hug, and sit down opposite her at a small table. She told me she'd been to rehab and moved into a halfway house, and she does look a lot healthier. She's got some color in her cheeks and she's not as painfully thin.

But I'm still wary of her, so I don't really know what to say.

"How are you doing?" she asks, a huge smile spreading across her face.

"I'm alright—apart from being in jail."

"Well, it's good to see you, you look great."

"I doubt that." Even with the crappy mirrors in here, I know my hair has gotten thinner and I've put on weight. "But you look ten times better than the last time I saw you."

"Getting clean has been really good for me," she says. "I'm such a different person now. It's like I'm learning how to live again, focusing on what's important—I really wanted you to see how much I've changed."

As she's talking about how great recovery has been for her, I try to block out the fact that she's out there, free and happy about turning her life around, with no idea what it's like for me in here. So I'm trying to appreciate being out of the dorm and seeing different faces, only half-listening to her go on and on about why I should get into a program.

"I really think you should sign up for some kind of rehab when you get out," she says. "You're not going to be able to do this on your own."

I know she means well, but sitting here in a jail jumpsuit, it's hard to listen to her tell me what to do—especially since I was on my way to meet her when I got arrested.

"Listen, after spending the summer in jail, the last thing I want is to be locked down in some program, being told what to do and when I can do it. Maybe I'll go to some meetings, but I'm not gonna spend another four months stuck somewhere talking about how much I fucked up when what I really need to do is get on with my life."

Tracy just looks at me for a minute, not saying anything, but it's obvious she doesn't want to let it go. "So what are you going to do when you get out? You can't go back to the projects—you know they'll drag you down just like they did before."

"I'm not going back there. I've got a friend in here who's going to help me get an apartment."

I'm starting to get irritated—I really don't want to get grilled about my plans or what she wants from me, so I change the subject and point out a guy I know who's talking to his parents. The dad's wearing a suit and tie and the mom's dressed like she just came from church. This kid went to a good school in Manhattan but he acts like he grew up in the ghetto. It's strange seeing people with their families, realizing that they have these other lives outside of jail.

We're only allowed an hour for visits, so considering how long I waited, it goes by pretty fast. I tell Tracy about my daily routine and all the different people I've met in Rikers. She tells me about the women in her program and how hard she's trying to turn her life around. She's made it clear that she wants to get back together when I get out of here, but as much as I want the best for her, I can't see that happening. Our relationship went south pretty much right after I met her, but I'd already let her move in, thinking she'd help cover my mortgage—which she didn't for most of the time she was there. "I can forgive, but I can't forget," I've told her, but she doesn't want to hear it, and I don't have it in me to be totally blunt.

Once the CO comes over and says, "Time's up!" I give Tracy a quick hug and thank her for coming to see me.

"I'll try and come again," she says. "Hang in there, you're gonna be fine. Call me later, okay? I'll write you!"

After our visit, I have to strip for another cavity search, which is even more thorough this time. Since I missed dinner, I get a sandwich instead, but I just pick at it. I'm too caught up thinking about the wreckage of the last few years to eat.

BY MID-JULY, THE summer heat has turned this place into a pressure cooker—it's got to be nearly a hundred degrees some days. The smallest thing seems to set people off. If it's not the phones, it's the TV, and if it's not the TV then it's the fucking fan. With all the fights breaking out, the whole jail seems to be ringing with alarms all day.

Today they brought in a kid who's a Blood—fuck knows how that happened 'cause usually the gang unit checks everyone out, so they can keep people from rival gangs separated in different dorms. All afternoon this kid's been swaggering around, throwing gang signs at all the young Crips, winding everyone up. I was sure all hell was going to break loose, but some of the older guys were able to keep things under control.

Then around nine thirty, just as I'm asking Jimmy if I can borrow his reading glasses—he managed to work through the bureaucracy and get a pair—I hear shouts coming from the bathroom. Everyone runs toward the wall separating the showers from the rest of the dorm, watching through the windows. There are about half a dozen guys going at it, pummeling each other and shouting insults. Two COs are in the middle of it, trying to get some order, but they're all slipping and sliding on the wet floor. I'm waiting for the pin to get pulled or security to burst in, but before that happens they manage to break it up. All we get is a lecture about keeping tempers in check so they don't have to come down hard on us, like in some of the rowdier dorms.

But the next morning, we're woken up by the sound of a dozen guards marching in.

"Okay, fellas—get dressed, sit on the end of your bed, face the window, NO SHOES," one of them orders.

The search guys lead us into the dayroom, where we have to stand with our hands on our heads while they bring us out one by one and rifle through our stuff. Pulling off bedsheets, looking under mattresses, leafing through books and magazines, tossing things everywhere, then they take us each into the bathroom to frisk us for contraband or weapons. The whole time, other guards are looking under and around everything with flashlights and little mirrors on sticks—behind the TV, on top of window ledges, under the beds. I'm used to getting treated like dirt, but today I'm not in the mood to deal with this shit, lying on my bed facedown with my hands behind my back while everyone else goes through the same routine.

After the search, sanitation comes in and sweeps whatever got tossed on the floor into garbage containers—magazines, family photos, food we bought from commissary, books. They don't give a fuck, it's all gone. Once they leave, the atmosphere in the dorm is even more toxic.

"This is just gonna set people off again," Jimmy says. "Let's get out of here—they're gonna call yard soon."

Once we get outside, Jimmy and I walk around in circles for a bit, but it's hot and sticky so we end up lying on the grass looking up at the sky, trying to pretend we're anywhere else.

"I'm fed up being surrounded by the lowest common denominator mentality in here," I tell him. "Inmates who are too fucking stupid to stay under the radar, asshole guards who overact just 'cause they can, medical staff that don't give a shit about us—this whole place is totally dysfunctional."

"Don't let it get to you. One more month and you're done."

"Yeah, and then what? You're not getting out until six weeks after me and I really don't know how I'm gonna deal with everything on my own."

"Listen, you're a smart guy, you've got a little cash put aside, you just have to get out there and hustle. Most of these nitwits only know how to make money in the criminal world—you've done well in the real world. You just need to stay away from anyone who's going to drag you back down."

I know Jimmy's right, especially about who I need to avoid. Some of my stuff is still at Joe's place—if it hasn't been stolen by now—so I'm worried about going back to the projects to pick it up.

"The thing is, I'm not sure how much I trust myself to stay on the right side of the tracks," I admit.

"If you can keep your shit together in here, Graham, you can hold on a few more weeks till I'm out."

Jimmy's not an addict, so he doesn't quite get that a lot can happen in a few weeks—or days. But what really scares me is the idea that I might be vulnerable for the rest of my life. The thought of having to deal with being in recovery every day, forever, is totally fucking with my head right now.

ONE MORNING I wake up from a drug dream that's so realistic it takes me a few minutes to realize where I am. I've had a few of these nightmares since I've been here, but this one lasted all night long. Every time I woke up I'd fall back into the same scene—smoking crack and shooting up in some random apartment with a bunch of junkies I didn't know.

The feeling that I've actually done drugs lingers with me as I lie in bed. I let it pass, but it felt so fucking real it scares me. The memories coming flooding back, my hands are shaking, and there's sweat running down my neck. For a while I just lie there, wondering what it would be like to get high right now.

To be honest, it's been a struggle to stay clean in here. There always seem to be a few people who are fucked up or coming down. Some hide it well, but others are so out of it, nodding off or stuck looking out a window, it can set me off. The cravings come roaring back and I'm salivating just thinking about a hit. Then I've got to drag myself back from those thoughts before they over-whelm me.

At first I couldn't work out how anyone was getting drugs in Rikers, but it didn't take long to catch on. Someone offered me methadone—they call it "keep" in here—which he got from one of the guys on the program. After a while it was pretty obvious who's got what: cigarettes, lighters, weed, pills, dope. Rumor has it most of the contraband comes in through workers or guards, but inmates usually end up selling it. A guy I know told me he had a bunch of Percocet so well hidden he'd beaten two searches, but then he got moved so he needed to find some way to get his stash to his new dorm.

Buying drugs in Rikers is a lot more complicated than it is on the street, especially if you're trying to maintain a habit. You've got to make all sorts of deals, like finding someone to put money on the seller's commissary account or getting a friend to pay a dealer on the outside, which gets you credit in here. I don't know who I'd get to do that even if I wanted to get high—which I don't. I've been clean for almost three months now, and I'm feeling pretty good about that. I'm starting to get that clarity of mind people talk about—which isn't always a good thing, but just being able to get through the day without that tedious routine of buying and using drugs is pretty fucking brilliant.

IN MID-AUGUST, ABOUT a week before I'm due to be released, I get a letter from my brother. It's the first I've heard from any of my family since I've been in Rikers. Anna sent me their addresses and phone numbers, but it's almost impossible to make international calls from here, and every time I tried to write, I just couldn't do it. I kept imagining my mum and dad in shock after getting a letter telling them I was in jail, and I had no idea how to explain how everything spiraled out of control. So I'm nervous about opening my brother's letter and reading what he wrote.

> *Hope you are doing okay, things are going as well as expected, and that you are getting healthy and stronger. I would have gotten in touch sooner but I had a lot going on. Me and R. have split up, I'm out of the house, and I did not really know what to write.*
>
> *We all saw Liam a few weeks ago, he was in Dublin for five days with his girlfriend. He's doing very well and really enjoying college.*
>
> *Anyway Graham, what we need to know is what's happening on your release i.e. deportation or not. If you do go back to Scotland please do not turn up on Mum and Dad's doorstep. I know that sounds very hard, but I think it would be too much for them. This whole episode has taken a terrible toll on them, and I think the shock would totally destroy them. It was for this reason that we decided not to tell them you were in jail. But if you do go back to Scotland, you could get in touch with them and make up some story as to why you are back (without the jail-deported part).*
>
> *I know this is a short note but we can catch up much better very soon. All the very best, and all my love.*

Reading it tears a hole in me—the familiar handwriting and the sort of unemotional distance. I fold up the small piece of paper and just sit on the edge of my bed for a while, trying to let the words sink in.

I used to be so close to my brother. We ran together, shared apartments in Scotland, and had a lot of the same friends growing up, but the last time I saw him was in 2008, when he came to New York to visit me. It was a few months after I'd met Tracy, and things were really going off the rails. I tried so hard to keep it together while he was here, using just enough to keep myself level, but I'm sure he knew something was up. We didn't talk about it—I don't think either of us wanted to go there—but it wasn't like how we usually are together. Once he left for the airport I just felt this emptiness, like it wasn't ever going to be the same between us. I went straight out and got completely fucked up.

After that we just drifted apart. I can't even remember the last time we talked. I had no idea he and his wife were breaking up, or that Liam was going over to visit everyone in Dublin. It makes me realize how much I've isolated myself, totally shutting out my whole family. Still, it's a bit harsh that my brother's telling me not to show up at Mum and Dad's.

Actually, I'm surprised he thinks I'm getting deported. I know Homeland Security put a detainer on me, so I'll probably have to meet with immigration before I get released, but everyone in here seems to think I'll be fine. I've got a green card, and I was only convicted of a misdemeanor, but now that the whole thing is looming up on me, I'm starting to worry that the jailhouse rumor mill might be wrong.

The day I'm supposed to be getting released, I'm in outtake, already back in street clothes, thinking I'm minutes from freedom, when two guys from immigration show up and pull me out of line. They shackle my hands, my feet, and my waist and exchange some paperwork with the guards. I'm in shock. I thought I might have to meet with immigration when I got released, but I never expected anything like this.

All the other guys are shouting at me, asking if I'm being extradited, or if I'm a terrorist, while the two agents in black uniforms

are going through my bag. They're pulling out clothes and magazines and books, saying, "You can't take this . . . you can't take
this," throwing everything except my wallet, checkbook, and letters into the garbage.

"But that's my stuff," I protest. "I need it."

"You won't need any of this where you're going," one of them
says, then they haul me through outtake and out the door.

Part Three

US

"With liberty and justice for all."

—Francis Bellamy

CHAPTER FIFTEEN

August 2010
Varick Street Processing Center, Manhattan

In the Homeland Security van on the way from Rikers Island to the processing center on Varick Street, my ankles are still shackled and my handcuffs are attached to a chain around my waist. All I know is that we're heading for lower Manhattan on the Brooklyn–Queens Expressway, a road I've taken home from LaGuardia Airport many times.

We pass Greenpoint, then Williamsburg, and I can see the Brooklyn Bridge up ahead. The neighborhood where I've lived for twenty years is so close I could walk there. But the van flips a right onto the Manhattan Bridge, and just like that we cross the East River, leaving Brooklyn behind. My stomach is churning and my back is dripping with sweat.

There's another guy in the back of the van who looks Mexican, probably in his twenties, but he doesn't speak English so I can't talk to him. We're separated from the two agents by a metal screen—it's like we're in a cell on wheels. They don't say much except that they're with Immigration and Customs Enforcement, and that I should sign the paperwork they've got with them, saying I agree to leave the United States.

"It'll be a lot easier for you if you sign," one of the ICE guys says. "If you don't, it can take a long time to see a judge."

"Can I talk to a lawyer?" I ask.

"You don't get a lawyer—you're not a citizen."

"Well, can I call someone?"

"Once you sign the paperwork, we'll give you a five-minute call."

"What about bail?"

"You've got a drug conviction so that's not an option."

I can't fucking believe this. No right to a lawyer, no phone call, no bail? After four months at Rikers, I'm used to being treated with total indifference, but these guys are so cold you'd think I killed somebody—not got caught with a couple of dime bags of dope.

"I don't understand what's going on. Am I getting deported?"

He doesn't give me a straight answer, just repeats what he already said: that if I sign the papers, this will all be easier—whatever that means.

"Well, I'm not signing anything in a van crossing the East River. Who can I talk to when we get there?"

"You'll be processed at Varick Street," he says. "I'm just trying to make it quicker for you."

None of this makes sense so I stop talking and look out the darkened window. For some reason they haven't been pressuring the other guy to sign anything, probably because they don't speak Spanish—or maybe he already signed.

Driving through Chinatown, we pass a bunch of stores I've shopped at, buying lighting gear for photo shoots, or cheap produce and Chinese buns. Then the van turns right, heading toward Soho. I used to work at a photography gallery near here, after I first moved to New York, but now it feels like all those years have fast-forwarded to this instant.

When we pull up to Varick Street, the van backs into a loading dock. Once the heavy garage door closes, the driver tells us to get out. Another white van is unloading half a dozen other immigrants, all shackled and chained. A different agent in a black military-style uniform yells at us to line up and face the wall.

Once the freight elevator arrives, he orders us to get in and turn toward the back. "Don't look at me, don't look at each other, don't talk!"

As the elevator rumbles upstairs, my nose bumps against the metal. I can sense everyone else's fear. When the doors open, we're led down what looks like any office corridor, except we're shuffling with shackles around our ankles and the only sound is chains. Then a guard directs us into a huge, brightly lit room— ICE's processing center. I can't believe how many people are bustling around.

ICE agents in black uniforms are taking fingerprints and photographs, officers in white shirts are rifling through paperwork at rows of desks, and dozens of detainees are moving from one place to another, looking completely dazed. The whole thing feels like some kind of industrial production line, and we're on the conveyor belt.

Along one wall, there's a row of cells with signs on the doors that seem to list what everyone inside is being held for or where they're going—court appearances in Manhattan or different detention centers in New Jersey. A guard tells me to kneel on a chair—so he doesn't have to bend down to remove my chains— then I'm put into a large holding cell with a mix of other immigrants: Mexicans, Russians, South Americans, Africans, and a few other Europeans like me. Some people have come straight from Rikers, others were picked up from construction sites or workplace stings. Mostly men, but I spotted a couple of Asian women on the way in here, crying as they got led around.

The cells don't have bars—we're locked behind heavy metal doors with small windows that face the processing room. People take turns pressing their faces against the reinforced glass, trying to figure out what's going on. We must be a few floors up—I can see Houston Street through a window on the opposite side of the cell, and a park about a block away. I used to walk by that park on the way to visit a friend.

There are a few metal benches, mostly occupied by other detainees, and a toilet in the corner of the cell. I'm starving, but we must've missed lunch—probably not that edible anyway, based on all the foil packets and bits of food on the floor.

Most of us have no idea what's going on or where we're headed, but anyone who's been in the system for a while offers up an opinion about my case: *You've got a drug charge? You're getting deported. . . . It's a misdemeanor? You can beat it. . . . Heroin possession? ICE will make it an aggravated felony, even if it isn't. . . . You should sign out. . . . You should fight it. . . . If you spent less than a year in jail, you'll be fine.*

People are talking about good judges and bad judges and who knows the best immigration lawyer and how long it can take to fight a deportation order—nine months, eighteen months, six months, *two years.* My head is spinning, trying to take it all in.

After a couple of hours, the door opens and my name is called. I'm led to a desk where a middle-aged guy in a white shirt and khaki pants is sorting through papers, barely looking up when I sit down. He starts reading me the notes written in my file.

"You came here from the United Kingdom in 1992. . . . You got your green card in 1999. You were arrested in 2006." He glances at me, as if to drive home the point. "Then arrested again a few more times . . . You were convicted of drug possession in May and served four months at Rikers Island."

After finishing his spiel, he looks up and asks, "Do you agree with the charges?"

"What charges? I had a misdemeanor—I already served my time."

"Do you agree with the immigration charges?" he asks again.

"I don't know what you mean," I say, not sure if he's asking about my conviction in May or whether there's some new charge from immigration.

"You're not a citizen, you were convicted of a crime, you're deportable. Do you agree?"

"No—I don't agree. I'm a permanent resident, I have a green card. Can I speak to a lawyer? Or do I get to see a judge?"

"You don't get a lawyer for immigration proceedings," he says, getting impatient. "But you'll see a judge after you sign these papers."

"Why would I sign something I don't agree with? Don't I have any rights?"

He won't give me a straight answer and doesn't offer me any options. He just keeps asking me to sign paperwork agreeing that I'm deportable—which I refuse to do.

"If you get deported," he asks, turning to another page in his stack, "which country would you like to be deported to?"

"What do you mean, *which country*?"

"You're in the European Community, so you can choose where you want to go—as long as they agree to take you."

"Are you telling me I'm getting deported? I don't understand what's going on."

"If you get deported," he repeats, "where do you want to go?"

"I don't want to get deported—I want to stay here. I've been here for eighteen years, my son is here, I can't leave him."

"So we'll put the United Kingdom then," he decides, totally ignoring me. I sit there in silence while he finishes filling out forms.

After he's done, he hands me over to another agent to get fingerprinted and photographed. Then I'm led to a different desk where an Asian guy presents me with more forms to sign: confirming that the photograph is me, that I refused to sign the waiver giving up my right to see a judge, and other documents full of legal jargon I don't understand. He doesn't question me or leave any opening for me to question him, just silently passes papers across the desk.

By the time we're finished, he's got a stack of paperwork that he clips together, then stamps DEPORTATION ORDER in big letters across the top. It's obvious that he couldn't care less about me—there's no sign of empathy, no emotion.

I can't fucking believe this: I'm getting kicked out of the country. Once it hits me, I can't help it—I put my head in my hands and start to cry.

"I've got a kid here, I've lived here for almost twenty years, my work is here, my whole life is here," I'm pleading. "How can you do this? Isn't there some way I can stay or file an appeal?" But it has no impact on him, he probably sees this every day.

He tells me I can make a phone call, but when I dial Anna's number I already know she's not going to be home. I don't leave a message, worried it'll count as my call, so I try Tracy—the only other number I know. She doesn't answer, but I leave a message saying I got picked up by immigration and that I'll call again when I can.

I don't want the other detainees to see me crying, so I wipe my face with my sleeve as I get led back to the cell. Immediately they start bombarding me with questions.

"What happened?"

"Are you getting deported?"

"Did you get offered a bond?"

I don't feel like talking so I just mumble something about things not looking good. I don't really have any answers—I'm still trying to figure out what's going on.

As it all sinks in, I feel like my whole life is suddenly being taken away. I'm trying to imagine going back to Scotland, or maybe London—where I'd go, what I'd do, how I'd manage. But it's too overwhelming. I can't bear to think about it. I close my eyes, as if I can block out everything that's happening.

IT'S DARK OUT by the time I'm taken back downstairs in the freight elevator, then loaded onto a bus heading for the Hudson

County jail in New Jersey. There's no traffic in the tunnel or on the Pulaski Skyway, another route I know well from trips to Newark airport. But the bus pulls off the highway in Kearny—ironically, home to a bunch of Scots who came to America to work at a thread mill. I used to bring Liam here, to buy him Scottish soda and candy. Apparently it's now a big hub for sending immigrants back.

Once we arrive, it's too dark to see much as we're led to intake. Detainees returning from court appearances get processed first, then the rest of us are unchained, strip-searched, and issued orange prison uniforms—plus a T-shirt, underwear, a roll of toilet paper, some soap, and a little toothpaste. Then we're all put in a holding cell.

A guard asks if anyone is a vegetarian and I raise my hand, hoping to avoid the so-called meat I saw working in the kitchen at Rikers. So when everyone else gets a bologna sandwich, I'm given processed cheese on white bread, slathered with mayonnaise. It just tastes like a bland mush in my mouth.

This place looks like the kind of jail you see in movies, with two tiers of cells full of inmates who are locked down most of the time. I'm taken to a cell where a Hispanic guy is already asleep on the top bunk, so I crawl into the bottom bunk and actually manage to sleep for a few hours.

When I wake up, I have no idea where I am. My cellmate is brushing his teeth at the sink and I can hear somebody shouting, "Trays, trays, trays! . . . If you want to eat, get up and get it. If you stay in bed, you don't get fed." Then it hits me—I'm not at Rikers. My morning haziness quickly shifts to panic and dread.

After a guard buzzes our cell open, I follow the line of inmates heading to breakfast, hoping for a strong cup of coffee—which I already know I'm not gonna get. We're still in intake, separated from detainees fighting their cases, so we're all in a state of confusion. There's no one from ICE to talk to, just guards who are much colder and more distant than any of the COs on the island. We only get let out of our cells for meals and a little time in a concrete yard facing the New Jersey Turnpike. There's just enough room to walk in circles, staring at two soccer balls impaled on the razor wire above our heads.

The Hudson County jail is mainly a transit hub, so detainees come and go constantly. The second day, the Hispanic guy disappears, replaced by a Gulf War veteran from Guyana. He tells me he's got a green card and has lived in America most of his life, but he got in a bar fight after he came back from Iraq and ended up with an assault charge—for defending Bush's decision to go to war. His kids, his wife, and his mom all live here. He doesn't know anyone in Guyana, where he might get sent any day.

Everybody has some equally depressing story. One guy keeps saying, "I'm an American, my mother is American. They can't deport me—I've never even been to Africa." He's nineteen years old and got picked up because he missed an appointment with his probation officer.

Other than a few conversations about how people ended up here, I don't talk much. I feel completely cut off from everybody I know. I keep worrying about what Jimmy's gonna think when he doesn't hear from me—probably that I relapsed—and how Liam will react once he finds out where I am. It crushes me to think I may not see him anytime soon. I still don't know if Anna told him I was in jail.

I wish I could call somebody, but the money left in my commissary account didn't follow me here, so I can't buy a phone card. I could call collect, but not to a cellphone, which rules out trying to reach Tracy. And Anna is never home when we're allowed out of our cells. It crosses my mind to try Susan, but I don't know her number—and at this point, I'm not sure she'd want to hear from me. She'd probably just tell me that she warned me this could happen.

My only link to the outside world is the telly in the common area, which we get to watch for a couple of hours after we eat. It's usually tuned to some mind-numbing show like *America's Funniest Home Videos,* Court TV, or Jerry Springer. Mostly the other detainees just trade rumors—we're all getting shipped to Texas or Louisiana, or we'll be deported from New Jersey as soon as ICE gets us travel documents. Since I lost my passport during the chaos of the last couple of years, people keep telling me I'm gonna get stuck here longer, waiting for the British government to issue me a new one.

No one really knows what the fuck is going on, and the guards don't seem to know anything about our cases. They treat us like we're worse than criminals—like shit on the bottom of society's shoe, something offensive to be scraped off and thrown away. At Rikers, a lot of the COs would bullshit with us and some of the female guards even flirted, but here there's none of that—they don't interact with us at all. I'm bouncing between anger and total despair, wanting to scream or weighed down by depression.

Days pass—five or six, I lose count—and then it's my turn to get woken up at 4 A.M. to be transferred. I'm herded to outtake with about twenty-five other detainees, all bleary-eyed and anxious. At first they don't tell us what's happening or where we're going.

It takes hours to process us and sort us into groups moving to different detention centers. I end up on a rickety metal bus heading for Pennsylvania—once again shackled and chained. But it's a beautiful day in late August, the first time I've been on a long drive in ages, so the bars on the windows don't keep me from taking in the view. As we're speeding along the highway, I'm thinking about possible photography projects, wondering what Liam is doing right now, trying not to dwell on everything I missed in the haze of addiction.

I'm in a seat by myself, but other people are talking to each other and shouting questions at the driver and the guard—asking where we're going, what's going to happen to us, and how long it'll take to get there. The guard says all they know is that we're going to York County and tells us again that everything will be easier if we just sign the papers.

Around noon, we pull off the highway and stop at a McDonald's. The driver gets off and goes inside. When he gets back on the bus, the smell of fries wafts back toward us—my stomach grumbles in response. But they finish their burgers before passing out our packed lunches: a cheese stick, some pretzels, a little sandwich, and a juice box.

I manage to jab the tiny straw into the juice pack, but with my hands chained to my waist, I can't get the straw close enough to my mouth to drink it. The bus is back on the highway by the time I get the plastic wrapper off the cheese, so when we hit a bump I drop it. Other people are complaining: "This is bullshit . . . how the fuck am I supposed to eat . . . these chains are too fucking tight." All we had for breakfast was a mini box of cereal and a small carton of milk, so this kiddie snack we can't eat just adds frustration to everyone's hunger.

That's when the hopelessness of my situation really hits me: I'm shackled in a bus being shipped from New Jersey to somewhere in Pennsylvania and I have no control over a fucking thing. I can't tell anybody, nobody knows where I am, and I have no idea what's going to happen to me.

This sick, chilling feeling stays with me for the rest of the ride, settling in once we pull up to our destination. York County Prison is a low-lying gray building surrounded by fences with barbed wire, but otherwise it blends in with the suburban offices and trees. It's the kind of place you wouldn't notice if you didn't look closely—which just adds to the feeling that I've disappeared.

It can take a full day to get processed into Rikers Island—all the paperwork is done by hand—but this prison has its intake system down to a science. Everything is computerized and the staff is way more efficient. Within a couple of hours I'm back in an orange prison uniform with a wristband sliding up and down my arm. It's got my name, photo, ID numbers, and a bar code so I can be tracked.

For all its backward bureaucracy, at least Rikers Island still felt like part of the world. You could see the Manhattan skyline, boats on the East River, planes taking off and landing at LaGuardia. Here I feel like I'm trapped inside a machine designed to move people through detention centers and spit them out of the country. We're all tracked by our alien number, which is how the government refers to anyone who isn't a citizen—as "aliens." It feels like we've been totally removed from the world we used to know.

The dorm I'm taken to is an open rectangular room made of gray concrete blocks. There are two rows of metal bunk beds topped by thin plastic mattresses, with gray metal lockers next to each bunk. The only light comes from dim fluorescent tubes— there aren't any windows except thin slits at the top of the room. At Rikers, light poured through the windows, I could move around between buildings, each dorm had its own personality. This place feels soulless, just gray and cold.

Even though it's late August, it's freezing inside. Other detainees are walking in circles with dingy blankets wrapped around their shoulders, the corners gathered in their hands. We're in the heartland of America, but it looks like some kind of Third World refugee camp. I'm the only white person—everyone else is Hispanic, African, or Asian. I overhear bits of broken English, but I'm not in the mood to talk.

At 6 P.M., dinner is brought to the dorm on hospital-like trays. Since I said I was a vegetarian, I get a baked potato, a soy patty, and white bread—no vegetables or fruit, nothing nutritious. Without any money for commissary, I can't buy coffee or oatmeal or peanut butter—nothing to supplement the practically inedible prison food.

After dinner, I lie down on my bunk, wrapped in a worn sheet and thin blanket. I just want to fall asleep, but the TV is blaring and even at night the lights are barely turned down from their dim daytime setting. I toss and turn, trying to find a position that's slightly more comfortable, but every thought that enters my mind makes me more and more anxious.

Mostly I keep thinking about how long people have told me they've been locked up fighting their cases. I'm not sure I can spend a whole week in this place, never mind months or years. I'll sign the papers if it comes to that, and I guess that's the point—to make us feel so isolated and traumatized that we beg to leave.

My SECOND NIGHT at York County Prison, I'm woken up by guards rousing people at 4 A.M. They're walking around the dorm pointing flashlights in detainees' faces, saying, "Pack up . . . pack up . . . pack up." Lying there with my eyes half-open, I wait for them to approach me.

I can hear the sounds of lockers opening and shutting, people whispering, the metal bunks squeaking, feet in prison-issue slippers padding around the floor. After I close my eyes for a few minutes, the footsteps come nearer—it must be my turn.

"Yo, Scotland!" someone says. I open my eyes: It's one of the young black guys I met at Hudson County, who also got transferred here.

"We're getting moved," he says. "Probably to Texas or Louisiana, but I'm not sure. They're not telling us much except that we should pack up to leave."

I'm still groggy, wondering why the guards haven't approached me.

"Thanks for the boxers and T-shirt," he says. He wasn't issued any underwear when he got to York—supposedly, they'd run out—so I'd given him one of my two sets.

"No problem," I tell him, propping myself up so I can shake his hand. "Good luck, maybe I'll see you down there."

"Yeah, maybe—if I haven't been moved somewhere else by then."

The next morning, the dorm is practically empty—most of the bunk beds stripped, the mattresses folded in half. I ask one of the guards where everybody went.

"Don't worry," he says. "We'll be filled up again by dinner."

It's a real mind fuck, all these people getting taken away in the middle of the night. It's the kind of thing you see in movies or hear about in repressive countries. I'm sure most people have no idea it's happening here.

OVER THE NEXT few days I get to know some of the detainees who come and go. Since I don't speak Spanish and many of them don't speak English, there are a lot of people I can't talk to, but some of these guys have stories that are way more depressing than mine.

A blond guy from Lebanon tells me he's getting deported for insurance fraud, after putting his aunt on his company's medical plan so she could get kidney dialysis. He already spent two years in jail, paid $130,000 back to the insurance company, lost his house and his business—and now he has to move his American wife and kids to the Middle East, where he hasn't lived for twenty years. He fought the deportation order for eleven months before losing his case.

An old man from El Salvador tells me in broken English that he once owned a car dealership but lost everything fighting to stay here, so he's getting deported with just $190. When I ask him what he's going to do, he tells me he'll buy some flowers and apples and sell them on the street until he makes enough money to get a room. If that doesn't work out, he's not sure how he'll manage.

A middle-aged Italian guy won't talk to anyone except to say he got busted for a DUI. He seems like he's got money—he has a green card, so he probably had a decent job. Whenever people try to engage him, he acts like he's in a state of shock.

I get why he's keeping to himself. Every time I get to know somebody, they end up getting transferred somewhere else, so after a while I stop making the effort. It's too upsetting to make friends at dinner and then wake up to find out that they're gone.

There isn't much to do except pace around or play cards, but with just one deck we all have to take turns. There's also a chess set that's seen better days—a piece of toilet paper wrapped with Scotch tape fills in for a missing rook. I can't remember the rules so I just watch other people play, trying to memorize how all the broken pieces are allowed to move.

Time passes so slowly I want to cry every time I look at the clock. When I'm sure an hour has gone by, it's only been fifteen minutes. If I think it's almost lunchtime, the hands point at 10 A.M. Just waiting around with nothing happening is really fucking with my head—I feel like I'm about to erupt.

It's been nine days since ICE picked me up at Rikers, and I *still* haven't seen a judge. I finally managed to get through to Tracy—we get a free call each week—but her halfway house has a lot of rules about when people can go out or use the phone, so I don't know how much she'll be able to help. I'm desperate for her to try and find me a lawyer—she owes me money, so I told her to use that until I can get ahold of my checks.

ICE makes it difficult to navigate the simplest things, like sending mail or getting money for commissary or making calls. We're all totally in the dark, relying on rumors other detainees spread around. Everybody's got an opinion but nobody really knows—and no one from ICE is around to tell us what's going on. The guards all work for York County so they know even less about immigration than us.

The only way you can communicate with ICE is to fill out a blue slip with a question or a comment and drop it in a box, but that's a fucking joke—I've already done that. No one ever seems to come and open it, and even if they did, I'm sure they'd just dump the whole box straight into another box that never gets looked at, or they'd send one slip back with a vague answer.

All this frustration is eating away at me and I'm lying on my bunk fuming when one of the COs shouts, "Who's MacIndoe?"

I sit up, startled.

"That's me," I answer, suddenly hopeful. *Maybe they realized they made a mistake—or maybe Tracy got through to a lawyer.*

"Here," he says, handing me a small piece of yellow paper. It has the seal of the Department of Homeland Security in the left corner and says "I.C.E. Detainee 'MESSAGE Form'" across the top.

The handwritten note reads: "Susan Stellin called," along with her phone numbers, home and cell.

Honestly, I'm a bit disappointed at first. I know it sounds crazy, but for a minute I actually thought I was getting released. But then I start to think that Susan might be able to get me out of this jam—I just don't know if I have the guts to call her.

Other detainees start crowding around me, asking questions: "What's it say? . . . How come you got a message? . . . I didn't think we could get messages here."

I didn't think so, either—no one's gotten a message while I've been in ICE custody.

"It's my ex-girlfriend's number," I tell them, a bit stunned.

Walking back to my bunk, I stare at the piece of paper. It says the call came at 9:58 this morning, September 1. Just looking at it makes me feel relieved that at least someone else knows where I am, but I have no idea why Susan wants me to call her—or how the fuck she found me. After everything that happened and how much I know I let her down, I'm not sure I can ask her to help me. She already did so much and I totally shut her out.

That's why I don't head straight for the phone. I need to pull myself together before I can face her. All these memories come flooding back, feelings I'd locked away, all the pain I caused, my broken promises. My mind is all over the place, trying to work up the courage to call her.

But by the next afternoon, desperation and curiosity get the better of me. I wait in line for the phone, my hands shaking when I pick up the receiver. I press the buttons for a collect call, then slowly enter Susan's home number.

"Please state your name," the recorded voice says.

"Graham," I answer.

The line starts ringing. I have no idea what I'm going to say if she picks up.

CHAPTER SIXTEEN

August 2010
Cobble Hill, Brooklyn

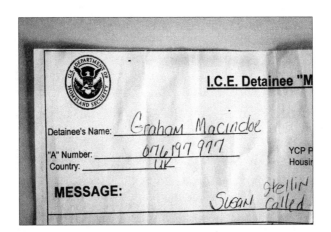

After Anna emailed telling me that Graham was at Rikers, I looked up his release date on the Department of Correction website, kicking myself because I hadn't thought to check it the whole time I'd wondered if he was dead.

My relief turned to fear once I read what the inmate locator said. Graham was supposed to have been released from Rikers that morning, but instead he'd been handed over to Immigration and Customs Enforcement—the Homeland Security agency rounding up and deporting four hundred thousand people every year.

Now I debated whether I wanted to be the bearer of bad news, but I sent Anna another email, letting her know that Graham had been picked up by immigration and explaining how she could find out where he was.

He's not showing up yet in the ICE system, but here's a link to a database where you can check the status of anyone detained by immigration. Maybe he'll get lucky and they'll just release him, but if you hear from him and he wants help finding a lawyer I can probably track down some names. If there's anything I can do, let me know.

A friend who worked for Human Rights Watch had told me about ICE's online detainee locator, which had just launched earlier that summer. Before that, families had a tough time finding out where their loved ones had been taken—often, after agents showed up at their homes with guns.

But there was still something disturbing about tracking a human being like a missing package or lost luggage. I didn't just want to know where Graham was; I wanted to talk to him and find out what was going on.

Anna's response was not particularly reassuring.

I remember the lawyer saying Graham would most likely be picked up by immigration and Graham mentioned immigration had been in touch with him at some point, so maybe this is all a part of that process. He seemed pretty convinced he wouldn't be deported based on what he was arrested for. Let me know if you find anything else out and I'm sure he or a lawyer will be in touch when he's ready or allowed to.

Based on what I had read about ICE, I wasn't so sure that Graham would be allowed to call a lawyer—or anyone else, since Anna didn't hear from him over the next few days. She worked in an office where it was tough to make calls about her incarcerated ex-husband, whereas I could work at home and was used to pestering people for information, so I offered to keep trying the ICE phone numbers we found.

By that point, the online detainee tracker indicated that Graham had been taken to the Hudson County Correctional Facility in New Jersey. When I finally got through to a curt employee at the jail, she told me he was allowed to have visitors, but he first had to put my name on his approved visitors list. The only way to ask him to do that was to send him a letter—which I promptly did.

"I have no idea whether this letter will get to you, or if someone else might read it, so I won't go on and on," I wrote, already feeling guarded about our monitored communications. *"But I hope you'll call me—collect, whatever. I know it's a lousy situation in there, but it will get sorted out. And since I thought you might be dead, I was happy to hear you're alive."*

A few days later, that envelope came back marked *"RTS"*—return to sender—*"No longer on A3W,"* the wing where Graham had temporarily been housed. By the time my letter arrived, he had already been transferred.

I also left voicemail messages for the deportation officer and the social worker I was told had been assigned to Graham's case. Neither of them called me back.

Anna didn't have much better luck on her end.

"Not looking good," she wrote me, a week after we had first been in touch. *"Graham has been moved to York County, PA, which is a prison, not a detention center. I'm now wondering if he still has access to a commissary account, if I can send him some money, as maybe he can't get a phone card. I think ICE beats to its own drum on what anyone in their custody can do—really kinda scary how under the radar they operate."*

I didn't want to worry Anna by telling her how awful some of those prisons and detention centers were; I'd read reports about immigrants getting mistreated and abused, or even dying because they were denied medical care. But the more time that passed, the more I started to panic. I had spoken with a lawyer who told me that ICE usually transferred people to remote prisons far from their home states—far from their families and the advocates who could help them. It was essentially a domestic form of rendition, sending detainees to states like Alabama and Texas, where the judges were much less sympathetic to immigrants.

As one New York lawyer I'd spoken with put it, "They don't think like us down there." He made it clear that Graham needed to hire an attorney soon—before he got moved again.

Finally, on September 1, I got through to a woman at York County Prison who had somehow maintained her humanity in the dehumanizing place where she worked: She didn't cut me off or transfer me to a voicemail black hole, and she wasn't immediately dismissive when I asked if she'd pass Graham a message.

"We don't usually give messages to inmates," she told me, sounding a bit apologetic.

Sensing a lack of commitment to that policy, I pressed my case. "I'm sure he hasn't called because he doesn't remember any phone numbers. They're all stored on his cellphone, and that was taken away. All I'm asking is for you to give him a slip of paper with my name and number."

"And you are . . . ?"

"His girlfriend." I thought it might complicate things if I said I was Graham's ex.

"Well, we aren't supposed to give out information to anyone who isn't a family member."

"I understand that," I said, already prepared for this objection. "But I'm not actually asking you to give *me* any information—I'm just asking you to give *him* my phone number. His parents are in Scotland so he can't call them collect, and his son is at school so he can't answer his phone in class. I'm sure you can imagine how worried he is about his dad."

My appeal to family ties worked: She agreed to pass Graham a note with my number. I just wasn't sure if he'd actually call. We hadn't talked in so long I had no idea if he'd even want my help. Then again, his present situation was so dire I figured he'd grab any lifeline that floated his way.

So why was I bothering to throw Graham that line, after all the times he'd pushed me away? Obviously I still cared about what happened to him, and it was shocking that he could just disappear into this shadowy system—with none of the rights even mass murderers get if they're U.S. citizens. Even though I'd warned Graham about this possibility and knew *theoretically* it might happen, it was chilling to actually experience that fear: knowing someone who had gotten picked up by government agents and taken away.

But there was another motivation that didn't really sink in until later that night, when I couldn't sleep wondering if Graham had gotten my message. If he did call, I was finally going to get something I'd been wanting for years: the chance to have a conversation with him totally clean. In some sense, that anticipation overshadowed the fact that he was in prison.

I worked from home the next day, trying to distract myself while I waited for the phone to ring. When it finally did, at around four in the afternoon, a recording asked if I'd accept a collect call from "Graham"—his Scottish accent rolling the *r* in his name.

Suddenly nervous, I didn't know what to say.

"I got your message," Graham said, sounding a bit defensive. "How'd you know I was here?"

"Anna told me—well, actually, she told me you were at Rikers, so I looked up your release date, but by then ICE had picked you up and taken you to New Jersey. There's a website where you can track detainees. I sent you a letter, but you'd already been moved to Pennsylvania. I finally managed to get through to a woman who I guess did give you my number."

I felt like I was rambling, so I stopped talking—leaving an opening for Graham to launch into one of his rants.

"This whole thing is a fucking nightmare. The day I'm supposed to get out of jail they tell me immigration has got a hold on me so I'm not getting released. Then these ICE officers come get me and put me in shackles—my hands chained to my waist, my feet chained together, like I'm a fucking serial killer or something. All the guys in outtake were looking at me like I was Charles Manson."

Shackles? It sounded even more barbaric than I'd imagined. "What did they tell you when they picked you up?" I asked. "Have you seen a judge?"

"Are you kidding? They don't tell you a fucking thing. I haven't seen a judge. I don't get a lawyer. They just come at four A.M. and take you away. Hundreds of people come and go every day in this place, mostly Mexicans—I'm the only white guy. And these ICE officers are so fucking racist. While everyone's lining up one guy says, 'See this line? Don't cross it. Wait till you get back to Mexico and you can try jumping the border again.' It's unbelievable how nasty they are."

"Are you okay? I mean, obviously you're not okay, but are they treating you decently?" I didn't know how to ask, *Is anyone beating the shit out of you?*

"I'm alright—it's not violent or anything, but this place makes Rikers Island look like the Hilton hotel. It's fucking freezing in here, I've not got any commissary so I can't buy a long-sleeved shirt, or anything half-decent to eat. The food is shite, and there's no outside time. You're stuck in this dorm with nothing to do, nothing to read. Just Jerry Springer on the telly all fucking day. How often is that show on?"

At least Graham hadn't lost his sense of humor, but being in jail had clearly amplified his swearing. In some sense, he didn't sound all that different off drugs.

"I'm trying to find you a lawyer," I said, shifting the conversation to practicalities. "I've got some names of firms that specialize in deportation cases. The thing is . . ." I hesitated, thinking it was a bit crass to bring up money.

"What?"

"Do you have any money left? I know you sold your house, but I don't know how much these lawyers charge, or if you even want to fight this. Maybe you'd rather just go back to Scotland."

"I've got money—I can pay for a lawyer. But I can't spend a long time in this situation. I've met people who've been in here for *years* fighting their cases. That would do my state of mind serious damage. I'd rather sign out if I'm gonna get stuck in this place."

"I don't think it takes years to see a judge. You're supposed to get an initial hearing within a couple of weeks, but if you agree to leave, you're exiled forever. You can't ever come back to the U.S.—

not to see Liam, not for work. You don't even get to pack up your stuff. They basically just put you on a plane."

Graham was silent; I wondered if I was being too blunt. Hoping to soften the blow, I added, "I really think you should talk to a lawyer before you decide what to do, just to find out your options. Or I guess I should talk to a lawyer—you can only make collect calls, right?"

"You should call Tracy."

Tracy? The mention of her name totally threw me. "Why would I call Tracy? I thought you finally got rid of her."

"I did, but she came to see me when I was in Rikers. She's living in a recovery house—she's been clean for a while now. I talked to her and she was going to call a lawyer."

I wasn't quite sure how to interpret this news. From everything Graham had told me about Tracy, I didn't want anything to do with her—and I wasn't sure I wanted anything to do with Graham if she was back in his life. After they broke up, she had even called me at one point, leaving crazy messages demanding I call her.

"I can't believe you've been in touch with her," I said, more bothered by this revelation than I was letting on. "Please tell me you're not back together. . . ."

"She'd like to be with me, but no—that's not happening. Please, just call her. She owes me two thousand dollars so you can get some of the money for the lawyer from her. I can't access my bank account—they took my checkbook, my wallet, everything."

This was not at all how I pictured our conversation going. The fact that Graham had called Tracy made me wonder if he really was free of that life. *Why would he have called her, instead of Anna or me?*

"Why didn't you tell me you were at Rikers?" I asked—it sounded more like an accusation than a question. "I didn't know what had happened to you. I actually thought you were dead, and it turns out you were talking to the most dysfunctional person you've ever been involved with."

"I didn't call her. She found out where I was and came to visit. I didn't call you because . . . I don't know. I was ashamed, I didn't want anybody to see me there. But I asked Anna to tell you where I was—I thought she had. I'm sorry, I should've written to you. I didn't even write to Liam, or my family. It's hard to explain, but I was coming out of a really fucking dark place and I didn't know how to deal with that."

Just as I was mulling over that explanation, a recording interrupted us, saying our time was almost up. There was a twenty-minute limit on prison phone calls—which wasn't entirely a bad thing, since it cost about a dollar a minute to talk.

"I've got to go," Graham said, adding "thank you"—almost as an afterthought, I noticed. I was starting to remember what it felt like to get sucked into his chaos, a gravitational pull I wondered if I should try to resist. But there was no time to deliberate over what I should do: I couldn't call him back or email him later, after I'd thought about it. I had to decide in that instant.

"I'll call a couple of lawyers," I told him, brushing aside my reservations. "Call me tomorrow."

Before he could answer, our call got cut off. I sat there for a while longer, just holding the phone. The sensation I always got after talking to Graham was back: that buzz, that hum—like the electricity had just come back on after the power went out, making you notice how quiet it had been when everything was off.

I lay back on my bed, staring at one of the pictures Graham gave me when we were together, which was still on my wall. It was a black-and-white photo of a skinny guy with his hands in his pockets, by the street photographer Leon Levinstein. With just his torso and legs visible, he looked a lot like Graham.

"I'm not the only person who keeps their pants up with a too big belt and their hands," he'd written on the cardboard backing.

"*Think of me every time you look at it. With love, Graham XXX.*"

I knew I was getting pulled back into that vortex—not of Graham's addiction, but a whole other drama. Maybe Graham had detoxed, but it was hard to tell if he had changed, and that uncertainty made me feel very conflicted.

A week later, I got the letter he started writing me from York County Prison that night, just after we talked. It came in an envelope stamped with a warning: THIS CORRESPONDENCE ORIGINATES FROM AN INMATE INSTITUTION. As I tore open the envelope, I wondered if the mailman thought I'd taken up with a prison pen pal.

Dear Susan,

> *Firstly thank you so much for doing everything + anything you have + will be doing for me. I'm really touched + sort of humbled mixed with a wee bit of shame that you've had to put yourself to this effort on my behalf—but trust me I'm glad you are + I was so happy to talk to you on the phone tonight. Everything just sort of seems fucked up here—it's really frustrating, no one tells you anything, nothing gets done in a timely or organized manner, it seems so easy to fall through the cracks. One minute I'm on Rikers Island the next ICE picks me up + I'm in Jersey, don't see a judge, then 3 days later brought here to York PA + being told all the time that I'll be going to TX or LA in a few days . . . I've got a funny (well not funny given the situation) idea I'll be packed up tonight/tomorrow morning. They always do that stuff between 2 AM & 4 AM for some reason or other. I think it's so that you get even more fucked up when you wake up in the morning to find the guy you'd just made friends with has gone—psychological torture.*

Anyway, this place here is a nightmare. A second seems like a minute, a minute seems like an hour, an hour like a day and a day seems like a week. Rikers Island seems like a dream compared to this. In fact the last 2½ months there was probably the happiest I've been in a long time. I was with some good people. I had a job in the kitchen, I was on the card playing team, I read lots of books, I was in a good dorm. The Bloods liked me, the Crips liked me, the Mexicans cooked for me most nights 'coz I brought up lots of food from the kitchen every night. My section in the dorm was really good—I had some great laughs—not to say jail is good 'coz it's not. It's just that you can make the best of it—I could move around all over the building. But here there's no movement, no books or mags, everyone is from South America or Mexico. I'm just the lonesome white boy.

Well, I went to bed now it's Friday + obviously I didn't get packed up last night. But I woke up this morning at 6 am by the TV at volume 20—now 6 am is unacceptable. TV's not meant to go on 'til after breakfast at 8 am. So I put up with it blaring the early news + ads in English when I decide to get up + see if it was the CO and lo + behold there's this little Mexican guy sitting on a table watching the TV. He looks at me and asks if I speak Spanish or English— I tell him English and he looks at me and says "No hablo English!" My question at that point (though I didn't ask) was why are you watching TV so loud when you don't understand?

I know I need to make a decision about fighting this case and I know that you've picked the best law firm and I appreciate that very much. Part of me wants to call it quits + just go back to Scotland or London, start up my career there—new clients, new jobs, fresh start. Sounds appealing doesn't it? But also I would like to have the freedom to be able to go wherever I want + I know I can hunker down and get through another 3-6 months—as painful as it may be. But I'd hate to spend the time & money to find that I'm gonna get deported anyway.

I'm trying my best to get access to my checkbooks so I can send you a check for the lawyer but I understand if you can't get the cash and you don't want to front it for me—don't feel bad. I got me in this situation—no one else—so I've got to take the rough with the smooth and at least that will leave me no choice but to ask for final deportation order. Things will work out for the best either way. I can't let the word worse be in my vocabulary. I am sorry I didn't keep in touch with you—I was selfish, I suppose + a little lost + out of control (not in a crazy way but not in control of simple things that I should have been in control of—you know what I mean!) I keep singing the Frank Sinatra song—My Way in my head and U2 Beautiful Day + knowing one day I'll be on the outside walking down a street— somewhere—with a spring in my step and a smile on my face.

Oh yes—I've started playing chess! I'm not great but have won a few games.

Susan, all I can say is thank you, thank you, thank you from the bottom (+ top) of my heart.

Much love Graham xxx
P.S. I'll write more in a bit

The letter included a drawing of the dorm—little rectangles for all the bunks along the walls, round circles for the tables and chairs, and an open area with showers and toilets. There was a television, a desk where the CO sat, and an enclosed area where the inmates could work out. Graham had marked his locker and bunk and noted the drawing was "not to scale."

It was simultaneously depressing and comforting to be able to visualize the place where he was locked up. I had a flashback to my claustrophobia at Rikers Island when I bailed him out. But as I finished reading Graham's letter—for the second time—the main thing I was thinking about was that he was already using the word *love*.

I wasn't sure how I felt about that. It did occur to me that Graham was just using me because I was the only person who could really help him. And to be honest, I don't think he understood why I had tracked him down. But one of the reasons I was willing to get involved in his case was that I thought I had the upper hand. If I found out Graham was lying to me, or dealing with him got to be too chaotic, I was willing to walk away this time.

CHAPTER SEVENTEEN

September 2010
Cobble Hill, Brooklyn

Three days after I first talked to Graham at York County Prison, I met Tracy at a park in Brooklyn to get the two thousand dollars she owed him. I hadn't exactly warmed up to her in the days I'd been dealing with her, so I was irritated even before she was late.

Despite Graham's assurances that she was living in a halfway house, off drugs, she still acted erratically: ignoring my messages, not calling when she said she would, and threatening to use the money to hire a lawyer she'd found—someone with minimal experience fighting deportation. Somehow Graham talked her into bringing me the cash instead, but as I sat there on a park bench watching parents play with their kids, I wasn't convinced that she'd actually show up.

By that point, I had spoken with Graham a couple more times—and Anna, and the British consulate, and several lawyers—so I was already stressed about the mess he was in, wondering if it was too late for anyone to help.

Michael, the attorney I'd settled on, had told me that Graham was eligible for "relief from removal," but that his odds of winning depended on which judge heard his case. The firm had a good track record with the judges in Pennsylvania; in Texas or Louisiana, not so much. But our phone call was on Friday and now it was Labor Day weekend, so I couldn't meet with Michael until Tuesday. Since Graham had already been packed up once to be transferred—then inexplicably pulled out of line—he could be gone even before I signed the retainer.

So I was checking my watch and worrying that he was already heading south, when Tracy finally appeared. "Susan?" she said, extending her hand. She looked like all the middle-aged moms in the park—not at all Graham's type, but healthy enough that it was plausible that she really was clean.

I made an effort to be friendly, explaining what Michael had told me, and why I thought his firm was the right choice. "There are a lot of attorneys who take advantage of immigrants in desperate situations—or just haven't dealt with deportation. Graham needs someone who specializes in these types of cases."

"Well, he's really lucky that *three* women who love him are helping him out," Tracy said. "He's just *so helpless* right now."

I assumed she was referring to the fact that she and Anna and I were all pitching in to cover the deposit until Graham could access his money—except in Tracy's case, it was actually a debt she owed him.

"I'll do what I can to help," I said, unable to resist adding, "He really should've spoken with an immigration lawyer while he was at Rikers, but hopefully it's not too late."

After she handed me an envelope full of cash—like some sort of drug deal—I hoped to be done with her. But Tracy had no intention of going away.

"Thank you for doing this for us," she said.

For us? I didn't ask what she meant because by then it was clear: Tracy thought she and Graham were getting back together. Even though I didn't totally trust him at that point, I was pretty sure that wasn't his intention.

Still, her comment bothered me long after I walked away. I was already wary about getting too involved in Graham's case—and so was Anna, whom I'd been in touch with almost every day. We were both freaked out by what was happening to Graham, but neither of us wanted to pressure him about what he should do: agree to leave the U.S. forever, or fight to stay.

"I don't think he should feel it's giving up if he decides to go," Anna had told me, worried about the psychological toll of spending more time locked up. "It can be a more positive thing than being worn down."

Since I was the one talking to Graham, I made sure to pass along her message. But I encouraged him not to rush into any decision, writing him a letter explaining why.

> *Mostly, I worry about how you'd handle it if you go from prison to an airport in Europe with just the "small bag" they'll allow us to bring you. That's a harsh transition, and if it comes to that, having more time to adjust to what that's going to feel like emotionally—and figure out where you'll go and who you'll stay with—could make the difference between you being ok vs. being completely overwhelmed, depressed and adrift.*
>
> *I also think you should speak with Liam, or write him and find out how he feels. Anna told me she'd talked to him and that he'd understand either way, but this just feels like a big decision to make without really working things out with your son.*
>
> *But if you decide not to fight this, or if you start to feel like you really are cracking up, you shouldn't feel like you're letting anyone down.*

I genuinely meant that—Anna was right, I didn't know what prison was like. She had been in touch with Graham while he was at Rikers and I hadn't, so she had a better sense of his state of mind. But the truth is, I would've been disappointed if Graham had signed out. Because I finally understood something about him that I'd missed or hadn't wanted to see when we were together: If he was going to make it, he had to choose to fight for his life.

Maybe his mind had been clouded by chemicals, or he was too

stubborn, or success had come too easily and he'd lost that scrappy work ethic, but for whatever reason he'd never been willing to put in the effort to save himself. ("I wanted the same from recovery that I got from drugs—I wanted it all instantly," he'd tell me, years later.)

It's not that I thought my help or anyone else's didn't matter; it was a crucial part of a complex mix. But nothing was going to make a difference unless Graham jammed a spike into the side of the cliff he was slipping down and put all his energy into stopping his fall. He had to find that desire.

That was something David and I had discussed years earlier, during one of our many email exchanges. I had asked him why he thought some people changed and others didn't. He wrote back: *"I think my short answer would be—suffering, desire, the sense that something is wrong, a capacity for close relationships, the willingness to say things that are difficult to say, and finding good allies. If any of those are missing, in my experience, it ain't gonna work."*

When I asked him what he meant by desire, he answered, *"I mean wanting something very intensely and with longing—having something that you want to get and that you don't want to live without, so that you become willing to alter existing habits and conditions, so that they become less important than getting what you want."*

That's what Graham had been missing, and that's why I thought he should stay and fight. Because if he got exiled from the U.S., the emotional trauma would've been too much for him. I knew there was a good chance he'd relapse and end up alone on the streets—and deep down, so did he.

ONE OF THE most maddening things about Graham's situation was his limited ability to communicate with the outside world.

Once I'd racked up a hundred dollars in collect calls from prison, Verizon wouldn't let me accept any more. ("That's our policy," a representative curtly explained.) So I had to set up two accounts with the York County Prison phone service provider: one for my home number and one for my cell. Each account required a deposit (using separate credit cards), and I had to constantly monitor both balances, paying a service fee every time I added money—and every time he called. But I never wanted to add too much money because if Graham got transferred, I would've had to start over with a different provider.

That's partly why I ended up being Graham's main link to the outside world: I had the obsessive, detail-oriented gene necessary to navigate these hurdles, and as a reporter, I already spent most of the day close to a phone.

So on the Monday of Labor Day weekend, before I headed out to a barbecue, I filled Graham in when he called—that I'd gotten the money from Tracy, that Anna and I would cover the rest of the deposit for the lawyer, that she'd told Liam and his family what was going on. Even though I'd covered some of this in my letter, I had no idea when (or if) he'd actually get it.

"What did Liam say?" Graham asked.

I felt awkward being the go-between for such a sensitive topic, but Graham was desperate for news about Liam, so I shared what little I knew. "Anna said he was okay about it, but I don't think she told him all the details. He's back in school now, so she doesn't want him to get caught up in everything that's going on. Even Michael said these cases are always stressful."

Graham was silent for a second, letting that sink in before asking, "So what are my odds of winning? Please be honest with me because I really don't want to spend money and time fighting this if I'm just gonna get deported anyway."

"Basically, Michael said you're eligible for 'relief from removal,' but you still have to persuade a judge that you deserve a second chance. On the plus side: You've only been convicted of a misdemeanor, you're a legal permanent resident, and you've got a son who lives here. The main negative is that you've been arrested for drug possession multiple times so it's clear you've got a drug problem, and it'll be tough to prove you were rehabilitated washing dishes at Rikers."

"What the fuck was I supposed to do? They didn't offer me shit up there. There wasn't any fucking rehab."

Ignoring that outburst, I plowed on. "The thing is, I know I said before that you should take time to decide, but we really need to get the ball rolling—before you get transferred again. I made an appointment to meet with Michael tomorrow morning and pay the deposit, if that's what you want—"

Graham interrupted: "Did you ask how long it's gonna take?"

I hesitated, knowing this would be hard to hear. "You should see a judge soon, but it could take three to six months before you get a final hearing."

"Fucking hell. Are you serious?"

"Maybe longer. Michael said it's hard to predict."

"There's no way I can deal with that. I'd go out of my fucking mind. I actually dream about being back at Rikers. I'm not kidding—that's how bad this place is."

"Well, that's the worst-case scenario. It may only take three months, and if you decide to sign out, Michael said they'd prorate their fee."

"What do you think I should do?"

I didn't want to make the decision for Graham, but the strange thing about these conversations was how much more direct we both were—without drugs or denial clouding what either of us said.

"You're the one who has to live with the consequences, Graham. But if you want my honest opinion, I think you should fight it. I think you have a better shot at rebuilding your relationship with Liam if you're here. I know you can call and email and he can visit, but it's not the same. And as miserable as you are now, it's not going to be that easy if you're sent back to Britain. All you're allowed to take is a small bag of clothes—no laptop, no phone, no cameras, nothing electronic. I don't even know how you'd get access to your money. I'm sorry to be so blunt, but you can't idealize flying off into the sunset and starting over. They literally put you on a plane, and once you land you're on your own."

I paused, waiting for Graham to say something. When he didn't, I asked, "Do you have any idea where you'd go?"

"I don't know." He sounded so defeated I felt bad about pressing on.

"I mean, Scotland or London? Or could you stay with your brother or sister in Dublin?"

"I have no fucking idea what I'd do," Graham snapped—like I'd just poked an animal trapped in a cage.

"Then I guess it can't hurt to sit tight until you see a judge. If nothing else it'll give you time to come up with a plan. All it's really costing you is money, and you've wasted so much on drugs I can't believe it's not worth it to spend—"

"Alright."

At first I thought Graham cut me off because he didn't want to be reminded of how much money he'd blown, but when I asked what he meant he said, "Hire the lawyer."

Which is what I did the following day. After Michael escorted me into his office, past all the framed legal certificates and plaques hanging on the walls, I pulled out my notebook and a pen—so I could summarize our conversation for Graham later.

"Graham wanted me to ask about bail," I said, reading from the list of questions I'd jotted down.

"Very few immigrant detainees get bond," Michael answered, eyeing my note-taking warily. "And he isn't eligible because he's got a drug conviction."

"So a citizen who murdered somebody can get out on bail, but Graham—who already served his sentence, for a *misdemeanor*—has to stay locked up?" In my role as Graham's proxy, I found myself channeling his temper (minus the swearing).

"I know it doesn't sound fair, but the laws have gotten a lot stricter lately."

"What about getting his checkbook? Graham said it's with his property at York, so doesn't ICE have to give it to him, so he can pay for his defense?"

"He's in prison and he's not a citizen, so I'm afraid he doesn't have a lot of rights in this situation—but we can ask."

I shook my head in disbelief. As much as I knew about how badly immigrants were treated, a lot of this was still news to me.

Michael told me he'd send Graham a form so he could grant me or Anna power of attorney over his finances, but Graham would have to get it notarized in prison and we'd have to get it approved by his bank. Then he introduced me to his paralegal, Maria, explaining that Graham could call her collect anytime (*You'll regret that*, I thought) and that she'd handle the paperwork for his case.

Maria was reassuringly efficient—making phone calls, faxing documents, putting things in motion—but a bit deadpan as she answered my questions. Her take on Graham's arrest record: "I've seen worse." Where he was being held: "It's not as bad as other prisons." The fact that ICE hadn't officially charged him yet: "That's not good. It could be a sign that they plan to move him."

"What should I put as your relationship?" she asked.

"My relationship?"

"With Graham."

"Oh. How about guardian angel?" I joked, finally eliciting a smile. "I guess ex-girlfriend sounds too bizarre, so why don't you just say friend."

After Maria finished filling out forms, she handed me a two-page list of documents Graham needed to submit, explaining that she'd also send a copy to him. At the top it said: *"Preparing for your final deportation hearing may be the most important thing you do in your life!"* As I scanned the list—pay stubs, bank statements, proof of stable residence, marriage certificate, college diploma, inmate record, letters from family, friends, and employers discussing "your good moral character," etc.—I could feel my hope seeping away.

"Um, just looking at this list, I'm wondering how Graham is supposed to get all these documents if he's in a prison in Pennsylvania?"

"Someone will have to do it for him," Maria said.

Someone? Almost everything Graham owned was in storage. The key to that storage unit was being held by the New York City Police Department, along with his laptop. Even if Anna and I could get his key and find half of these documents, the firm also needed Graham's last seven tax returns, which I was pretty sure hadn't all been filed.

"The thing is, he sold his house before he got arrested, so all his stuff is in storage. And to be honest, he was really a mess the last few years so I'm guessing he may not be totally up-to-date with his taxes."

"The judge is going to have a serious problem with that," Maria said.

I felt like telling her to tear up the retainer I'd just signed and give me back the check I'd just written. There was no way Anna and I could gather everything on this list. But before I hit the eject button, I figured I should at least talk to Graham, so I thanked Maria for her help and headed for the exit, clutching the thick folder of documents she gave me.

As I waited for the elevator, all I could think about was something Anna had said: "Once the lawyer is hired, it's out of our hands."

I never thought it would be that easy—that we could just hire an attorney, give Graham the firm's number, wish him luck, and hope for the best. But I certainly didn't expect to get drawn into anything like this nightmare. And I definitely wasn't going to deal with his taxes.

ON THE WAY home on the subway, I mulled over what I was going to say to Graham: *Sorry to get your hopes up, but I just can't take on such a huge challenge. . . . All your stuff is in storage, and I'm sure it's a mess. . . . I know I said you should fight it, but maybe a change of scenery would actually be good.*

I felt guilty that I couldn't help him, but by that night I was sure he'd understand. Except once again, Graham didn't call. At first I was irritated: even off drugs, in prison, with nothing else to do, couldn't he follow through on a simple task? But when he didn't call the next day or the day after that, I started to worry, convinced he was on his way to Texas. Yet when I called Maria, she confirmed that the ICE database said he was still in Pennsylvania. She had no idea what might've happened.

On Saturday morning, my phone finally rang, followed by the prison preamble.

"Sorry I haven't called," Graham said. "I was in the hole."

"The hole?"

"The box—solitary. They packed me up to ship me out a few days ago—again—but for some reason they didn't put me on the bus. Then the guards didn't know what to do with me so they threw me in the hole."

"Shit. Did they say why?"

"Are you kidding? No one except you has told me a fucking thing. I haven't seen a judge, there's no counselor to talk to, I haven't gotten anything from the lawyer—"

"You didn't get the package they sent? It should've gotten there by now."

"No, only a letter from you. And I still don't have any money on my commissary so I can't buy stamps or envelopes or paper or a thermal top—it's fucking freezing in here. Everyone walks around huddled under a blanket."

"Wait—Anna put a hundred and fifty dollars in your account, like ten days ago."

"They told me my balance was zero."

Weeks later, Graham would get a printout showing that someone from ICE withdrew Anna's deposit, then a day later voided the withdrawal. This happened twice—both times, just before inmates were allowed to place their commissary orders for the week. Mail delivery was equally unreliable. Besides the lost package from the law firm, some of the letters I sent came back saying the forwarding order for "Mariners Choice Marine" had expired. It took me weeks to figure out that ICE had listed the wrong address for York County Prison on its website, and the boating company down the street had apparently moved.

At first I chalked up all these problems to the incompetence of a big government bureaucracy, but after a while it started to feel like a deliberate campaign. The pricey phone calls, the blocked commissary deposits, the out-of-state transfers, the erratic mail—the whole system seemed designed to isolate detainees, so they'd give up and agree to leave.

"I'll ask Anna to find out what happened with her deposit," I told Graham. "And I'll call Maria and see if she can send another package. But you should try calling her, too—just don't go off on any rants. I know you're frustrated, but it's not going to help your case if you piss off the people who are supposed to defend you."

"I'm not going to yell at anyone," Graham insisted, noticeably softening his voice. "But I'm pretty fucking fed up. My situation has only gotten worse since I've been here. I feel like I'm trapped in one of those mazes where every time you turn a corner and think you're getting closer to the exit, you hit a dead end. And even if I wanted to sign out, I don't have a fucking passport, so everyone says I could get stuck here for months waiting for a new one."

That was my opening to tell Graham there was only so much I could do for him, that maybe he should throw in the towel and sign out. But I was so shocked by the way he was being treated, just as the September 11 anniversary and all its bombastic patriotism rolled around, I couldn't do it. I didn't think I could live with myself if I turned my back.

Graham had been plunged into the kind of nightmare most Americans think only happens in other countries—usually, not democracies—where people get thrown in prison with no rights. But now it was happening here, to someone I knew and still cared about, all over a civil immigration matter. *Graham had already done time for his crime.*

As the injustice of his situation became clearer—the privatized prison companies profiting from locking people up, government officials lying about the immigrants they were deporting (Graham was hardly a "serious criminal")—my motivation kept shifting, moving from worry and concern to outrage and anger. So when Graham told me that he'd been thrown in solitary confinement *because some guard didn't know what else to do with him,* I got drawn into his battle. And to be honest, at that point it became mine.

Of course, not everyone who knew me understood why I was helping Graham, or believed me when I tried to explain my intentions.

"I'd rather see you invest that energy in trying to meet someone else," one friend told me.

Other people were less direct, but the message was still clear: I must be nuts to rush to the aid of my junkie crackhead ex-boyfriend, especially now that he'd landed in prison. And that was fine—I expected a few raised eyebrows directed my way. But after describing Graham's plight and trying to justify what I was doing for him, I finally realized why it made some people uncomfortable: because they wouldn't have done it. And that was fine, too—but it still bothered me. No matter what Graham had done, I didn't think he deserved what was happening to him.

The person I leaned on most was my friend Alex, who was shocked by Graham's situation and didn't question why I'd gotten involved in his case. If it hadn't been for her support, I'm not sure I would've seen it through to the end.

"I feel like you're just beginning on this journey," she told me, one night when I was feeling overwhelmed. "You've elected to do it, you feel compelled to do it, and your gut is going to have to tell you if you're okay with it."

"Yeah, but am I crazy to be doing it?" I asked.

"I think you're being driven for reasons we don't fully understand," Alex said.

ON SEPTEMBER 13, three weeks after Graham was taken into ICE custody, he finally saw a judge—but the law firm wasn't notified about his hearing in time, so it was postponed until the end of the month. Maria told me that that was still good news: It meant that he wouldn't be transferred out of Pennsylvania.

With that worry off the table, we moved on to preparing Graham's case. After hiding so much for so long, he had to open up his whole life to my scrutiny—which was terrifying for him, but tantalizing to the sleuth lurking in me. He gave me the password to his email account, permission to access his storage unit, and a notarized letter saying I could pick up his property from the police. Somehow he managed to get ahold of his checkbook, so he also sent me a bunch of signed blank checks—a risky move, but it took so long to get the power of attorney approved, it was the only way I could access his money.

None of this was easy—each task had some complication we had to solve—and we still had to deal with his taxes.

I called Graham's accountant and explained what had happened to him—one of many times I'd have that conversation, paving the way for Graham to follow up with a letter. She told me she didn't think she could do much to help, since he'd blown a chance to work things out with the IRS, then shared her own frustrations with his slide into addiction.

"Can I ask you something?" she said, not waiting for my consent. "Why are you doing this for him?"

When I hesitated, she chimed in with an answer: "Well, it must be love."

"I don't know about that," I stammered. "I mean, obviously I still care about him, but the main reason I'm doing this is that he's in a horrible situation and I think it would be devastating for him if he got deported."

Then I thanked her for whatever documents she could find and hung up, unnerved by her romantic assumption.

Love? Graham was now a twice-divorced, unemployed, recovering addict with a prison record—who'd lost his brownstone and ruined his credit. I really didn't swoop in to save him because I thought we'd get back together. For one thing, I had no idea if he'd end up winning his case. And even if he did get to stay, Graham still had a lot of problems he needed to address. From what I could tell, he'd gotten clean but he hadn't really dealt with the emotions that made him turn to drugs for relief, and being in jail certainly hadn't helped with that challenge.

Maybe I still loved him, but from everything I wrote or remember feeling at that time, I had two major reservations about Graham. First of all, I wasn't sure if he'd be able to stay clean over the long haul, and more importantly, I didn't know if I could ever really trust him.

THE DAY AFTER Graham got out of solitary confinement, I went to the Brooklyn Book Festival downtown, hoping to meet Piper Kerman—author of the memoir *Orange Is the New Black*. She was taking part in a panel discussion titled "Exposing a Difficult Past," talking about the year she spent in a women's prison. Since I was having trouble talking about Graham's difficult present, even to friends, I was riveted by everything she said.

Afterward, I lined up with other fans waiting for Piper to sign our books. When it was my turn, I was nervous to admit—out loud, in front of strangers—that my ex-boyfriend was in immigration detention, but I blurted out Graham's story and she nodded sympathetically, saying that she'd heard those facilities were pretty grim.

I asked if she had any advice about how to help Graham maintain his sanity, especially since just a few days in solitary had rattled his already fragile state of mind.

"Letters," Piper said. "Send him lots of letters."

So I did. And he wrote back—surprisingly thoughtful, confessional letters. And that old-fashioned correspondence was how Graham and I really reconnected, our unlikely present circumstances churning up our unresolved past.

"Thanks for your letters," Graham wrote me, early on in our postal exchange. *"They make a bad day a bit better and an okay*

day even more okay. I must admit that if it weren't for your inter-
vention in this whole mess I would probably just be trying to go
back to Scotland—cut my losses + start all over again. It might
still come to that, but hopefully not. So I'm gonna be grateful to
you one way or another 'coz you took a lot of time out of your life
and in a selfless way thought about my wellbeing + future—a rare
+ beautiful thing. But if it gets to be too much don't be scared to
say enough is enough, okay? I'm saying that truly but hoping it's
not the case!"

I *was* scared to say "enough is enough" but I wasn't afraid to
be blunt about other things, like telling him he needed to come up
with a plan A and a plan B for his future (in America or Britain),
step up and be a better dad to Liam, and consider some kind of
drug treatment program wherever he landed. Graham was adamant that he didn't want to go to a halfway house—"I've had
enough of living with men snoring, farting, and burping all night
long," he told me—so I pressed him on what changes he *was* willing to make.

> *What I wonder is really the same as the questions I was*
> *asking you a few years ago: What do you want, what's it*
> *going to take to make it happen, and are you willing to do*
> *those things? It's that last part I'm not sure about with you.*
>   *I still have this nagging feeling you're looking for an*
> *angle or a shortcut. And honestly, that's what weighs on me*
> *as I'm doing all this to give you one last chance—and I do*
> *think it's your last chance, Graham. Because if this hell isn't*
> *enough motivation to get you to make some serious*
> *changes, to let go of your pride and your stubbornness and*
> *get some help so you actually have a shot at staying clean,*
> *no matter what side of the Atlantic you end up on, I think*
> *any relapse, if that happens, is going to lead to a bad end-*
> *ing. That would be a particularly crushing blow, but it's a*

risk I'm taking—once again betting on you and hoping that
this time you'll prove me right.

It's not that Graham was reluctant to be honest about his struggle with addiction; he'd write pages and pages about how it had
taken him down. He was finally acknowledging all these things he
couldn't see or admit when we were together, so I was getting the
truth I'd been so desperate to hear. It didn't matter that it had taken
years to get there. I'd rush to open the mailbox every night, still trying to come to terms with the fact that I had a pen pal in prison—
the same way Graham couldn't believe he was inmate #160863.

> *Sometimes I think to myself "How the fuck did I end up*
> *in this situation?" And you know what? It's an easy answer:*
> *addiction, selfishness + lies—in a nutshell.*
>
> *Addiction is a motherfucker. Coz you don't think it'll af-*
> *fect you when you start doing drugs, you convince yourself*
> *you can quit anytime you want (especially if you've kicked*
> *before). You don't want anyone to know so you lie about*
> *it—the whole situation gets depressing + unsurmountable!*
> *So you get high to take away the pain of not being able to*
> *quit—and on the few occasions that people reach out + try*
> *+ help, you push them away usually lying to them coz your*
> *so embarrassed + ashamed + the admission of addiction—to*
> *the addict—it's like an admission of failure. You see your-*
> *self as being weak, lacking in spirit, strength, morals, faith,*
> *whatever + it leaves one open to being judged by people*
> *who've never been in your shoes. Then fear and self-*
> *loathing send you back to what you know will take that*
> *away and to people who do know—other addicts. They un-*
> *derstand, they'll take my side, they're my pals—that's how*
> *your mind convinces you to use again, to run from the truth*
> *right back into the arms of the devil.*

Anyway, it is what it is and I'm alive + not dead, I can think clearly + not in a blur, I can be honest + not lie. And for all that I'm grateful. This losing my freedom has taught me a lot. A 78-year old heroin addict that I used to spend hours talking to used to say to me "Graham, everything happens for a reason" and it drove me crazy 'coz of course everything happens for a reason or it wouldn't happen. But now I'm sort of understanding what he meant by that. I'm in jail for a reason—and not the obvious one—getting arrested for drugs—no I'm here to save my life 'coz if I didn't get put in jail who knows what could have happened to me!

Getting arrested probably did save Graham's life, but prison was definitely wearing him down. On the phone, he was often angry, ranting about the disgusting food, the crushing boredom, and the racist comments some of the guards made. As one of the few white people in immigration custody, he often benefited from that prejudice, but he still identified with the other detainees, dressed in the orange jumpsuits they had to wear.

"We look like people from Guantánamo Bay," Graham once told me.

I knew he was far better off than any of the Gitmo detainees—and so did he—but I still couldn't get that image out of my head.

Hoping to lift his spirits, I tried to balance out my lecturing letters with reading material that offered more of an escape: copies of articles I thought he'd like, news about the photography world, jokes a friend used to email me, and *New Yorker* cartoons—like one of a guy telling his therapist, "I do count my blessings, but then I end up counting those of others who have more and better blessings, and that pisses me off." And sometimes I just injected a little humor into how I described all the shit I was dealing with on his behalf—a joking tone tinged with a little resentment.

After a failed attempt to retrieve Graham's property from the police, I sent him a play-by-play of my maddening outing.

> *11:00 a.m.—Change into skirt and heels—helpful for upcoming errand.*
>
> *11:15 a.m.—Catch cab to go to Gold St. to pick up your property. Cab driver has no idea where Gold St. is so I have to direct him. At end of ride he says, "Wait, you're going to the police station!?!" then wishes me luck.*
>
> *11:30 a.m.—Lazy police officer won't look at all the paperwork I show him. Because he just sees the pink voucher for the knife, he says that's arrest evidence and I need a release from the DA. Sends me to the courthouse for that.*
>
> *12:00 noon—Arrive at courthouse. As usual, get treated nicer than everyone else because I'm a) white, b) female and c) wearing a skirt. Nice guard practically offers to escort me upstairs. Sit down to wait in another dismal hallway with wooden benches. Annoyed guy at the window keeps turning around complaining that the clerk is on the phone, having a personal conversation. I get even more annoyed than him about the mind-numbing bureaucracy and ask woman next to me—who seems like a lawyer—if she knows why I need this DA release. She looks at the form and tells me it's arrest evidence but that I shouldn't need a DA release for the other stuff. I silently curse lazy officer at property pick-up and thank her.*
>
> *12:45 p.m.—Back to Gold St. Same idiot yells at me to wait outside. I finally get allowed in and he tells me I need a voucher for your bag, laptop, keys, etc. or at least a voucher number. No amount of pleading (or the skirt)*

*will convince him to look up one number plus or minus
the number on the voucher I do have (for the knife),
which I shouldn't be given anyway at this point because
I'll use it on someone. He tells me I need to go to the
police precinct and they can look up the number for me.
Hey, guess where the 76th precinct is? Right by my
house!*

*2:00 p.m.—Enter police precinct, where nice but slow-
moving older lady at first reacts as if I've asked for
something impossible, like a ride to the moon, but finally looks through all my paperwork and goes and gets
a binder with all the voucher forms for May arrests. She
uses the eraser end of a pencil to flip through the pages
(slowly), stops to take a phone call, steps away to speak
to the sergeant, finally finds your form and by now likes
me enough to make a photocopy for me. She even takes
the time to check and see where your property is: 508
Pearson Place, in Queens—not Gold St.*

*2:30 p.m.—Get home and call # for Pearson Place, which it
turns out is near the 7 train. Nice guy on the phone
checks to see if your stuff is there, which it is, except for
the bike, which went to Kingsland Ave. and the 2
watches, which are at Gold St. Of course, Pearson Place
is only open M-F from 7:30 to 2:30, but he confirms
that your laptop, cameras, keys, etc. are in fact there.
Why would they send the watches somewhere else? No
idea. He assures me it will only take 15 minutes, not 2
hours, to find your stuff once I show up.*

But when I went to Pearson Place a couple of days later, it
didn't take fifteen minutes—it took almost an hour. Once I got to
the right window, at the right warehouse, I couldn't catch the eye
of anyone drinking coffee, chatting, or reading the paper in the

room beyond the partition where I was standing, until someone finally noticed me and said (to no one in particular), "You have a customer." The overweight officer who eventually sauntered over looked at the form I handed him, pulled on a pair of rubber gloves, sighed, and said, "This is going to be mass confusion."

After he walked away, I watched him fiddle with the knobs on a box across the room, wondering what he was doing—*maybe the box had codes to wherever property was kept?*—but it turned out to be a radio, which I realized when the Beatles song "Got to Get You into My Life" came on and everyone started swaying to the beat. Then he disappeared, leaving me to ponder the big stuffed dog in a cage on the floor with a sign saying PEARSON—BAD DOG and a withered plant (also in the cage) with another sign warning, DO NOT WATER OR TOUCH PLANT.

It took him so long to come back with Graham's bag, I had plenty of time to conclude that this was probably where people who couldn't get demoted any further ended up. They knew they were being punished, and the only power they had left was to punish whoever showed up at their dreary workplace. But I still wanted to shout, "I'm not a criminal, so stop treating me like one!"

BY LATE SEPTEMBER, I felt like I was doing time with Graham. For a month I'd been juggling work and friends with this parallel life—taking care of someone in prison—and that burden was starting to weigh me down. There were a few friends I confided in, but I hadn't told my family yet. I had the courage of my convictions, but I didn't want to deal with anyone else's doubt—which doesn't mean I didn't ever waver.

"I'm seeing the point where this gets to be too much for me," I wrote in my notebook one bleak afternoon. *"I don't know if it's the taxes or sorting through all these depressing papers or if it was*

Graham annoying me on the phone yesterday—but I'm getting irritated. And the thought of this taking many more months makes me think of that infamous quote by the BP head after the Gulf oil spill: I want my life back, too."

But when I wrote Graham that night, I didn't mention feeling responsible for his well-being, or my anxiety about not knowing who he really was. I knew there was only so much he could handle behind bars. So I sometimes held back about my own frustrations and insecurities—but not entirely. I needed him to know how this was affecting me.

> *Your last letter was a bit of a downer. The one about all the people you'd met and what minor offenses they'd committed that were going to change their lives forever. Not that you shouldn't write about it, but sometimes I think you don't realize that it's not easy to be immersed in this and then hang up the phone and finish an article or go out to dinner or listen to a band.*
>
> *Another trippy thing is flipping through all your papers: the marriage certificates, divorce settlements, little scraps of paper with names of rehab centers, lists of how many bags of crack or heroin you bought, all the to-do references to your taxes—and one note that says "Learn Spanish" that made me laugh. Plus all the drops of blood on your bills and unopened mail you just couldn't face. None of it is really a surprise at this point, but it's sad to be sorting through all the artifacts of your unraveling. And then when I talk to you on the phone, it's like I'm speaking to someone else. Maybe you don't appreciate that yet, but you already sound so different—in a good way.*
>
> *Even if it seems like you couldn't possibly put up with months of this, just remember you're going to be in a much better place when it's all over, free of many of the burdens*

*you couldn't deal with for so long. That's what I keep
thinking as I'm sorting through everything—how chaotic
your life was these past few years. Well, longer. I guess I always knew that much of this started when you were with
Liz, but now it's really clear that it way pre-dated me showing up on your doorstep.*

The truth had trickled out letter by letter, but by then Graham
had admitted that he'd been using long before we started dating. It
hadn't been a relapse, and it had nothing to do with my inability to
tell him I loved him. Even though I already knew both of those
things, it was still important to hear Graham say it. He had always
hoped that love would save him from addiction, so I wanted him to
know that wasn't going to happen—with any woman, not just me.

*Here's another observation (you'll probably wish that
I'd go back to being silently brooding): I don't think there's
a woman on this planet who could possibly fulfill the expectations you have for a relationship—and yet, probably
when you least expected it, I showed up for reasons maybe
neither of us will ever quite understand. I think you'll find
that if you're more grounded in yourself and can keep all
these insecurities at bay—not to mention getting drugs out
of your life—you'll have a better shot at getting the love
you want. OK, I'm done lecturing now. . . .*

All in all, Graham took my admonishing letters fairly well.
He'd been off drugs for five months, and I was starting to see how
much of a difference it made. There were still flashes of anger, but
also this sense of acceptance I didn't think I'd feel if I were in his
shoes. One of the letters he sent me, written on the back of a "notice of hearing in removal proceedings," sounded like he'd been on
some kind of Buddhist retreat.

I'm sitting with 13 other people waiting to go into court and it's amazing how patient you get after months of dealing with a bureaucracy that cares nothing about how long you wait for anything—from sick call, to mail, to notary public, to laundry—you name it. I used to get mad but now here I am sitting in this holding cell on a metal bench dressed in orange and I'm patient—It's a sort of serenity that comes from knowing that anger, frustration, self-pity, blame—all do nothing to help your state of mind when you're incarcerated. You can only fuck up your own head + that (in my case) has had enough of being fucked up, confused, medicated + convinced by it's own self that what I'm doing/have done is/was OK. Now I have what people call clarity of mind.

It's a weird thing 'coz memories come flooding back to me and leave me full of regret, sadness, pain + anger—but also I have many good + happy memories. It's just that in the present situation the ones that hit home + kick you in the arse are the bad ones. I've lost a lot Susan—financially, emotionally, relationship-wise, friends—but I've learned a lot too. Anyway I've got to go into court now. This is on a poster in the councilors room:

We do not see things as they are.
We see things as we are.

Because of the weird time warp we were in—letters arriving a week after we'd talked—I already knew that the hearing had gone well. Graham told me that the judge said he didn't see any reason why his request for "relief from removal" would be denied. But that preliminary opinion hinged on all the paperwork we had to gather, so I moved on to the next item on my to-do list: retrieving Graham's stuff from the housing project where he'd been living. It was only six blocks from my apartment, but it might as well have been an ocean away.

All I knew about Graham's former roommate, Joe, was that he was a black man in his fifties who used to work for the city but was on disability because of some health problems. "He's really protective of me," Graham warned—and he wasn't kidding. It took weeks of phone calls to get Joe to agree to let me come over, and when I arrived, everyone hanging out by the entrance seemed just as wary.

A feeling of neglect permeated the whole building, as if the people who lived there didn't deserve bright hallways or an elevator that didn't groan like it was about to break down. Once Joe let me into his apartment—clean enough, but still dark and shabby—he whisked me straight into the bedroom and pointed to a pile spilling out of the closet and onto the floor. It was way more than I expected: clothes, cameras, shoes, negatives, notebooks, CDs, and a box of papers. Picturing Graham holed up there, like an injured animal that had crawled out of sight, was even more depressing than picturing him in jail.

After I stuffed what I could into the bags I had brought—discarding XXL hoodies and bootleg DVDs—Joe led me into the living room, where a large gray-haired woman sitting on the couch glared at me like I'd come to evict her.

"Hi," I said, awkwardly. "I'm Susan."

"A little late for that," she snapped. "You walked right by when you came in. Never seen anybody so rude."

I apologized profusely—thinking it was really Joe's fault, for not introducing me—and she warmed up after I told her why I was there. Everyone, it seemed, had a soft spot for Graham. After I packed up some more things Joe had hidden, he helped me drag everything downstairs. I just hoped there wasn't a stray crack pipe or dope bag in any of the clothes I had grabbed. I'd checked the pockets, but not that carefully.

While Joe and I waited for the car service I'd called, a guy named Tye came over to chat. He was a bit younger than me, in good shape and sharply dressed—he didn't strike me as a crackhead or a junkie. I knew Tye was friends with Graham, but that didn't stop him from giving me an earful about how bad Graham was at the end.

"If he hadn't gotten locked up, I don't know what would've happened. That boy was heading down a path where there was no turning back."

Just as he was going off about Tracy and all the shit she had pulled, a skinny woman named Kia walked up and chimed in: "That bitch was a nightmare. He had to sell his house just to get rid of her, and then she *still* wouldn't leave him alone."

I was surprised by how much they all cared about Graham. Clearly, he wasn't just some white guy who came to the projects to buy drugs—he was embedded there, they were all friends. But if he did win his case, they didn't want to see him end up back in their midst.

When I mentioned I thought Graham should do some kind of outpatient program once he got out, Tye said, "Hell no, he had his chance at that outpatient shit. Graham is way beyond that. He needs some serious fucking rehab." Kia and Joe both nodded their heads.

I knew they were right, but that consensus still threw me. If Graham's pals from the projects could see the depths of his addiction—but he resisted getting help—what were the odds that he'd ever stay clean? That was the main thing I worried about as I ran all over the city, trying to give him that chance. Even if he won his case, all that effort might still go to waste.

ONCE I GOT home, I had just enough time to sort through Graham's stuff, pull out any papers that seemed useful, and dump the rest in the basement before my parents arrived. Since they had no idea I was back in touch with Graham, I'd asked him not to call while they were in town.

For the next three days, I lived life solely in the outside world. We went to the opera (passing back and forth my parents' huge binoculars), walked all over the city, and celebrated my dad's birthday—this time, meeting my friend Alex and her husband for dinner. It was one of our better visits: The weather was perfect, no one was sick, and we didn't argue about politics or family dramas.

The day before they left, we were having brunch near Graham's old house when my dad said, "Oh, I forgot to tell you—remember the caretaker at that condo we stayed at in Florida? He got deported."

I froze, my heart racing as I listened to him describe what happened to this guy.

"Can you believe they made him leave the country?" he asked, after wrapping up his story. That opening was too tempting for me to resist.

"Actually, I can. I wasn't planning on telling you this, but Graham is in immigration detention right now. They're trying to deport him because of a misdemeanor."

Without missing a beat my dad asked, "Who's Graham?"

"The guy I was with a few years ago," I said, surprised by this memory lapse. "You were at his house for my book party, just down the street from here."

"Oh, right."

After I told them what had happened to Graham—the arrest for drug possession, the summer in Rikers, the transfer to immigration detention, and how I found him—I gulped down half a glass of water, bracing myself for their reaction.

"Well, of course you should help him," my mom said.

"Why wouldn't you?" my dad asked, reaching over for a bite of my cold pancakes.

That was not at all the response I expected. I thought my parents would caution me about getting too involved with Graham, especially given how badly our relationship had ended. My mom knew I had bailed him out of Rikers—I'd shown her the story I'd written about that, and reading it had really upset her. That was partly why I hadn't shared much about Graham's later decline: all the arrests, his escalating drug habit, or my efforts to help him.

But now they didn't seem judgmental about what I was doing for him, and maybe that shouldn't have been such a surprise. I was raised to believe you helped out someone in need; my mom especially had set that example. But it was still a relief that they thought I was doing the right thing. Finally, I didn't have to justify or hide what was going on in my life, and that meant a lot to me.

CHAPTER EIGHTEEN

October 2010
York County Prison, Pennsylvania

I'm playing blackjack with some Russian guys—all card sharks so I'm losing badly—when the CO tells me I need to go downstairs to meet with ICE. This can't be good. I just saw them at my hearing a few days ago, and that was stressful enough.

My lawyer was on speakerphone, so it was just me, the judge, a court officer, and two guys from ICE, in a tiny courtroom inside the prison. I was panicking 'cause everyone told me this judge is tough, but he said he didn't see any reason why my deportation order shouldn't be canceled, and the ICE lawyers didn't object. I felt this huge weight lift, thinking I might actually have a shot at winning, so I'm nervous about why they want to see me again.

"What's this about?" I ask the CO, knowing he probably won't have a clue.

"No idea. They just want you down there."

When I get to the ICE office I'm told to sit and wait. There's nothing to do except stare at all the posters on the walls—about safety, terrorism, and what to do if you're feeling suicidal. Eventually an officer comes out of a back room, hands me some papers, and says, "You need to sign this."

"What is it?"

"A new charge. You're ineligible for cancellation. Just sign at the bottom saying you understand and I'll send a copy to your lawyer."

I can't fucking believe it: It's the gun charge from 2006, which I finally pled guilty to in 2009—after more than two years of hearings. I was fed up going to court every six weeks, so I took the deal in exchange for a conditional discharge.

"I'm not signing anything until I talk to my lawyer," I tell him, so he makes me put my thumbprint on the letter to confirm I got it.

Back in the dorm, people crowd around me asking what ICE wanted. I feel like screaming at everyone to get the fuck away, but I know we're all in the same boat. When I mention the new charge, the Irish guy in the bunk next to me says, "I thought you were good with the judge?"

"Me, too, but they must really want to get rid of me."

"They want to get rid of all of us. I'll probably be gone by next week."

He's getting deported because of a bar fight eleven years ago—even though he's got a green card, has a wife and three kids, and has lived here since he was one. That's how heartless these fuckers are.

I really want to talk to Susan, but her parents are in town and she needs a break from dealing with my shit, so I call the law firm instead, going off about the new charge as soon as Michael picks up.

"One minute I'm thinking I can win this thing, the next they're telling me that no matter what the judge said, they're still going to find a reason to deport me. I'd rather sign out now if this is all just a losing battle."

"I'll have to read through the paperwork once I get a copy," he says. "But I doubt this is going to impact your case. Some of these ICE lawyers like to make it tough on us—try not to worry about it, we'll deal with it."

Easy for him to say. I spend the rest of the weekend convinced that ICE is going to trawl through my record and drag up every little run-in I've had with the police. I've heard so many stories about people getting stuck here for years, I almost feel like jacking it in. But I can't imagine getting sent back to Scotland with my tail between my legs—I don't even know who'd take me in. I've lost touch with everyone I know there, so how would I explain all the shit that's happened to me? But the main issue for me is Liam. If I get deported, I can't ever come back to the U.S.—not even for a visit. The thought that I'd hardly ever see him again is the main thing keeping me here.

But I also feel like I owe it to Susan. I still can't quite wrap my head around what she's doing for me, or why she's taken on this massive task. Maybe she feels responsible 'cause there's no one else in my life who could do it—I don't know, it's humbling but sort of overwhelming. After all the shit I put her through, I'm not totally comfortable letting her go to all this trouble, especially if it looks like I can't win.

Once I talk to her, after her parents leave, she tells me not to get too stressed about the new charge—basically repeating what Michael said. Her other news is good and bad: She met with a new accountant and it sounds like the tax stuff is manageable, but I'll probably owe a lot to the IRS.

"So what if I pay thousands of dollars to the government and then they *still* deport me? I don't want to land on somebody's doorstep totally broke. They're gonna take everything they can get from me and then tell me, 'Now get the fuck out of here.' It's really not fair."

"You're still going to have plenty of money," Susan says, cutting me off. "You didn't have much income the past few years, but you drained your IRA so there are penalties for that, and then you owe taxes on your house sale. But you're in a lot better shape than most people these days. Frankly, I'm surprised you've got *any* money left."

Susan is always setting me straight like that. She seems a lot more sure of herself than she used to be, and she doesn't put up with any of my self-pity—kind of like Jimmy. She's really helped me keep it together in here.

After we hang up, I feel like I didn't get a chance to say everything I wanted to tell her, so later on I start writing her another letter. It's been kind of therapeutic to get all this stuff off my chest—coming clean about the lies I told and apologizing for how much I hurt her. As crazy as it sounds, I think all this writing has really helped us understand each other and deal with the past.

Susan's letters to me have been funny and supportive, but they can also be hard to read. Sometimes I wait till the end of the day to open them, needing that quieter time when I can really absorb what she's written. Whenever she describes what she went through, I feel guilty about how much I strung her along—even in the throes of addiction, I knew I was keeping her in it. She was that last branch I was hanging on to, trying to stop myself from falling into the abyss. It was selfish, but it was almost a survival instinct: As long as I didn't let go, I thought that there was still hope for me.

But as much as we've written to each other lately, it stills feel like there's this issue we haven't addressed. It seems a bit presumptuous to come right out and ask if she's thinking we might get back together, especially since I'm sitting here in prison and might get deported. And if I'm way off the mark, I'd feel like an ass. But she's said and written a few things that made me wonder how she really feels about me—like telling me the other day, "I'm not doing all this so you can run back to Tracy the minute you get out of there." I couldn't tell if she was threatening to pull the plug because she thinks all her efforts will go to waste if I end up with Tracy, or if she was implying that in some way, she's expecting something might happen between us.

Then in one of her letters, she told me my accountant had asked why she's doing all this for me, and when Susan didn't answer, my accountant said, "It must be love." Susan wrote me, *"I guess on some level it is,"* but I couldn't work out exactly what she meant. So when I sit down to write her—blocking out the telly, the phone calls, and the card games around me—I pretty much get straight to the point.

> *You know what's sort of funny? You using the word love—or at least partly agreeing with it—because during our relationship it was a word that you found so difficult to utter. I remember on one of the last days we were in Hawaii me saying I love you (and I did) and you just being silent and me getting upset and leaving you to go for a walk on the beach. I was mad 'coz all I wanted was for you to turn to me, hug me and say "I love you" but it never happened and in some ways I understand why and on the other hand I don't! You also wrote that you thought that I was just looking for someone to love as if it could be anyone and that's not true. I don't love easily but when I do I do so for real.*
>
> *Anyway, I'm not sure why I'm bringing this up, I think maybe because of the way our relationship ended—it was bad I know and I accept most of the responsibility for it and I'm sorry I lied to you so many times. I didn't want to hurt you—I wanted to love you and you to love me back. But somewhere in the insanity of addiction I'd convinced myself that if you couldn't say you loved me then I'd just keep using (not quite as literal as that but that's what I'm working out in my head now). I've also come to the conclusion that I was running from my addiction and in a way using you in the process—I'm trying my hardest to come clean here Susan, or as open + honest as I can be at this time.*
>
> *I know that no amount of sorrys will make up for how I hurt + disappointed you and my selfishness was—well it was selfish! You deserved more from me—even though I*

thought in my messed up head I was offering you every-
thing and all I wanted in return was your love + everything
would be rosy!! How fucked up is that? Every time you did
anything that pissed me off, depressed me, confused me I
ran to the one thing that I thought gave me comfort and to
the people who would tell me it's okay, we're on your side,
fuck it, get high—who needs love when you have the perfect
affair at your fingertips. That's right, when you're in a rela-
tionship using drugs is like having an affair. You can't/won't
admit it, you keep it secret, you run to it when your lover
pisses you off—and it's always there. Addiction won't desert
you, leave you, disappoint you. It's very reliable especially if
you can afford it.

Anyway, as you said maybe after all this is done and I'm
clean, sober, straight thinking I'll be able to find the love I
have been looking for. At this point Susan, I don't really
know what I need, want, expect, desire—yeah I've got little
thoughts in my head and happiness is better shared than
alone and I'm a romantic at heart but you're right maybe I
have to work out what my insecurities are—not totally sure
yet. Anyway I'm sort of blabbering on, probably not mak-
ing total sense just trying to open up and express my-
self. . . .

By the time I'm done I've written thirteen pages, full of the
usual bad spelling and shitty grammar. It's the most focused I've
been in a long time, and getting it all out feels like an achievement.
After years of lies and denial, I want Susan to know that I can
admit where I went wrong, and that the fight she's signed up for is
worth it.

Sometimes the words just flow out of the pen—other times I
can't even come up with a sentence. I've been working on letters
to a few friends and my old boss, asking if they'd write a letter to

the judge for me, saying I'm a good person who made some mistakes but deserves a chance to stay in the U.S. In some ways, that's a lot harder than writing Susan. She already knows where I am and how I ended up here. With everyone else, I have to start off with *"I hope this doesn't come as too much of a disappointment to you, but I'm in a prison in Pennsylvania being held by immigration. . . ,"* then explain everything that happened after I disappeared.

That is really fucking painful. Especially since if I'd asked any of these people for help years ago, I might not be in this situation.

A FEW DAYS later, just after breakfast, the CO says to me, "MacIndoe! Get ready—you're going to the dentist." He tells me my oral surgery got approved, but the dentist is in town, so I've got to strip down to my uniform and boxers—no T-shirt or thermals. I guess if I try to escape, I'll be running around almost naked.

I can't believe this actually got approved—I've had a cracked wisdom tooth for ages. I didn't really feel it when I was using, but in Rikers I kept getting these crazy toothaches and the dentist there told me I had to see an oral surgeon. That was never gonna happen, so I've been dealing with these brutal waves of pain the whole time I've been locked up. The Advil I managed to get just doesn't cut it.

Once I get downstairs, two officers are waiting for me—both with guns strapped to their belts.

"You the guy going to the dentist?" one of them asks. "I don't know how you managed to swing that."

As he shackles my hands, feet, and waist, I wonder if it's because the dental assistant here is Scottish—maybe she pulled a few strings.

The dentist's office is in a strip mall, and as soon as they take me out of the van, people look at me like I'm some violent felon. I don't really care—I'm outside for the first time in months, feeling the cool fall breeze on my face. I want to stop and take it all in but the guards quickly lead me through the parking lot and into the office, my chains rattling the whole way.

One of the guards takes my paperwork up to the desk while me and the other one sit down. Everyone in the waiting room is staring at me, probably not what they expected when they set off for the dentist this morning. A woman in a skirt and cardigan pulls her two small kids a little closer and whispers something to them. The boy doesn't take his eyes off me for a second.

"It might be a while," the guard says when he comes back from the desk. "There are a few people ahead of us."

I'm surprised they'd have me sit in the waiting room instead of whisking me in and out, but I guess even a shackled prisoner can't get quicker service at the dentist.

"So is that a Scottish accent you have?" the big guard on my right asks.

"Yeah, they're trying to deport me back there, but I'm fighting to stay."

"I'm Scottish," he says—in a totally American accent.

"Really? You don't sound Scottish."

"Well, my family's from there—back in the day. Me and my wife go to the Highland Games every year."

For the next half hour, he tells me all about his Scottish heritage and asks me a million questions about haggis, whiskey, and castles. He says he's lost a lot of weight lately, and it's a pain 'cause not only does he have to buy new clothes and a smaller uniform, but now his kilt is too big so he can't wear it.

I like this guy. He's funny and down-to-earth, which is refreshing but also a bit strange. It's almost better when the guards are assholes—it's easier to dislike them. As I tell him my story and how hard it's gonna be if I get separated from my son, it's obvious he feels bad for me. The other guy I'm not too sure about. He just seems bored and impatient.

But I actually don't mind the wait. This is the first real interaction I've had with a guard who treated me like a human being, not just a criminal. I'm sharing all these personal details with him, and he's telling me about his wife and places they want to travel. By the time I get to the dentist's chair, I feel like I've been hanging out with a new pal.

The dentist gives me a couple of shots, then waits for the Novocain to kick in before trying to lever the broken tooth and roots out of my jaw. It's tougher than he expected and my mouth fills with blood as the tooth cracks and splinters.

My eyes are closed tightly when I hear a commotion by the door. I look up and see the Scottish guy stumbling toward a chair, with the other guard holding his arm.

"Shit, I just about fainted," he says, looking down at the floor. "I hate the sight of blood."

I almost start laughing, but my mouth is still pried open and there's a tube jammed in there sucking up debris.

It's funny how much this whole outing lifts my spirits, even though getting a tooth pulled is no picnic. Then again, I'm in chains and these guys have guns. If I tried to make a break for it, I wonder if the Scottish guard would shoot me.

AFTER BEING IN Pennsylvania for six weeks, I finally get through to Liam. I've written him a few letters, but I don't know if he got them 'cause he hasn't written me back, and since he doesn't have an account with the prison phone company, I can only try him when I get my free call every week. I've been out of my mind worried that he might not want anything to do with me—but this time, he picks up after a couple of rings.

"Liam, it's Dad."

"Oh," he says. "I didn't recognize the number."

It's been so long since I've talked to him, I have no idea where to start, but I only get five minutes for these calls so I can't exactly beat around the bush.

"I'm in a prison in Pennsylvania," I tell him. "Actually, immigration detention. Have you gotten any of my letters?"

"A couple. Mom told me what happened, but I'd already heard some of the messages you left on the machine so I knew you were at Rikers Island."

Just hearing him say that makes me cringe.

"I'm sorry I didn't call you sooner. Your mum wanted me to wait until she talked to you first, and then things got pretty rough after I got picked up by immigration. To be honest, it's been kind of a nightmare, so she didn't want you to be dealing with that once you were back at school."

"I know. . . . I was really worried about you."

Liam's voice sounds a little off—I can't work out if he's upset or if it's the crappy connection. I feel so distant from him I just want to reach through the phone and hug him.

"Listen, I'm really, really sorry about everything I've put you through. I know I wasn't the best dad the last wee while. Everything sort of spiraled out of control and I couldn't reel myself in. . . . I guess you know why, but that's not an excuse."

"You don't have to explain anything," he says, which we both know isn't really true. But I don't want to dwell on my situation right now—I want to hear about him.

"What's been going on with you? I heard you went to Ireland with your girlfriend over the summer."

"Yeah, we went to Scotland, too."

"Is this the same girl you've been dating for a while?"

"Yeah, but we're at different schools now so we don't see each other as often."

It's weird to think of him grown up and traveling with a girl-friend, visiting family I haven't seen in so long. I ask him how everyone is—he fills me in on his cousins and how my parents are doing, then asks me what it's like in prison. I tell him it's really boring, but not as bad as what he probably imagines. He sounds different—more mature, I guess—which makes me realize how much I've missed out on over the last few years.

There's still a million things I want to say when the CO tells me my time's up.

"I have to go—I'll try to call you next week," I say quickly. "I love you."

"I love you, too, Dad."

Before I get a chance to wish him a happy birthday—he'll be twenty soon—Liam hangs up. I put the phone down, wipe my eyes with my sleeve, and get up to leave. The CO looks at me and glances away—as if he's uncomfortable seeing a grown man cry. But I'm sure that happens all the time in here.

As I walk back to the dorm, I wonder what Liam is thinking—if he's told anyone I'm in prison, or if he's too embarrassed to admit that his dad is locked up. Even before I got arrested, I figured he didn't want any of his pals to know what a mess I was, so I used to cycle to the soccer fields in Red Hook and watch him play—but from a distance, so he wouldn't see me. That was the only way I could feel connected to him.

Now I just want to be able to hang out with him like we used to, but I know it's not gonna be the same even if I do get to stay. He's grown up now, with his own life to worry about, so I've got to get to know him in a whole different way. Susan keeps reminding me that it's not gonna happen overnight, and I got a letter from Anna saying I need to give everyone time to catch up. She was nice about it, but it's still frustrating. I've wasted so much time already, I just want to move on and fix things.

When I talked to my brother the other day, he seemed eager to accept me back into his life. At first all I wanted to do was tell him how sorry I was, but he made it easy on me—he's always been really forgiving. He said if I didn't win my case I could come stay with him and he'd help me find a job, which was a huge relief. I'm not sure I'd want to live in Dublin, but at least I won't be out on the street. Mostly he was worried about what I was going to say to our parents.

"Mum and Dad are pretty hurt," he told me. "They're still there for you, but only if you've changed. After everything they've been through, they can't face another disappointment. It's too much for them at this stage of their lives."

I appreciated his bluntness, but it made me realize that talking to my parents was gonna be a lot tougher than I'd thought. For weeks I couldn't make international calls 'cause commissary kept telling me they were out of phone cards, but now that I've got one I don't have any excuse not to call. I'm sort of hoping it'll go better if my brother fills them in first. Talking with him went better than I expected, but all these conversations are really draining. There's only so much I can deal with at once.

A FEW DAYS later, Susan tells me she's going by my old house to pick up some of my stuff. The new owners let me leave some things in the basement, but I never went back to get it, so Susan got in touch with them and they said they'd put it all out in the front yard. They're gonna get rid of whatever doesn't get taken.

I call Susan around the time she was going over there, to figure out what she should save.

"I'm here," she says. "And so is Tracy—with a U-Haul. She's acting like everything is hers, so you're going to have to tell me what you want."

That doesn't sound good. We both knew Tracy would be there,

but I thought she only left a couple of boxes in my basement—not enough to fill a truck.

"Listen, I honestly can't remember what's there, but the only thing I care about is my film. There should be dozens of rolls of exposed film in a bag with a tripod, and maybe a couple of light stands."

"Well, I don't see anything like that. It mostly looks like junk you picked up on the street. Broken chairs, bike parts, old magazines, some huge speakers. Wait a second—Tracy just grabbed something that might be the bag you want."

I can hear Susan and Tracy arguing, but I can't make out what they're saying. I'm trying to imagine the scene in my front yard in Brooklyn, with stuff strewn all over and two women fighting—just when the neighbors probably thought they were done with my drama.

"I'm sorry, I can't find your film," Susan says, finally coming back on the line. "One of the new owners told me someone broke into the basement a few months ago and took some stuff that was under a tarp. Maybe the film was in a bag that got stolen."

Those rolls of film must have hundreds of self-portraits I took, trying to document my slide into addiction, so it's devastating to hear they might be lost. I have no idea what I'd ever do with them, but those photos are a record of what my life got reduced to—the endless repetition and isolation of getting high.

"Don't worry about it," I tell Susan, relieved that I've still got a lot of digital shots on my computer. "Maybe the film is somewhere in my storage space. Just take whatever looks like photo equipment or anything you want. The rest I can live without."

That part is true. I've lost so much and been living with so little, everything else seems inconsequential.

"I'll take whatever I can fit in a cab," Susan says. "But you really need to deal with Tracy. She seems to think she's saving all your stuff for you and once you get out you're going to pick up right where you left off. You're not doing her any favors by not being honest."

I know Susan's right—I probably haven't been as up front with Tracy as I should be, but I've been going to some AA meetings in here and listening to everyone talk a lot about forgiveness. If I want people to accept that I've changed and not hold all the shitty things I've done against me, I feel like I have to do the same for Tracy. It doesn't seem right to totally cut her off.

It's just hard to explain that to Susan, especially since I'm not sure exactly what's on her mind. After she got the long letter I wrote her, she told me she doesn't expect anything from me, except that I do whatever it takes to stay clean. I was relieved about that—it takes some of the pressure off me—but I feel like that might not be all she really needs. It's impossible to bring up all these feelings and emotions without getting drawn back into thinking about our relationship, and there's definitely something changing between us. I just have no idea where it's gonna lead.

ONE NIGHT RIGHT after dinner I get a call from the CO telling me to pack up—I'm getting moved.

"Where to?" I ask, a bit nervous. *People don't usually get moved at this time.*

"You're going to IB3-10. It's up the stairs and along the corridor, opposite the kitchen workers' dorm."

"Man, you goin' on the snitch program!" someone behind me shouts.

"What the fuck is the snitch program?"

"Oh, you know—you got to tell on everyone about all the things they're doin' wrong."

"Well, I'm not a snitch," I say, wondering if he's talking about the Freedom Program—I had an interview to see if I could get on it the other day. It's a four-month rehab meant for county inmates, not immigrants, but I was telling my CO about my situation and he told me I should apply. *Maybe I managed to talk my way in.*

When I get to the dorm, the first thing that strikes me is how quiet and orderly it is. There's not the usual prison chaos—and not an unmade bed in sight.

I'm introduced to a guy called Mr. Torres, who shows me my bunk and hands me a bulky red book with an American eagle and the words *Freedom Program* on the front, along with a six-page list of rules (single-spaced!). Some are pretty obvious—no shaming, no arguing, no disrespectful comments or allowing doors to slam—but others seem a bit picky: *"If you sneeze, cough, wipe your nose or put your hands in your pants, you have 10 minutes to wash your hands."*

As I flip through the book—hundreds of pages about recovery, writing exercises, and a detailed schedule, from 6:30 A.M. to 8:00 P.M.—I start to wonder if I'm going to regret this.

"Everyone has that look on their face when they first get here," Mr. Torres says. "But trust me—once you get the hang of it, it's gonna make you think different about things."

He gives me a quick rundown on the daily routine and explains what cognitive behavior therapy is—as far as I can tell, understanding how your negative thoughts lead to bad choices like doing drugs. Honestly, I'm a little stunned. I thought there would be a couple of meetings a day—not five groups, individual counseling, and self-analysis pretty much every waking hour. I can't imagine ever getting it, but I scribble notes and nod enthusiastically, hoping it'll become clearer as time goes on.

The next day, it feels like I've stumbled into the middle of a race everyone else has been running for miles. Most of the groups are led by other inmates, but two outside counselors come in every day. In the morning there's a workshop on anger management and another one on self-esteem. In the afternoon someone does a presentation on rational thinking and then everyone gathers around for a "feelings check." I'm shocked when a few really hardcore jailhouse guys break down in tears talking about what's going on inside their heads. I can't imagine anything like this happening at Rikers.

The mix in here is pretty different—there are a lot more white, blue-collar guys. Everyone in the program is mandated by the court, or they sign up so they can reduce their sentence—mostly for drug crimes, fighting, or DUIs. I can already tell it's nothing like the rehab I did in California, definitely a lot less pampering. Here there's always someone doing chores, but I haven't quite worked out how they're assigned.

After dinner my second night, I finally get a chance to call Susan—making sure I sign in on the phone sheet first. We're only allowed two phone calls a day, one before 5 P.M. and one after we eat.

"I'm in the program," I tell her.

"What? The connection is terrible so you have to speak up."

"I can't. I got into the Freedom Program—that rehab program I told you about—but there's a rule about talking loudly. They've got rules about everything—how you make your bed, when you can use the phone, how you clean up the bathroom sink. . . ."

"That's great!" Susan says, sounding a bit like a parent congratulating a kid. "I thought you said they don't take people from immigration?"

"They usually don't, but I must've convinced them I really need this. I've got a week to decide if I want to stick with it."

"Do you think you will?"

"Yeah, probably. I think it'll be good for me. But it's pretty intense. You have to address people as 'Mr. Jones' or 'Mr. Clark'—no first names. It's all about respect and taking responsibility and facing up to how your bad choices got you where you are now. It's really disciplined—you should see all the rules."

I want to say "fucking rules," but that's another thing: We're not allowed to swear.

"Well, it'll definitely help your case," Susan says. "I didn't want to make a big deal about that in case they didn't accept you, but it's really important to show the judge you're committed to staying clean. I'm doing a lot for you, but that part is up to you."

I tell her I know that—it's why I applied to this program—feeling a bit irritated that she's not giving me much credit for taking this step. She changes the subject, telling me she's going to search through my storage unit tomorrow, to look for some documents Michael and the accountant need. I know that's the only way she can pull together everything for my case, but I'm worried about what else she might find. Before I got arrested, I'd sometimes bike over to my storage space and hole up there surrounded by my stuff—flipping through photography books, trying to feel some connection with who I used to be. I'd usually end up getting high to block out the pain, so there might still be a pipe or a needle lying around.

"I hope you don't come across anything in there that upsets you," I tell her.

"I can't imagine there's much left that can shock me. Besides, I'm so busy reading your email, cashing in your frequent flier miles, and spending your money, I don't have time to dig through your boxes and read all of your letters."

Picturing notes from Tracy, arrest records, and notebooks full of whatever was going through my head at that time, I'm not so sure about that. "I guess I'm not gonna have any secrets left, am I?"

"Probably not. But your taxes will be done, and you'll be starting over with a clean slate. As far as I'm concerned, that's not a bad trade."

AFTER A FEW days in the program and all this talk about taking responsibility and making amends, I can't put it off any longer: I finally call my parents. These calls are never easy—I keep playing out the conversations in my head first, trying to imagine how everyone will react. But this time I'm practically shaking as I punch in the international codes and dial their number.

My dad picks up the phone attached to the old fax machine in the hall—I can tell by the delayed click.

"Hello?" he says—in that Scottish brogue I haven't heard in at least a year.

"It's me, Graham."

There's a pause before he says, "Your brother said you were going to call."

"I'm sorry I've not been in touch sooner," I tell him, my own accent coming on stronger. "It's hard to make international calls from here—it took ages to get the phone cards I ordered."

"Aye, well, I'm glad you got through. We've been waiting to hear from you."

It's uncomfortable at first, but we settle into a semi-normal conversation, mostly talking about how I've dealt with being in prison. Once I've reassured him that I'm okay—no one's beating the shit out of me and I'm not getting buggered—he says, "Let me get your mum on the other line. She'll want to speak to you as well."

I know her health's not great but when she picks up the other phone she sounds different—quiet and sort of frail. I tell her how sorry I am that I've caused them so much stress and try to explain what happened, but it's like she's not quite ready for that. She just asks how long I think my case will take.

"I don't know yet. I have another hearing next week, so I'll probably find out then."

"Well, you're lucky to have Susan," my mum says. "I don't know what you'd do without her."

"I know, she's been brilliant. I can't believe how much she's doing for me."

I try to reassure them that I'm actually pretty good, or at least a lot better than the last time they heard from me. It's hard to describe the Freedom Program to my parents—all the rules make it sound like I'm in some sort of boot camp, not rehab. But I tell them this is something I've needed for a long time, it's just a pity that I had to find it this way.

"Well, I hope it works," my dad says. "Because if you can't pull yourself together after this, then I don't know what could possibly help you. The last few years have been a nightmare for us—your mother can't deal with it, I'm worried sick constantly. It'll be the death of us if you don't get your act together."

I'm surprised by how blunt he is, telling me he's had sleepless nights wondering if I was dead or crumpled up in a doorway somewhere, and how much of a burden it's been for the whole family.

When he's done, I don't know how to express how sorry I am. I'm already choking up when my mum says, "We're still here for you, but you need to get better—get back to your old self. This has gone on for too long."

"I know," I tell her, the lump in my throat making it hard to speak. "This whole experience has been a real eye-opener for me. I promise you I'm not going down that road again."

My dad wraps up the conversation with news about my relatives and tells me I need to take the advice I'm getting in here seriously—because the advice I've been giving myself hasn't worked. I tell them I'm doing my best and promise I'll call again soon.

After I sign out on the phone sheet, I just sit there for a minute letting everything sink in. Sometimes it feels like I'm living a double life. It's as if people are talking about a person I don't recognize anymore, someone I never thought I'd be. But I know I have to accept that I was that person and I did do those things. As much as I wish I could take a lot of it back, I can't—it's all me.

———

A few days before my hearing, I call the law firm to check in and get hit with another surprise: Michael quit.

"So who's gonna handle my hearing?" I ask Maria. "I'm supposed to see the judge on Tuesday!"

"I'm not sure yet," she says. "But one of our other lawyers will phone in. Don't worry, they'll have all the notes about your case."

When I tell Susan—I have to wait until after 5 p.m. for my second call—even she seems rattled, promising she'll call the firm and find out what's going on. I get the feeling she must've read someone the riot act because the next time I talk to her she tells me one of the partners is going to step in.

The morning of my hearing, I'm a nervous wreck waiting to see the judge. It doesn't help that almost everyone seems to come out of the courtroom holding a deportation order. By the time my name is called, I'm so convinced that ICE is going to throw the book at me I'm already imagining trying to start a new life in Dublin.

The judge doesn't look up when I walk in. Neither do the ICE guys on the other side of the room. I feel such a weight in my stomach I want to stand up and shout, "Fuck it—just deport me!" But then I hear my lawyer introduce himself on the speakerphone and the judge makes a joke about him not handling a case in ages—like they know each other and used to cross paths all the time.

"I assume you won't be doing the final hearing," the judge says, then asks if someone whose name I don't catch is gonna take over. My lawyer says that's probably who it'll be.

I thought I'd get grilled about the new charge or at least get asked *something*, but it's all over pretty quickly. The judge announces he's scheduling my final hearing for February 24—four months from now—my paperwork gets stamped, and I'm back in the holding cell. I'm one of the only people who didn't get a deportation order, so I feel bad for all the guys who weren't so lucky. If you speak English and can afford a good lawyer, at least you've got a chance of winning. If not, you're basically fucked.

IT'S 7:30 A.M. and I'm standing in line with a dozen other prisoners, staring straight ahead with my hands behind my back. Everyone else in the dorm is looking on in silence.

I'm trying not to catch the eye of my bunkie, Mr. Walker, but it's practically impossible. He's giving me this long, hard stare and I'm trying not to laugh since that'll just get me in more trouble. I bite my tongue and look at my feet as all the guys in line next to me recite their negative behaviors.

When it's my turn, I take a deep breath, unfold the strip of paper in my hands, and start to read: "*Mr. MacIndoe— Manipulation. My name is Mr. MacIndoe and I manipulated the phone by not signing out. A manipulative person is viewed as sneaky, self-serving and uncaring. This is proof that I am trapped in the cycle of addictive thinking patterns. Until I show that I can leave the manipulative ways of my past behind, I cannot expect others to take my recovery seriously. Being that I am in the Freedom Program looking for change, I will take an honest look at where my manipulative behavior has gotten me.*"

I refold the paper and put my hands behind my back as the guy next to me chants about how he enabled someone else on the program by not addressing their irresponsibility—leaving a coffee cup on the table.

Addressing other people's negative behaviors—or *snitching*, as the rest of the prison calls it—is a big part of the Freedom Program. At first I wasn't comfortable doing it. I felt like I was turning people in for stupid shit. But after a while, I realized that the point was to help people become more aware of the rules and break down the way addicts enable each other—by turning a blind eye. So that's why I'm lined up reading a chant about my manipulative behavior, because someone addressed me for not signing out on the phone sheet.

I've been in the program for almost three weeks now and I'm starting to get it, but sometimes it's still really stressful. If you're not careful, little mistakes can snowball, and before you know it you've been addressed so many times you get kicked out. That thought terrifies me—not just because I want to prove I can do this, but also because of how it would look to the judge.

When everyone's done and we sit down for breakfast, I tell Walker he's got to stop trying to fuck with me when I'm chanting. "If you get kicked out of the program it just means you lose some of your good time. If I get kicked out I could lose my case."

"Oh, relax," he says. "You're going to sail through this and be back in New York before you know it. Then the next time The National plays there you're gonna get me tickets and introduce me to them."

That was how we first bonded—over music. He was listening to his radio and handed me his earphones, saying, "I love this band."

"I know these guys," I told him, instantly recognizing the singer's voice. "I took pictures of them before they were famous—I went to the bass player's wedding years ago."

Walker didn't believe me at first, but I finally convinced him that I wasn't bullshitting. Ever since then we've become really good friends. Even though he's a lot younger than me, he's sort of guided me through the program. He's smart and sincere but doesn't take it all too seriously—like he keeps drawing dicks on my assignments that I don't notice until I'm meeting with one of the counselors and have to shuffle papers to cover them up.

After breakfast we break into groups for a workshop called STAR, which stands for *Stop Think Act Review*—everything in this program has some quirky name. It's all about what to do when you're caught up in the heat of the moment so you don't make rash decisions. We're talking about how to step back and deescalate the situation when a guy called Mr. Hammond gets up and says, "Stop and breathe." We all look up at him as he puts his hands behind his back and shares what he's learned.

"I get angry way too easily, especially when I've been drinking," he says. "I make irrational decisions that always have bad outcomes. That makes me ashamed so I get even more angry and end up taking it out on my family. Now I realize I have the ability to take a deep breath and think about the consequences of my actions—weigh it up first and avoid my usual pattern."

What he says stops me in my tracks. Mr. Hammond isn't the type of person you'd expect to find in prison—a middle-aged white guy who's been locked up a couple times for DUIs. He's pretty quiet, but everything that comes out of his mouth in group is so enlightening he almost always gets a round of applause. Supposedly when he first got here he couldn't communicate a word about how he felt—he just looked angry all the time. Now that he's about to graduate from the program, he's the go-to guy for anyone who's feeling down or needs advice. I hope I can make changes the way he has, but it still feels like a lot to take in.

The other day I was meeting with my counselor, Mr. Dean, to talk about my progress. We were going over a paper I wrote about the "fishbowl technique."

"If I step back, slow down and think of the situation as if I'm looking at myself from the outside, I'll be able to hold back on the words and actions I use and also I'll be able to deal better with whatever the other person is saying or doing to provoke me," I'd written.

Mr. Dean explained how that relates to the ABCs—another recovery acronym we've been working on. There's an "actuating event," like an argument, you have a "belief" about what happened—thinking the other person insulted you—and then that belief has an emotional "consequence," like getting angry or depressed. You're supposed to step back, challenge your irrational thoughts, and change your behavior so you don't overreact.

"It's not about going from one extreme to another—you're not going to suddenly be happy," Mr. Dean told me. "It's about lowering your emotional state so instead of being angry, you're annoyed or you feel a bit down instead of depressed."

It made me realize I did that a lot—overreact. Someone would say something, I'd misinterpret it, and that would set me off. That kept me trapped in a cycle of feeling the same anger or disappointment over and over, so I'd drink or use drugs to make myself feel better, incapable of seeing how self-destructive that was.

That's what the Freedom Program is all about—being aware of yourself and others and thinking about the consequences of your actions before you act. I never would've expected to learn so much in this environment, but the way the other guys have opened up has been totally inspirational. Once I saw how they were making changes for the better, I started to want that for myself. It's the first time I've understood how recovery could work for me.

CHAPTER NINETEEN

November 2010
Cobble Hill, Brooklyn

After Graham told me he'd been accepted into the Freedom Program, I remember looking up at the ceiling and mouthing, "Thank you." It wasn't just that doing a rehab program would help his immigration case, or that it would give him a much better shot at staying clean. I was mostly relieved that for the next sixteen weeks he'd have a support system to rely on—besides me.

Graham had been struggling to stay afloat in a sea of emotions, as he reconnected with Liam and his family, dealt with the stress of being in prison, and coped with all the ups and downs of his case. So far I was the main person he was leaning on and I wasn't sure I could handle that much longer—especially since our relationship was becoming part of the mix.

A few days before he got into the program, Graham had blurted out "I love you" when we were talking, just after the prison recording announced our time was up. At first I was glad our call got cut off before I could answer, but I knew I couldn't leave those three words dangling without a response. I didn't want to get into another "She loves me, she loves me not" scenario, but it was too soon to be opening that door.

"I'm not going to tell you what you should or shouldn't feel," I wrote him later. *"I've learned by now (I hope) to let people be who they are. But I also know you well enough to wonder if you're already stewing about what I say back, and honestly, I'm not ready to take on that question right now. This is all incredibly intense, after having very little contact for a long time, and on top of*

that I'm surrounded by reminders of the life you've been living and that's like having a big caution sign flashing all the time.

"It's not that I don't think about what's going to happen when you get out—I do, and I actually find it kind of exciting that you're going to get this chance to reinvent yourself. But what I'm trying to say is that I'm OK with not knowing what's going to happen between us, and I hope you can be too—especially since you're in a situation with a lot of question marks surrounding your future."

Maybe I was overreacting to what Graham had said—later, he'd tell me he had no expectations about how I'd respond. At the same time, I was probably underestimating how much my own feelings had evolved. As I got to know the clean and sober version of Graham, I *was* falling for him again, but I didn't know if we'd have that same spark in person—we hadn't seen each other in more than a year. Graham had discouraged me from visiting him, saying the trip wasn't worth it for a half-hour visit, just to talk on the phone separated by a Plexiglas window.

But with each week that passed, I was becoming more and more invested in the outcome of his case. And with each setback, I was less confident that he'd actually win.

After Michael quit, the partner who handled Graham's hearing had warned me, "This is a winnable case, but it's weak." I flipped out, asking why Michael had said it was a "good case" when I hired the firm—and told Graham it was worth the fight.

"Immigration law is extremely complicated," he answered. "If you get twelve lawyers in a room, they may all give you different opinions about a case."

I didn't share the exact details of that conversation with Graham, which I was glad about later, when yet another lawyer took over and offered a more optimistic take on his odds.

"I think this will be a very good case," Armen, our third and final lawyer told me the first time we spoke on the phone. I liked him—he clearly cared about his clients, but he could also be calculating. In that sense, he was a bit like me.

"Graham's got multiple arrests for drug possession," he said, laying out how he saw the scales of justice align. "Even though they're all misdemeanors, they're recent. But we can argue that he's committed to turning his life around. He's in a rehab program, he's motivated to restart his photography career, and he has good relationships with his girlfriend and his son."

"Ex-girlfriend," I interrupted. "I know this seems strange, but we actually broke up a few years ago."

"Look, obviously you love the guy," Armen said, adding quite pointedly, "Having a support system is very important to this judge."

I got the message, so I didn't argue with him, especially since my feelings about Graham were all over the map at that point, bouncing between exasperation, worry, compassion, and affection, carried along by an undeniable undercurrent of love.

"I've been feeling the hum of that connection again," I wrote in my notebook in early November, confessing something I wasn't ready to admit out loud. *"Graham's softer side is coming back, that sensitivity I fell in love with—such a rare pairing with his tougher front. It really does seem like he's changing by the day. I've been talking to the people he's asked to write letters on his behalf, so that's helped confirm that I'm not crazy for believing he has a 'good heart,' as one of them put it. Clearly a lot of people would go out of their way for him."*

Over the past few weeks, I had contacted some of Graham's friends to get their addresses for him, and explain why they'd be getting a letter from prison. Since I hadn't met most of these people, it was a bit awkward at first—being the bearer of bad news, and then answering their questions about how he was doing.

"Is he okay in there?" one of his clients asked. "He's thin and not very muscular."

I tried to reassure her that Graham had bulked up since she last saw him, now that he was off drugs and eating again, and that this prison seemed much less violent than Rikers.

"Well, he's lucky to have you," she told me—a phrase I heard a lot from his friends, which was strangely gratifying to hear. Usually when someone said that, I wondered if the subtext was "He doesn't deserve you," but these were people who thought highly of Graham. That came through quite clearly in their letters to the judge, which they sent me before mailing them to Armen.

"Generous is a word that is particularly appropriate to describe Graham," one friend wrote, crediting Graham with helping launch his career. Another friend captured his love for Liam especially well: *"One of my first memories of Graham is of him pushing his son around London in his baby stroller, with little Liam eating plums on the train. This memory sits beside one from recent years of Graham on his patio asking his teenage son for a kiss on the cheek, a tender father and son moment—and coming from a Scot all the more telling, with Scottish men not renowned for outwardly showing physical affection."*

That anecdote reminded me of the first time I saw Liam in 2005, a few nights after Graham took my photo. I still remembered him as a carefree boy in a bathing suit in Montauk, so I was surprised when this tall teenager greeted me with a polite kiss on the cheek—this time, unprompted by his dad.

As I got to know Graham's functional friends, and finally connected with his family, I realized I never really knew the guy a lot of them talked about: the big brother, the earnest art student, the doting dad, the up-and-coming photographer. Addiction had spoiled maybe a decade of Graham's forty-seven years, but it didn't define him. Even I was guilty of seeing him mostly through that lens.

"I know this is hellish for him," Graham's sister emailed me. *"But I hope it's the catalyst he needs to get his life back. We all really miss the man he used to be."*

Thinking about that gave me hope that there might be yet another version of Graham: not the person he was (that guy wasn't coming back), not who I wanted him to be (that wasn't up to me), but someone none of us knew he could be—maybe not even him.

BY MID-NOVEMBER, GRAHAM had been in the Freedom Program for a month, and it seemed like he had wholeheartedly embraced it.

"I went to a brilliant AA meeting tonight," he told me, after a particularly good day (there were still plenty of bad ones). "Everyone came up to me afterwards and said they really liked what I shared."

"What was that?" I asked, always curious about his progress—but not wanting to seem too eager.

"Just that we've been talking a lot about pride in the program—the AA meetings are open to anyone in the prison—so I was saying how much the bad kind of pride kept me from accepting help. I always thought I could deal with things on my own. But I also had low self-esteem, so I was actually really down on myself a lot of the time. That's another reason I pushed people away—I didn't want anyone to see the real me."

"Well, you'd better brace yourself for my next letter because I wrote it when you were being a pain in the ass. I told you to stop feeling sorry for yourself and be grateful that you're getting free rehab while I'm out here doing your taxes."

"I already got it," Graham said. "Your letters make me laugh even when you're pissed off."

"Really? Sometimes I wonder if you get them and just want to rip them up after you read them."

"No, I really think about what you write. I mean, it's not always easy to hear about all of my failings, but you didn't tell me anything I hadn't already learned about myself the last few weeks."

Lately, Graham's letters to me had taken a more introspective turn—looking inward more than just looking back at the past.

> *It's really important for me to come to terms with who I've been & what I've done—good & bad—and see how that's moulded me as a person & what I need to change & what I need to hold onto & let enhance me. I know it's all a process & I'm sure that these last 6 months of sobriety & clearheadedness combined with this program will get me a long way on the path to true recovery. Coz to be honest, I'm tired of being an addict. It's not something I ever thought I would be & it surprises, angers & sadens me to see how it got me & where it took me. I had no idea that it was so powerful.*

Given how much the program seemed to focus on negative behaviors, I was glad to hear that Graham was also thinking about some of his positive traits. When I wrote him back, I mentioned a few things I admired about him.

> *Your strength and your adaptability and the fact that you've even managed to pull off a few jokes recently are all things I'd put on the keepers list. I think you've handled this situation better than most people could, so I hope you recognize that, even as you're examining lots of things you might not like about yourself.*

Sometimes it felt like we were communicating along parallel tracks: these thoughtful, heartfelt letters, and then our frantic phone calls, which were mostly about Graham's case or his taxes.

I always had a long list of questions I rushed to get through before our twenty-minute time limit was up: "How much rent did your tenant pay? Where are your divorce papers? Who has the closing statement from your house sale?"

Digging through Graham's storage unit for clues was a forensic nightmare—one of the chores I sometimes resented. *I didn't sign up for this,* I'd think, pulling a heavy box marked ACCOUNTS down from a high stack—only to find copies of old design magazines instead. Or I'd take a break to look at one of his photography books and an empty dope bag would flutter to the floor, marked with a stamp saying KISS OF DEATH. I'd already thrown away a needle and a crack pipe, scared that I'd get busted with drug paraphernalia as I carried them out to the trash. Each new discovery wasn't surprising; it was all just depressing, imagining Graham hanging out in that lonely lair.

But at least I'd found an accountant who deserves much of the credit for saving Graham's ass. The first time I went by his office, he calmly sorted through the mess of paperwork I handed him, making neat piles of invoices and bloodstained bills on his desk. Then over the next few weeks, he patiently made calls to the IRS, trying to sort out Graham's taxes. It helped that Graham didn't have much income during those missing years, but it complicated my life that his phone privileges could be taken away—when I needed answers to the accountant's questions.

"Sorry I haven't called," Graham said, after I hadn't heard from him in a couple days. "I was on a speaking ban."

"What happened?"

"I got pulled up for phone manipulation. If you dial and the person doesn't pick up that's supposed to count as your call, but someone saw me redial so I wasn't allowed to talk for forty-eight hours. I had to wear a sign around my neck that shows a guy's face with a zipper across his mouth."

Picturing that punishment, I had to resist the urge to laugh—it clearly wasn't funny to Graham. "I thought this was supposed to be a non-shame-based program?"

"That's bullshit."

"Isn't swearing against the rules?"

"Yeah, but no one's around who can hear me. That's the one thing I hate about this program—all the snitching. If you don't address people for things they're doing wrong you get pulled up for nonparticipation. We've got quotas—like cops!"

I didn't understand what many of the rules had to do with recovery, either; leaving a cup on the table or talking too loudly seemed like pretty minor offenses. But I reminded Graham that he had to "pick up his awareness," quoting the line they used all the time in the program. "If you get kicked out, it's going to look really bad to the judge."

"Trust me, I'm not gonna get kicked out. I've only gotten pulled up three other times—once for not wearing socks outside my living area, once for not signing out on the phone sheet, and once for leaving my locker open."

Still, it was something I worried about constantly. Not because Graham wasn't committed to his recovery—I had no doubts about that—but he'd always been a bit scatterbrained, in that distracted artist or ADD sort of way. Even without drugs clouding his mind, I wasn't sure that had changed.

For a while, I'd been wondering what Graham would be like back in the real world. It was one thing to stick with the program when he was locked up in prison—with fifty-five other guys constantly hawking him. But once he was free, how would he handle the day-to-day stress of managing his life?

That question became much more personal a few days later, when I was on the phone with Armen and he suggested—or really, decided—that Graham should stay with me after he got released.

"It's what the judge would want," Armen told me. "Graham needs to show he's got a stable place to live, and it sounds like you're his best option."

"What about what I want?" I protested, half-heartedly.

"C'mon, do you really want him to end up back in the hood?"

I had already figured Graham might end up on my doorstep, at least for a little while, so I told Armen I'd consider it. But I wasn't a total pushover, so in my next letter to Graham I let him know how I felt about that idea.

> *Everyone at the law firm is assuming you'll end up stay-ing with me, and if the judge needs to know that you won't be getting dumped out on the street, I'm not going to stand up and yell, "Objection, your honor! He doesn't organize his silverware and I can't live with that!" But that's some-thing we need to talk about. I don't know what you imag-ine happening, but I don't want to just stumble into this because the holidays go by in a blur and then suddenly you get an earlier court date.*
>
> *Like I've told you, I don't know what I want to happen—and I have no idea what's going on inside your head. Seriously, what do you picture when you imagine walking out of York County Prison? The only things you've mentioned are that you want to breathe fresh air and be able to walk to a deli and buy a Kit-Kat.*

Graham's letters to me had tapered off as he got caught up in the program, doing writing assignments about addiction instead, so I really didn't have a clue how he pictured his life after prison. Since he didn't have much control over his future, I think we were both reluctant to make any real plans.

But if he did win his case, I actually didn't mind taking him in.

In some sense, I already felt like Graham and I lived together. His mail came to my apartment, his laptop was on my coffee table, I'd even washed the clothes I picked up at Joe's place. I'd been through his email, his credit card bills, his medical records, and his bank statements; I'd read about every arrest on his rap sheet. I knew more about Graham than many couples know about each other after years of marriage—and it didn't hurt that he was basically in cohabitation boot camp, admonished if he didn't make his bed with military precision or left a blob of toothpaste in the sink. Frankly, everything Graham told me about what he was learning in the program tipped the scale in favor of giving him a chance.

When we talked about it, he assured me that he'd be a model "roommate"—neither of us really sure how to refer to his status.

"I'm happy to cook, clean, do laundry, pay rent, whatever you want. I don't know how long it's gonna take until I can get my own place—I'm sure my credit is fucked—but feel free to tell me if I'm overstaying my welcome."

"There's just one—or really, two conditions," I warned him. "If I start wondering if you're using, or if you lie to me about *anything,* I'm kicking you out. I'm serious—I'm going to have a zero-tolerance policy about that."

"I promise you, that's not gonna happen. After everything I've been through, I can't imagine what would make me want to go back to that life."

I actually didn't think it was likely, but if Graham did relapse, I was pretty sure I wouldn't miss the signs. Now that I knew what he was like off drugs, it would be a lot harder for him to hide anything from me—especially living together.

After reminding him that my tiny apartment didn't have much more privacy than a prison dorm, I threatened to go on a mail strike if he didn't write me soon, which did prompt him to send another letter.

*I'm going to start off by telling you how much I appreci-
ate all you've done for me. I know that when you do something you do so 100% and I know this is for you as much
as for me! Correct me if I'm wrong. I can't imagine what
your friends who met me must feel about you doing all this.
I'm sure some think your mad—but maybe not—I don't
really know them too well.*

*It's really weird but as painful as it is in jail you sort of
manage to make a little comfort zone for yourself. A few
good people, structure to your days and setting yourself little goals—like making it through the day with only 2 cups
of coffee when you really want six + seeing if you can get
through the week without chocolate, candy, or cookies!! It
all helps to make the hours, days + weeks come around just
that wee bit quicker. But when a day drags in jail it's like
torture. It pains me to see other people struggling, that sad,
empty look on their faces, don't do anything, get depressed, sleep all day, don't mix—it's hard in jail, away
from everything & everyone you love. I can't believe I've
been locked up for almost 7 months now—that's crazy—I
would never have thought I'd be able to deal with it—you
don't have a choice though except to make the most of it—
or give in to it!*

*But I'll say one thing—I've met a lot of assholes in jail,
but I've met some nice people + especially here in the program 'coz almost everyone is here by choice. And there's a
big dropout/kicked out rate so the people who make it
through the 1st month are almost all looking for change,
trying to better themselves. I don't know what the success
rate is but this program is no joke—it makes rehab in CA
look like a picnic party—really. I know I've been real down
about it a few times but that's sort of the way the program*

works—it certainly weeds out the people who are not pre-
pared to give in to the fact that they are powerless and can't
go on. I was getting deeper into a hole I may not have been
able to climb out of and in a way my arrest may have saved
my life! Who knows but here I am in York PA a much bet-
ter person—I feel—than I have been in many years + that's
a great feeling. This is like the best rehab I could ever have
gotten.

Anyway Susan it's sort of strange how this whole thing
has thrown us together again in this weird way—me in jail
you on the outside helping me. I've had many mixed emo-
tions because of it. I found myself feeling love for you (real
love—from the bottom of my heart) feeling pain for how I
fucked up what we had 'coz I know if I hadn't been using
things would have been different. I'm scared if/when I get
out what it'll be like to see you, look you in the eye, hug
you and hold you + thank you for helping save my life (to
some extent!) I thank you for giving me somewhere to stay
also. That must have been a hard decision + maybe a little
awkward. I know you like your own space + I feel a bit
weird about it but I'm sure you'll kick me out soon as I
start leaving things lying around and bringing in things on
trash night!

I've enclosed a list of bands, songs, singers for you to
make a CD to play when you come down for my hearing—
and if all goes well I can listen to it with you on the way
back to NYC.

Love
Graham X

That's the condensed version of his letter—it was about twice
as long, going off on tangents in Graham's rambling, stream-of-

consciousness way. I sometimes felt like we were having this bi-zarre, old-fashioned courtship by mail. Without any physical contact, it was a slow buildup, all of that pent-up emotion pouring out onto the page.

If I was still holding back, it wasn't for any of the reasons I was reluctant years earlier: I didn't care about his divorces, his check-ered past, or his rap sheet. And the more time he spent in the pro-gram, the less I worried about him staying clean. I even felt like I could trust him to be honest with me. After all that he'd exposed and confessed and revealed, I couldn't imagine him lying again.

In fact, the main reason I didn't want to get my heart set on a future with Graham had nothing to do with him or me. It was that no matter how much Armen told us Graham had a good chance of winning, the government could still decide to send him away.

AS THANKSGIVING ROLLED around, I was mostly grateful that my work on Graham's case was almost finished. I had gath-ered all the documents the firm needed, written my own letter to the judge, and made plans to pick up Graham's tax returns from the accountant. Armen was driving down to York for another cli-ent's hearing in early December, so he was going to meet with Graham and get him to sign them.

After putting my life on the back burner for three months, I finally felt like I could rejoin the free world. I spent Thanksgiving with a friend's family, made plans to go to Michigan for Christ-mas, and took my friend Alex out for a birthday dinner. She had been propping me up through all of my freak-outs and doubts, so we toasted the light peeking in at the end of the tunnel.

But just as I was feeling a sense of accomplishment about pull-ing everything together, Graham was slipping into a holiday funk. One night he called complaining about all the Christmas ads on TV making everyone miss their kids even more.

"It just takes one of your pals getting down," he said. "Then it spreads—like a cold."

I looked at the pine boughs and lights I'd strung across the mantel, the log burning in the fireplace, and the sugar cookies I'd just made, feeling a twinge of deck-the-halls guilt. But not enough to stop me from reminding Graham about a letter he'd sent me, describing how he'd spent last Thanksgiving and Christmas— lonely, depressed, dope sick, and broke.

"It's not just the holidays," he said, winding up to the real rea- son he was moping: "I got a letter from my sister that was pretty harsh."

"Uh oh . . . What did she say?"

"It was mostly about the past—how much I hurt my parents, and how painful it was for her and my brother, and why she finally had to cut me off."

I was a little surprised by that, since Graham's sister had sent me several nice emails and she'd written a letter to the judge sup- porting Graham's plea to stay.

"Well, I guess you've got to give everyone a chance to say their piece," I told him. "I've certainly done that, so I'm sure there were some things she needed to get off her chest. Isn't that what you've been talking about in the program—that it's better to address it, so you can move on?"

"I know. . . . It's just a lot of shit coming at me at once."

Later, Graham would show me his sister's letter and it *was* pretty tough—but it was also really encouraging and loving, talk- ing about what a great big brother Graham had been and how much she missed having him in her life. Reading it, I was actually a little jealous of the relationship she described—going to gigs and exhibitions, sharing flats in London, and the "loads of laughs" they had growing up.

But at the time, my message to Graham was basically: Buck up, there's no point wallowing in self-pity.

"See, it's already like a marriage," I wrote him. *"No sex, I'm doing your errands, and I'm bitching about your mood swings."*

I wasn't going to let Graham's gloom spoil my Christmas, but I did try to cheer him up by scouring the racks for holiday cards that weren't too inappropriate to send an inmate—like one showing a snowman finding two lumps of coal in his stocking, holding them up, and shouting, "I can see!"

In a way, that card pretty much summed up what Graham was getting for Christmas: enlightenment, courtesy of a rehab program in prison. What I got was a new appreciation for the freedom to drink champagne at parties where everyone complained about "just getting through" the holidays. For me, it was hard to take even little things for granted after seeing what it was like to have so much taken away.

AFTER ARMEN GOT back from Pennsylvania, I went by his office to pick up the tax returns Graham had signed—it was the first time we'd ever met. I had pictured sort of a smooth operator, but here was this guy-next-door in glasses who immediately showed me photos of his wife and kids.

"Do you think Graham would do a family portrait once he gets out?" he asked. "Of course I'd pay him, but maybe he'd give me a discount."

"I'm sure he would, but you know that's how I ended up getting involved with him—I asked him to take my picture, and look where that led."

Armen laughed, sizing me up from the other side of his desk. "You two make a good couple," he said.

"What do you mean?" I asked, expecting some observation about our shared sense of humor or opposites attracting.

"You both have the same intense look in your eyes."

By then I was used to Armen's matchmaking efforts, asking if I thought Graham and I would get married or referring to me as Graham's "fiancée." At first I assumed that was part of his legal strategy, but over time I realized he was sincere.

"Not to put too much pressure on you," I said. "But our future is really in your hands."

Armen told me he'd won nine out of eleven deportation cases he had argued in York; one of the losses happened the day he saw Graham. As he described how hard it was to be in the courtroom with this client and his devastated family, the head of the firm popped in—assuring me that the rehab program Graham was doing would really help his case.

"Is there any chance we could get an earlier court date?" I asked.

"I doubt it," Armen said. "The judges' dockets are really backed up—and Graham needs to finish the program before we'd even consider requesting an earlier hearing."

I thanked them and took Graham's tax returns to the IRS office across the street. I knew he was depressed about how much money he owed—to the government that was trying to deport him. It was tough even for me to write those checks, given how much it cost taxpayers to keep him locked up: about $150 a day. That would add up to more than $20,000 for Graham's whole time in detention—and for all the immigrants in ICE custody, about $2 billion a year.

A WEEK LATER, I flew to Michigan to see my family for Christmas. I always looked forward to spending the holidays at my parents' house, which was decorated as if Martha Stewart had just stopped by: three Christmas trees hung with ornaments collected over almost fifty years of marriage, electric candles in the windows, and white lights on the bushes outside.

My sister flew in from Los Angeles with her husband and one-year-old son, my brother and his wife drove over with their two kids, and I arrived from New York—once again, traveling alone. I was always self-conscious about not quite fitting into the family tableau, so it was even more alienating to be keeping a secret about my ex-boyfriend in prison. My parents knew about what I'd been doing for Graham, but my brother and sister didn't, so I took the phone into my bedroom and shut the door every time he called.

On Christmas Day, he phoned just as we were about to sit down for dinner.

"It's Graham—I have to take this," I whispered to my mom—who was tolerant about many things, but not having a holiday meal delayed. "He's alone, in prison, on Christmas. Can't you stall for five minutes?" Then I dashed upstairs, accepting the call as I passed all the nutcrackers lining the steps.

"Merry Christmas! We're just about to eat, so I can only talk for a few minutes."

"That's alright," Graham said. "If you have to go I can call you tomorrow."

"No, I can talk—just not for long. I know it's not much of a holiday for you, but do they do anything special, like hang decorations or cook a turkey for dinner?"

"Are you joking? It's just like any other day, except some people from the Salvation Army came and sang a song and gave us all a gift—a pair of socks, a little calendar, and a pencil."

"That sounds like something out of a nineteenth-century novel, where all the poor kids get an orange for Christmas."

"Trust me, I would've rather had an orange—a calendar is sort of the last thing you want when you're locked up. And I find it really bizarre that you can have a pencil in here, sharpened to an extremely fine point, but they won't give you a fork. It's really boring to eat your dinner with a plastic spoon every night."

I pictured the table downstairs, set with silver flatware (two forks), linen napkins, and the good china. I couldn't think of anything to say that would make being in prison on Christmas less miserable, so I rattled on about what we'd been doing, trying to avoid any more holiday references.

"Well, we're having a pretty low-key day here. I took my niece and nephew sledding yesterday. He's eleven now, so he's started rolling his eyes at me, but I think I've got another year left of him thinking I'm cool. His sister is already on to me—she's only six but she's going through a phase where everything is either fashionable or unfashionable. All my bulky winter sweaters are definitely unfashionable."

"She's probably right about that. . . . How's your sister?"

"Pretty good. Her son finally slept through the night last night—he's had a hard time adjusting to the time change, so they moved the Pack 'n Play into the closet."

Graham said he was glad he never had to fly across time zones when Liam was a baby—he was almost two when they moved to New York—and was telling me about the time the government accused him of harboring an "illegal alien," because of a problem with Liam's visa, when I heard my dad shouting my name.

"Sorry," I interrupted him. "My dad is calling me—dinner is ready."

"You should go eat. . . . I'm not gonna ask what you're having."

"Roast beef," I lied. "You wouldn't like it."

I hung up and went downstairs, feeling the dissonance between my furtive relationship with Graham and the picture-perfect holiday table. Then again, even Martha Stewart spent one Christmas in the clink.

My mom didn't look up from the platter of turkey she was serving, but before we ate she said a prayer, mentioning "everyone who couldn't be with us." I thought of Graham in his prison bunk, marking off December 25 on his calendar, no doubt glad that tomorrow was just a regular day.

ON DECEMBER 29, the day before I flew back to New York, I got an email from Armen: *"The judge wants to do this case on Jan. 5th. This caught us off guard but my boss thinks we should go full steam ahead. CALL ME when you get this message."*

"What does this mean?" I asked as soon as Armen picked up.

"I think it's a good sign. The judge probably had an opening on his calendar and this looks like an easy, grantable case so he moved it forward."

"But we haven't submitted everything yet."

"He said to send whatever we have, so Maria is going to FedEx a package overnight."

"But Graham hasn't finished the rehab program—you said that was important."

"Look, I have a good feeling about this. I want to get it over and done with. All the factors are in place."

What I really wanted to say was "But I'm not ready!" I thought I had two more months before Graham showed up at my door—not seven days.

Of course I couldn't call Graham to tell him the news, which I did share with my mom, who I'm sure didn't know what to think. Ever since their visit to New York, my parents had asked about Graham's case, but we hadn't really talked about where this was all going. I thought I had more time for that, too.

After a sleepless night, and a long trip back to New York, Graham finally called late the next day.

"You're not going to believe this," I said. "I've got another New Year's Eve surprise for you—well, a few hours early this time: Your hearing got moved up to next Wednesday!"

"What do you mean, 'it got moved up'?" Graham asked.

"The judge scheduled it for January fifth. You might be free in six days."

———

IT TOOK A few days for me to wrap my head around what that meant for me.

"*Maybe it's better to have less time to think about it and get nervous about what might happen,*" I wrote in my notebook. "*But now it's hitting me—what if the judge doesn't grant the waiver, or for some reason Graham doesn't get released on Wednesday? And then there's the big question—what's going to happen if he does walk out a free man? What's that going to be like, to suddenly be living together after not seeing him for a year and a half?*"

Fortunately, I didn't have much time to worry. I channeled most of my anxiety into making plans to drive down for Graham's hearing. I booked a hotel in York and a rental car to get there; I printed maps, directions, and confirmation receipts. Every few hours, I checked the weather forecast obsessively, tracking all the storms heading our way. New York was still digging out from an infamous Christmas Day blizzard, so I hoped another one wouldn't close the roads again.

The day before I left, Maria gave me a rundown about visiting the prison—and advice about what not to wear. "No revealing clothes," she said. "These guys won't have seen a girl in a while."

"It's a bit too cold for a miniskirt and a tank top," I joked, although I *was* trying to come up with an outfit that wasn't too dowdy, my niece's sweater judgments still on my mind.

Armen explained that I wouldn't be allowed into the courtroom during Graham's testimony, but I'd get called in afterward as a witness. Then he prepped me about what the ICE lawyers might ask.

"They won't be aggressive," he promised. "It'll just be easy questions like: How do you feel about Mr. MacIndoe? . . . What are your plans for the future? . . . What makes you think he's going to be reformed?"

"Those are easy questions?"

"Of course they are—you love him, you hope to spend the rest of your life together, and you're confident he's going to come out of this experience a changed man."

"Well, at least two of those answers are true. I'd like to see how it goes before making a lifelong commitment."

He seemed much less concerned about how Graham would handle the lawyers' scrutiny.

"He's going to be contrite and eloquent," Armen assured me. "He'll be fine."

Thankfully, the drive down to York was uneventful: clear roads, no traffic, and sunny skies most of the way. I hadn't had time to make a CD of the songs Graham sent me, so I listened to an acoustic mix he made for me in 2006. As each song came on— "You'll Think of Me," by Keith Urban; "You," by Evanescence; "Always on My Mind" by Johnny Cash—I felt the swelling emotions music always sparks on a road trip, thinking about how much had happened since then.

At that moment, I wasn't too worried about what was going to happen next.

Sure, it crossed my mind that Graham might lose his case—and even if he won, ICE could decide to appeal. If that happened, there was a good chance Graham might give up and agree to leave. And even if he did get released, we still faced plenty of hurdles. Graham might have a difficult reentry, we might not adjust well to living together, or we might decide we couldn't be a couple again.

But I didn't want to dwell on any of those worst-case scenarios— I'd spent too much time not taking chances because things might not work out. As I'd written to Graham at one point:

Somewhere along the way I realized that I'd be a much happier person if I could embrace all the uncertainty in my life. I had to embrace it, or else set up my life so it's more predictable. But I guess deep down I must not want that. I like thinking that anything could happen next week or next month or next year.

Then I quoted a few lines from *Letters to a Young Poet,* by Rainer Maria Rilke, about having patience with "everything unresolved in your heart."

"*Don't search for answers,*" Rilke wrote, "*which could not be given you now, because you would not be able to live them. And the point is to live everything. Live the questions now. Perhaps then, someday far in the future, you will gradually, without ever realizing it, live your way into the answer.*"

Graham and I were about to get an answer to the main question we'd been living with: *Was he going to be allowed to stay here?* The answers to all of our other questions hinged on whatever the judge decided.

THE HAMPTON INN I had booked was only a mile from the prison, so it was strange to pull off the highway and see where Graham had been living—knowing he'd never seen much of it himself. It was like any American suburb, a grid of roads lined with shopping centers and chain stores. After I checked in, I got back in my rental car and drove around the corner to the York Galleria mall.

After months of writing Graham's "alien number" on the letters I sent him, now I felt like a visitor from another planet, blinking at all the brightly lit stores blaring holiday songs. I took an escalator up to the food court, ate a Sbarro pizza while watching teenagers flirt, then wandered into the Gap and bought Graham a couple of T-shirts and some boxers. When I'd gone through his clothes, I realized I hadn't rescued any decent underwear from

Joe's place, so I wanted him to have something new to wear home. Yes, *home*. Buying Graham underwear felt oddly domestic—in a good way.

I was back in my hotel room flipping through TV channels when he called.

"It's so weird being here," I told him. "It's all really suburban—you'd never know there was a prison just down the road."

"Yeah, it's sort of bizarre to think that you're so close by after all this time. I can't believe we'll see each other tomorrow."

We both let that sink in for a second. I wondered how Graham would look—and what he'd think of me. In some of his letters, he'd joked about putting on weight and his hairline receding, even drawing a caricature of himself "fat and bald."

"How are you feeling about the hearing?" I asked, pushing that image aside.

"Pretty fucking nervous. I haven't been able to sleep the last couple of nights."

"Armen is really confident you're going to win. He told me to remind you to be totally honest with the judge and the ICE lawyers. The most important thing is convincing them you've changed."

"I have changed. I don't know if I'm a *different* person, but I think I'm a better person than I was when I got here."

Graham thanked me again for everything I'd done for him, and I told him how much I admired him for sticking it out.

"There aren't many people who could've gone through what you did in the last year and actually come out of it in a better place," I said, pausing slightly before blurting out, "I love you."

It was the first time I'd said it since we reconnected in September, but I wasn't sure if Graham heard me—we got disconnected as soon as the words were out of my mouth.

I sat there holding my phone for a minute, wanting to laugh at this final absurdity: The most important thing I'd said to him might've gotten lost in the ether—unless it got recorded as part of our last prison call.

THE NEXT MORNING, I ran into Armen in the hallway at the hotel.

"I'm ready," he assured me.

"Really? Because it looks like you're still in your pajamas." He was wearing a T-shirt, sweatpants, and slippers—and looked like he'd just woken up.

"Relax. I'm going to get some breakfast, then I'll change into my suit and meet you in the prison parking lot at eight fifteen. You know how to get there?"

"I have directions I printed out, a Garmin, a local map, and my cellphone—I'm pretty sure I'll be fine."

An hour later, we walked into the visitors' waiting area at the back of the prison, which looked like a cross between a garage and a middle school gym. It had a concrete floor, cinder-block walls, and a few rows of plastic chairs facing the guard's desk. About ten other people were already waiting—to visit inmates, I guessed. At 8:35, Armen got buzzed into the prison, so I put my purse in a locker and sat down to wait for my turn. It was unnerving that the courtroom was located behind bars.

Just before nine, everyone else stood up and got in line on the right side of the room. One by one, they dropped their keys on the guard's desk, walked through a metal detector, picked up a spray bottle, and squirted it at a paper towel. I saw the first woman wipe the phone in the booth where she sat down on a stool.

From where I was sitting, I could see a couple of inmates on the other side of the glass, but I couldn't hear what anyone was saying. Mostly I just watched the clock on the wall. A stream of visitors came and went, many of them crying as they hurried toward the doors behind me. A cold wind blew in whenever anyone arrived or left.

After an hour, I went to my locker and got my notebook and a magazine out of my purse—I needed to do something to try to distract myself. *"9:35,"* I wrote. *"Trying to read a magazine. Can't concentrate on the words. 10:06 This is taking longer than I expected. 10:15 Still no sign of Armen. Just thought of that poem I wrote when I was little, 'I hate waiting . . . ' Wonder if I still have that somewhere."*

By ten thirty I felt like I was going to throw up. My mouth was dry, my head was spinning, my hands were shaking—I couldn't figure out why I hadn't been called into the courtroom yet. Every time the door to the prison buzzed, my head snapped in that direction, but it was always someone in a uniform coming or going.

When Armen finally appeared, a few minutes later, he wasn't smiling and he didn't give me the thumbs-up sign. He just held up his hand with his palm stretched out toward me—as if to say, "Hold on."

CHAPTER TWENTY

January 2011
York County Prison, Pennsylvania

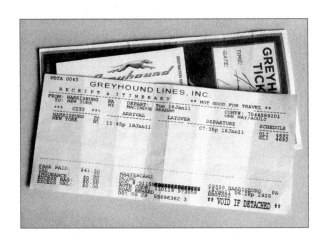

The morning of my hearing I get called down to court hours early—as usual—but this time I almost don't mind the wait because they bring us Rice Krispies and real milk for breakfast. I've been eating corn flakes and rice milk every single day for four months so I'm savoring each spoonful, hoping it helps settle my stomach.

I'm a nervous wreck. I've hardly slept since Susan called to tell me my hearing got moved up. All I've been able to think about is getting out of here—wearing my own clothes, breathing fresh air, and eating whatever I want. But bringing the case forward meant rushing to get everything ready at the last minute, which means Liam won't be here. Armen finally got through to him, but he's away with his girlfriend for the holidays and couldn't get to York in time. Maybe it's better that he isn't going to see me in prison. I'm not sure that would've been good for either of us, especially if I don't win.

When I spoke to Armen the other day, he was confident that the judge was going to grant me relief. Susan said the same thing, but she sounded a bit more cautious—maybe because she's got more at stake. If I don't win, I know it's going to be devastating for her, but right now I'm trying to keep my mind focused on the best-case scenario: *I'm walking out of here today.*

By the time I finally get escorted into court, my palms are sweaty and my heart is pounding. I look around for Susan, but it's just Armen, the judge, and the two guys from ICE. The courtroom is small and dark—with the seal of the Department of Homeland

Security above the judge's bench, next to the American flag. There's no public gallery, so it's deadly quiet. That just adds to the feeling that this is all happening in secret, inside a prison, totally out of sight. I sit down at a table next to Armen, who leans over and tells me to relax. Before I get a chance to ask him where Susan is, the judge jumps right in and starts reading my file.

He rattles off everything I've ever been arrested for—minor drug possession charges, but they still sound pretty bad when you hear them out loud. *They know all this already,* I tell myself. *The only thing that matters is what I was convicted for—and they were just misdemeanors.* It's a relief when Armen finally gets a chance to talk. He does a great job of describing my relationship with Liam, my career as a photographer, and everything I've been doing to turn my life around.

"Your Honor, Mr. MacIndoe has been in a very strict rehabilitation program here at York County for the past three months. He has really demonstrated his commitment to his recovery and becoming a productive member of society again."

He mentions all the letters of support I got from friends, family, and clients and tells the judge I'm in a stable relationship and will be living with my girlfriend once I'm released. I wonder what Susan would think if she heard that—I still can't figure out why she's not here. One of the guys in the holding pen said his whole family came for his hearing, so I wish I had at least one person to show I've got some support.

At one point the judge starts talking about my website and asks the ICE lawyers if they've seen it. He tells them there's a great picture of Peyton Manning—I took it for an ESPN ad—and says they should check it out. For a second he sounds more like an agent trying to talk a client into hiring me, not a judge deciding my fate.

Just when I think I might not get a chance to say much, the ICE guys start hitting me with questions: Why did I use heroin? . . . Where did I get it? . . . How often did I buy it? . . . How much did

I spend? Armen told me to be totally honest, and that's been drilled into us in the program—*don't justify or make excuses, take responsibility for what you've done*—so I answer everything they ask, straight up.

I wish they'd call Susan in as a witness—she'll tell them how much I've changed and how hard I've been working. But the ICE lawyers and the judge just keep grilling me, asking how I became an addict, if I ever hung out with drug dealers, and how I planned to stay away from them if I go back to Brooklyn. I have no idea how much time passes—it feels like I've been answering questions for hours.

I glance at Armen, but he warned me that once he'd had his turn he wasn't allowed to speak, so he just nods as if to say, "Carry on." Finally, when I think there can't possibly be anything left they haven't asked about, the judge flicks through papers like he's ready to wrap this up. I'm sitting there totally exhausted as the judge types at his computer and occasionally looks up at me. The ICE guys are doing the same.

After what seems like the longest few minutes of my whole time in prison, the judge says my name and case number along with some legal jargon. I'm practically shaking—Armen puts his hand on my shoulder and gives me a little smile. Then the judge announces he's recommending cancellation of removal and asks if the ICE lawyers have any objections.

My mind is racing—*Don't object, just let me go*—but one of the ICE guys says he's got some reservations. I obviously had a bad drug problem, he's saying, and even though he's impressed by my rehabilitation and he's willing to accept the judge's recommendation, he wants to make sure I have no open cases or warrants before signing off on my release.

I look at Armen in a panic, not sure what that means. "Am I getting released?"

"These guys are being tough," he says quietly. "I have to get another document from the court in Brooklyn showing you don't have any open cases. I'll try to get it faxed over this afternoon, so you might still get out today."

"What happens if there's an open case? Is this going to be like that additional gun charge they threw at me?"

"There isn't an open case—we already submitted several dispositions to the judge. They're just making us jump through hoops before they let you go."

Before I get a chance to ask anything else, a guard leads me back to the holding pen. I don't know whether to be happy or pissed off. The fact that the judge went in my favor is brilliant, but I've heard so many stories of people getting hit with additional charges I'm worried that these ICE guys are just buying time to dig up something else. And what the fuck happened with Susan? I still have no idea why she wasn't in court.

I'm desperate to get back to the dorm and call her when one of the court officers opens the door and shouts, "MacIndoe—you've got a visit!" At first I'm thinking it must be Armen, but the CO leads me past the lawyers' rooms toward another part of the prison. I've never had a visitor here, so I'm a bit thrown.

It looks like a scene out of a movie, with a row of men in orange uniforms sitting at booths talking into phones. When I get to the numbered booth I've been told to go to, Susan's already there. She smiles as she sees me and picks up the phone.

I'm not sure what I look like after being locked up for eight months—probably a bit puffy and pale, with less hair—but Susan looks way cuter than I remembered. She's wearing a dark gray sweater, belted at the waist with a lacy top underneath, and her curly hair is pulled up off her face. The attraction I felt the first time I took her picture comes back in an instant, hitting me a lot harder than I thought it would.

I know I signed my letters with love and I told her I loved her— and I meant it. I loved her for everything she'd done for me. But until I saw her, I didn't know how I'd physically feel. It's like a part of me that had been shut down for so long has suddenly come back to life. I just want to be able to touch her, hug her, smell her, and feel that closeness—which makes it even more painful to be separated by a thick Plexiglas window.

These "no contact" visits are so fucking cruel. At least at Rikers you could sit at a table with the person and feel like a human being for an hour. Here all I can do is put my hand up to the window. Susan puts hers up opposite mine. We joke and flirt and I keep thinking, *Shit—now I'm really in love with this girl.*

She tells me it doesn't look like Armen can get the paperwork faxed over today, so it might take a few more days to get things sorted out. I can tell she's disappointed, but in that positive way she's been this whole time she smiles and says, "Listen, we won. That's the important thing. A week ago you thought you'd be stuck here until the end of February, but pretty soon you're going to be free."

WHEN I GET back to the dorm, everyone is in group so I sit down in my usual spot. Walker is mouthing to me, "What happened?" but I just shake my head and he looks confused. While they're all talking about rational thinking, I sit quietly, not really listening to any of the shares. There's so much bouncing around in my head—the hearing, seeing Susan, what's going to happen next—I can't focus on anything else.

The minute group breaks Walker rushes over and asks, "So what did the judge say—are you going home?"

I tell him that the judge wanted to let me go, but one of the ICE lawyers asked to see some more paperwork first, so I don't know how long that'll take. "But at least I got to see Susan—we had a visit afterwards. She looked fucking brilliant. I didn't think I'd be so blown away seeing her."

"Listen, they all look good when you're on this side of the glass," Walker says.

"Oh really? I guess that's why every time your girlfriend visits you come back acting like you've just had a date with Pamela Anderson."

"Well, you should both be staying away from any pussy," another guy chimes in. "You know how that shit works—too much sex makes you lose sight of the bigger picture."

We've all had it drummed into us: Don't fall in love, don't get involved with another addict, don't go running back to your ex. If you're leaning on someone to get you through your recovery and it doesn't work out, then you're a lot more likely to relapse.

One time early on in the program, when we were talking about relationships and I'd mentioned Tracy and Susan being back in my life, the first thing out of the group leader's mouth was "Ditch the both of them." Everyone else seemed to agree.

But that was a while ago, and a lot has changed since then. I've tried to be more up front with Tracy about why I can't be with her, but I haven't really told her what's going on with Susan. Maybe I'm being a coward, but there's been so much thrown at me, I just couldn't deal with it all at once. And honestly, it wasn't until I saw Susan today that I realized how I really felt about her—and it's not love I need reciprocated to make me feel good, or something I'm clinging to 'cause I think it'll keep me off drugs. It's a way deeper understanding of what love really means, and it's pretty clear Susan feels the same way about me.

The night before my hearing, when we were talking on the phone, I could tell something was different. There was this feeling of anticipation—like everything was about to change—then she said, "I love you," just as I was about to hang up. That was the first time she'd said it since all this started, and hearing it gave me a huge lift. It wasn't a surprise that she felt it, but I couldn't believe she said it. Then when we saw each other today, I just knew. The way she looked at me, this was for real.

THE NEXT FEW days it's impossible to concentrate on the program. Between phone calls with Susan and Armen and talking to my family, all I can think about is the fact that I should be out of here by now. Except in this fucked-up system, everything moves in slow motion—no matter how urgent it is to the person locked up.

It turns out there was an open case, an arrest that got merged with my conviction last year, so Armen has to fax paperwork to the judge showing that was part of the time I already served. Then I'll either have another hearing or the judge will just issue a written decision—hopefully next week. But of course I keep worrying ICE is gonna throw another spanner in the works. Susan is trying to be positive, but I think she's just as fed up as me.

She's sick, I'm sick, everyone in here has got a cold or the flu. It must be obvious how anxious I am because one of the counselors pulls me into his office before he leaves on Friday and suggests I use this time productively—asking if I've got a "sobriety plan."

"Well, to be honest, I thought I had seven more weeks to figure that out. I'm sure I'll go to some meetings and I'm gonna reach out to a friend who's been clean for a while."

"Do you have a place to stay?"

"With my girlfriend." For the past few months I've been calling Susan my ex, but now that doesn't seem right.

"Does she live in Brooklyn?"

"Yeah, but in a different neighborhood from my old house—further away from the projects. I know what you're gonna say. . . . I should be avoiding people, places, and things that are triggers."

"It's a cliché but it's true: The minute you're around those people, in those places, and you see those things, you're gonna be tempted to use."

"I'm not going to be around people I did drugs with. First of all, Susan would never put up with that, and I've worked way too hard to get to this point to risk throwing it all away. Besides, if I get arrested again, it's all over for me."

We talk a little more about the warning signs of relapse before he heads home, giving me a last bit of advice: "Use the Red Book whenever you feel vulnerable. Just pick it up and read a few sections. Everything you need is in there."

The rest of the weekend I try to keep what he said in mind, participating in the program as much as I can. When we do our weekly feelings check on Sunday, I'm thinking it might be my last one, so I raise my hand to share. Walking to the front of the room, I'm not sure what I'll say.

"It feels weird to still be here knowing I'm probably going home soon," I start off, looking around at all the guys I've gotten to know. "I was pretty bummed when I found out I wasn't getting released right away, but the last few days have given me time to think about what I've gotten out of the program. There were definitely a few times I felt like packing it in—I'm sure you can all relate to that." A few people smile and nod. "But I'm really glad I stuck it out. I'd been resistant to this sort of thing for so long, and now I realize it's exactly what I needed. I'm actually a bit disappointed I'm not going to finish the whole sixteen weeks, just to have that sense of accomplishment."

I catch Walker rolling his eyes—*I should pull him up for disrespect!*

"Anyway, I will say I'm glad my time in prison is almost over. I never thought I'd be able to deal with being locked up for so long. Even though I'm nervous about going back out to the real world, I'm determined not to screw up again. So for all you guys who are early in the program, you might be overwhelmed now, but trust me, you'll be feeling really great when you get to this point. Stick with it—it's worth it."

Some of the guys tap on their tables as I walk back to my seat, which is how people show respect for your share. I wonder if I sound like one of the old-timers I used to look up to when I first got here. I know a lot of it is typical recovery talk—the old me would've shrugged off this sort of advice—but I meant what I said. I do believe people can change.

January 10th, 2011

Susan,

Well here I am almost a week after court still stuck at York County Prison—and I'm now starting to get pissed off—I just want to be out of here. I was okay at first but now it's that not knowing how long it's going to be. A few days, weeks—more than a month—I don't know and it's starting to wear on me. Also, coz I didn't sign out on the phone sheet—again—I've got a 48 hour speaking ban coming up. So I'm hoping I can get this resolved 'coz I'm getting sort of fed up + my mind keeps thinking of being outside + not in jail or on the program.

I've been told that when you get out you get a check & not cash so I won't have money to stay anywhere or get a bus home—I'm sort of in a dilemma about what I'll do. I can't get a wire transfer 'coz I have no I.D. I don't have a jacket and it's 19 degrees F outside. All this is sort of getting me down right now. It's really fucked up that they bring you down here from NYC & then just release you to the streets 250 miles away with no money or transportation.

Anyway by the time you get this I'll have spoken to you and maybe we'll have a better idea about how I can deal with this situation. It must be weighing heavy on your mind too. And on that note I have to say to you—again—thank you. I never thought the day would come (even though I'm not out yet) where I'd beat this immigration case and I know that without your help I would probably have little or no chance to have done so. I realize how lucky I am & how much you did for me—giving me the strength to sit tight & fight this case—despite all the obstacles. So, Susan, I want to say to you from the bottom of my heart THANK YOU.

Love Graham. X

ON TUESDAY NIGHT, I call Susan after dinner, hoping she's got good news for me.

"I just got off the phone with Armen," she says. "The judge scheduled your hearing—it'll be Friday at eleven A.M. He said it should be quick, but it takes a few hours to do the paperwork, so you'll be released by six."

"Are you sure about that?"

"I wrote it down. Armen's exact words were *He's going to be granted relief.*"

I don't say anything at first, not sure how to respond.

"C'mon—Graham MacIndoe is never speechless. You won your case! How do you feel?"

"Relieved, I guess, but I'm not gonna be totally convinced until I actually walk out of here. This last week has been really brutal."

"I know, but it's just three more days. Armen said he'd let Liam know."

"I spoke with Liam earlier—I told him I should be getting out soon."

"What did he say?"

"He sounded excited to see me—happy I'm not getting deported."

"Me, too," Susan says. "I had my doubts a few times, but I wouldn't have pushed you to stick it out if I didn't think you could win."

"I'm going to be sort of indebted to you the rest of my life, aren't I?"

"Maybe not that long. . . . But my birthday is coming up soon, so you'd better do better than a lingerie catalog this year."

FRIDAY MORNING, I'M back in the holding pen. Susan told me not to worry—it's just a formality and should be over in minutes—but it's hard not to be nervous. When I get brought into the courtroom, everyone is in their same places, except Armen is on speakerphone this time.

The judge starts by saying how impressed he is by my determination to turn things around and how he hopes my photography career will pick up where it left off. I'm used to judges coming down hard on me, so I'm not quite sure how to react. He looks through the new paperwork, asks the ICE guys if they're satisfied, they say yes, and he gives his final ruling: I'm being released.

That's it. The stress of the last ten days—or really, five months—disappears in an instant. *This is for real. I'm going home.*

"Thank you," I say to the judge.

"I hope I don't see you in front of me again," he says, then I'm escorted out of court—for the last time.

I feel like running back to the dorm, but that would get me a violation, so I walk as fast as I can, passing guards and inmates who must be wondering why I'm grinning.

When I get buzzed through the door, a meeting has just finished so I tell everyone it's official: I'll be out of there by dinner. Walker gives me a high-five, then a bunch of other guys shake my hand. I go through my locker and start packing up what I'm taking with me—a few books, all my letters, the Red Book, and my program notes. Everything else I give away.

I'm already imagining the drive back to New York with Susan— I hope she brings some music or made a CD with the suggestions I sent her. I'm picturing roadside stops for food I haven't tasted in ages and just looking out the window, sipping a good cup of coffee. Friday seems like a good day to be going home. It'll be the weekend tomorrow so maybe I can see Liam, or hang out with him and Susan. My mind races, just thinking about all the things I can do.

The afternoon drags as I wait for the call—it's always around four o'clock, but I try not to worry when it doesn't come. *I saw the judge sign the papers. He handed them to the court officer. Armen heard everything on the phone.*

By five I'm in a total panic. *Something's wrong.*

I pace back and forth, then ask the CO if he can find out what's up. He just gives me some bullshit about maybe they're running late. There's nothing reassuring about this statement, so I pick up the phone to call Susan—not even bothering to sign in first. "They haven't called my name yet!" I practically shout.

She tells me the van hasn't dropped off anyone at the parking lot yet and suggests I talk to my counselor—not that he'll have a fucking clue. After dinner, which I can't eat, I phone Susan again. I don't care that I've already used up my one call for the night.

"I'm sorry," she says. "I don't know what happened, but the van came and the driver told me you weren't on the list for release today. I've been buzzing intercoms and trying to talk to someone for the past hour, but no one knows anything."

"What do you mean I wasn't on the list?" *This can't be happening.* It's like some sick joke someone's playing just to fuck with me.

"That's what I'm trying to find out," she says. "Armen said he's never heard of anything like this—once the judge signs the order, you're supposed to get released. But everyone's already left for the weekend, and just to be totally honest with you, it's possible no one from ICE will be in until Tuesday."

"Tuesday?"

"Monday is a holiday—Martin Luther King Day."

"Are you telling me I might have to spend another four days in here?!" People are looking at me like I'm crazy—I'm talking loud enough to get a double speaking ban.

"It's possible. I'm going to stay in York tonight, so maybe I'll have better news in the morning, but it doesn't sound like ICE releases anyone on the weekend. I'm really sorry. Believe me, I'm just as frustrated and pissed off as you."

Except you're not in prison, I want to say. Susan sounds exhausted, so I tell her how bad I feel that she came all this way for nothing. She says to call her in the morning—maybe Armen will have heard something by then.

I save my ranting until after we hang up, then pace around the dorm complaining to anyone who'll listen about how unfair this is. Walker takes me aside and tries to calm me down.

"I know it's bullshit," he says. "But it's got to be some bureaucratic fuckup. You saw the judge sign off on your release—you know you're going home."

"Yeah but I want to be out of here NOW," I say, almost bursting into tears. "I've already been waiting nine extra days. What the fuck can be the problem this time?"

"You know how it is—no one gives a shit about any of us in here."

When I call Susan the next morning, she tells me it doesn't look like anything is going to happen until Tuesday, but says she'll come by for a visit before driving back to New York. I feel bad that this is the second time she's come down to get me—and gone home alone.

An hour later, I sit down in the booth opposite her and pick up the phone. "I hope you've got a joke for me," I tell her, forcing a smile.

"I never remember jokes," she says, leaning her head on her hand. She looks like she hardly slept at all.

"Well, here's one for you then: What's the difference between a Scotsman and a Rolling Stone?"

"I don't know. "

"A Rolling Stone says, 'Hey, you, get off of my cloud!' A Scotsman says, 'Hey McLeod, get off of my ewe!' "

Susan laughs. "I was expecting something dirty or tasteless— did you hear that one from your dad?"

"Yeah, but a long time ago. It's sort of a classic."

"By the way, the guard on duty is the one who took you to the dentist. When I told him who I was here to visit, he snapped his fingers and said, 'The Scottish guy? I really like him!' He seems nice—I think he felt bad that you didn't get released."

"Really? Tell him I said hi."

We chat for a bit longer—I think the guard gave us extra time. He nods at me when he walks over to Susan's side of the window and says something I can't hear.

"I have to go," she says. "It's almost lunch, so the visiting area is closing."

"I love you," I tell her, standing up while I'm still holding the phone.

"I love you, too—but you're a fucking pain in the ass, Graham MacIndoe."

"Yeah, but I'm worth it. You'll see."

THE HOLIDAY WEEKEND is the longest three days and four nights of my life. We have a light schedule—watching videos and going to a few meetings—but that's almost worse than being busy. I've got too much time to worry that ICE filed some last-minute appeal. Being in this limbo totally sets me back—I can't concentrate on the program, so I keep getting addressed for stupid shit. By Monday night, I've racked up a seventy-two-hour speaking ban.

Luckily, it doesn't kick in until later in the week, so I can still call Susan after dinner. All she's managed to find out is the name of the ICE officer she's supposed to call first thing Tuesday, so she tells me to try her again after 10:00 A.M. The next morning, I'm already dialing at 9:59. She says the ICE guy told her they were still deciding on Friday if they were going to appeal my case, but Armen told her that was bullshit—someone left early and didn't bother to deal with my file.

I'm still fuming when I get called down to process my release papers. The guy doesn't apologize or explain what happened, barely looking at me. I'm tempted to tell him how fucked up it is that I got stuck here an extra four days, but I don't want to rock the boat, so I just sign whatever he pushes in front of me.

When I get back to the dorm, I say my goodbyes—again—and sit on the edge of my bunk, waiting. I'm half-expecting ICE will find some reason to hold me longer, but Walker tells me to relax, it'll all be fine—then tries to wind me up by saying he'll see me at dinner.

"If I come back up here," I tell him, "you'd better stay out of my way 'cause I'm not gonna be happy."

Once the call finally comes, I thank him for helping me get through the program and give him a slip of paper with Susan's number. "I'll let you know once I get a new cellphone," I tell him. "But if you need to talk, you can call me here anytime."

"Take care, buddy," he says. "You'd better stay out of trouble— you're getting too old for this shit."

Before long I'm in a cell with a handful of other guys getting released. It feels weird to take off my prison uniform and put on the clothes I was arrested in—a grimy pair of jeans, a faded black T-shirt, and a baggy gray sweater someone at Rikers gave me. They smell like crack and the projects, mixed with the mustiness of dirty laundry that's been sitting around for months. I wish I had something else to wear—it's not a great look to impress Susan.

When the ICE guys show up and load us into a van, I think there's been a mistake—it's the first time I've been transferred without handcuffs and chains. But then I realize I'm not a prisoner anymore, I'm actually free.

Two guys hop out at the back of the prison and the rest of us get driven to the bus station in Harrisburg, sitting quietly with our stuff on our laps. Susan said the ICE officer she talked to promised they'd buy me a ticket back to New York, but when we get to the station the driver acts like that's news to him.

"You don't have someone picking you up?" he asks.

"No. I was meant to be released on Friday when my girlfriend came to get me, but she wasn't allowed to leave me any money so whoever she talked to said you'd buy my ticket."

"Hold on," he says. "What's your name?" Then he checks something in the van, walks me over to the Greyhound window, pays for the ticket, and hands it to me—without saying another word.

The bus station is one of those big old buildings with high ceilings and a waiting area with wooden benches. A homeless guy shuffles up to me and asks if I have a dollar to spare—I don't. All

I've got is some change in my pocket that somehow made it through the system, but I need it to call Susan. After I find a pay phone, I push some coins through the slot and dial her number.

"There was no recording saying this is a call from prison!" she shouts.

"Nope. I'm at the bus station."

"Did they buy you a ticket?"

"The driver didn't seem to want to, but eventually he did. The next bus to New York isn't until seven thirty so I should get to Port Authority by eleven forty-five. Sorry it's so late."

"That's okay, I'll meet you at whatever gate you pull into. So how does it feel, finally breathing fresh air?"

"Pretty fucking cold—and I'm starving. I think I've got enough change left for a cup of coffee, but that's it. It's crazy that ICE just dumps us out on the street."

"Well, I'll bring you a coat and you'll be able to eat whatever you want in a few hours. I can't believe I'm actually saying this—I'll see you soon! Just don't get arrested before you get here, okay?"

"Why would I get arrested?"

"Listen, I've just spent the past twenty-four hours trying to figure out how to get you back here without any money or ID, so I'm not being paranoid. Maria was the one who said it wasn't safe for you to take the train."

I promise her I won't do anything suspicious and assure her I'll be on the bus when it arrives.

I've got an hour to kill, so I wander over to a kiosk and buy a cup of coffee—which isn't great, but it's still better than the crap I've been drinking. Then I sit down on a bench and open one of the brown paper bags my stuff is in, pulling out a few letters to read. Thinking about what I've been through makes me feel like I've come out of some kind of time warp, still reeling from everything that's happened to me. After a while, I put the letters away and just watch all the people passing by—checking out everyone's clothes and wondering what music a guy with headphones is listening to, wishing I hadn't given my radio away.

When I hear the announcement for the New York bus, I jump up and get in line. I pause for a second after the driver checks my ticket, then move toward the back and choose a seat by a window. After sitting on hard metal stools and benches for months, even a Greyhound bus feels luxurious—a cushioned seat, a bathroom with a door that closes, and an overhead light I can turn on and off whenever I want.

Once the bus pulls away from the station, the engine rumbling, I look around at people's faces lit by the glow from their phones. It's too dark to see much out the window, except for headlights coming at us, neon signs in the distance, and piles of snow along the road. After we turn onto the highway and the bus picks up speed, I sink into my seat. It finally feels like this whole fucking nightmare is over.

DRIVING THROUGH NEW Jersey as we approach Manhattan, I see the skyline lit up in the distance—the Empire State Building, the Chrysler Building, all the lights of Midtown bouncing across the river. I wasn't sure I'd ever see this view again. I wish I had a camera, but I just watch all the buildings get bigger until the bus dips down into the Lincoln Tunnel.

When we pull into the Port Authority Bus Terminal, people jump up, grab their bags, and crowd into the aisle. I just sit there waiting for the bus to empty, wanting to relish the moment before I get off. The smell of exhaust fumes hits me as I walk from the garage into the building, holding a paper bag under each arm. This isn't quite how I pictured my homecoming, but at least I'm back in New York City. I look around for Susan—she's not here.

I'm standing in the dingy waiting area trying to get my bearings, sure this is where she said she'd meet me, then I see an escalator and wonder if she told me to go upstairs. When I get to the top, she's about twenty feet in front of me, talking on the phone.

I walk toward her thinking I'll surprise her, but just then she hangs up and turns around. I drop my bags and wrap my arms around her, whispering "thank you" in her ear. It's been so long since I've held anyone like this I just cling to her. Her puffy down coat is the softest thing I've touched in ages and her hair tickles my nose. When I step back, I'm grinning, she's grinning—a warm feeling surges through me. It's hard to believe we actually made it to this point.

"Sorry," she says, putting her phone away. "My mom called to see if you got here, but the signal was shitty downstairs so I came up here."

"For a second I thought maybe you changed your mind."

"You know, I did think about clearing out your bank account and disappearing, but if I got caught I'm not sure I could handle being in prison."

"Trust me, neither did I."

She hands me my favorite green jacket—it smells like laundry soap when I put it on—then asks if I want to get a cab or walk for a bit.

"Let's walk," I say. "But I might not make it too far. The furthest I've walked lately is across the dorm."

Out on Forty-second Street, it feels like everything is coming at me—crowds of people, street vendors shouting, the smell of food carts, billboards flashing, cars honking. It reminds me of how I felt the first time I went to Tokyo, especially once we get to Times Square. I feel like stopping random strangers and telling them I just got out of prison.

"This is too much stimulation—even for me," Susan says. "You must be totally overwhelmed."

"Yeah, maybe we should get a cab."

She raises her hand at the first free taxi that wheels down Broadway and we pile into the backseat, sitting close.

"Do you want something to eat?" she asks. "I brought you an apple and that Kit-Kat you've been talking about."

"Not just yet," I say, reaching over and holding her hand. "It's a bit of a mind fuck that twenty-four hours ago I was asleep in a prison bunk, and now I'm speeding through Manhattan."

Susan gives me a funny look, nodding toward the driver.

"What—am I not supposed to say I was in prison?"

"You can say it . . . maybe just not so *loudly*," she says, squeezing my hand. "Not everyone is going to be as accepting as me about that."

I'm sure the driver doesn't care where I've been, but I change the subject and tell her how different Manhattan seems. Even though I haven't been away that long, I hardly ever left Brooklyn before I got arrested, so it's like I'm seeing a whole new city. Big glass buildings seem to rise up every few blocks.

When we turn onto the Brooklyn Bridge, half my life comes rushing back—the excitement of moving to New York, Liam growing up, photo shoots, friends I haven't seen in ages, the blur of addiction, and that brutal day I got picked up by ICE.

"You okay?" Susan asks, nudging my shoulder.

"Yeah, I was just thinking about all the times I've crossed this river, especially the last one."

It's starting to hit me that I'm actually going to be staying with Susan—with nowhere to go if this doesn't work out. I'm comforted by her closeness and really want to lean over and kiss her, but I don't know if I should. It's a strange sensation—feeling like we've been together for years, but also like we're on a first date.

Once we pull up to her building, I make a joke about only having fifteen cents left in my pocket while she pays the fare. After we climb the stairs to her apartment, I put my bags down and just stand there, not quite sure what to do with myself. I can hardly remember the last time I was here.

"These are some of the things I picked up from Joe's place," she says, pointing to a pile of clothes lying on a chair. "And I bought you some new T-shirts and underwear—actually, when I went to York the first time. I wasn't sure about the size but you can exchange them if they don't fit."

"Thanks—I'm sure I'll need to buy a whole new wardrobe. I've put on a few pounds while I was locked up."

"Well, you still look a lot better than the last time you were here."

"Is it alright if I use the bathroom? I wouldn't mind cleaning up a bit."

"You don't have to ask me," Susan says. "I want you to feel at home—you can take a shower if you want."

In the bathroom, I hardly recognize myself in the mirror. Standing there looking at my reflection, I haven't seen my face so clearly in months. My skin is a bit sallow and I've got less hair than I'd hoped for, but all in all, not too bad.

Just as I turn on the shower, I hear Susan shout something about a toothbrush and a razor, which I spot sitting next to the sink. After cleaning my teeth, I shave with the new multi-blade razor she bought me. It feels brilliant gliding across my face.

Once I'm in the shower, I use every product Susan has— shampoo, conditioner, cleansers, gels, and soap that smells like lemon. The hot water spills all over me as I scrub and exfoliate until I've washed away all the dregs of prison. When I get out, my body is tingling and the fresh clothes feel soft on my skin.

Susan makes some tea, we sit down on her couch, and just talk for a while—about her family and her trip to Michigan, how excited I am to see Liam, and how tough it was thinking about what would happen if I got deported. By 2 A.M. I can barely keep

my eyes open. I keep yawning and Susan looks totally knack-
ered.

"I'm sorry, but it's way past my bedtime," I tell her. "I'm used
to lights-out at eleven."

"Yeah, this is pretty late for me, too."

I don't quite know how to bring up this topic—it's a bit
awkward—but I finally ask, "So where am I sleeping?"

Susan smiles and looks at me for a minute, like she's enjoying
drawing this out. "Well, since you just got out of prison it doesn't
feel right making you sleep on the couch. . . ."

"I don't want you to give up your bed."

"I wasn't suggesting that," she says, giving me a flirty look.
"But you can sleep with me if you want."

So I do—and after that night, I never leave.

◄◄•►►

I WISH I could say everything was brilliant after I got out of
prison, but the truth is, picking up the pieces of my life and putting
them back together was a lot harder than I expected. Then again,
I wasn't sure what to expect after I got off that bus. No one really
prepares you to be thrown back into the real world—and I was
only locked up for nine months. But with the years of addiction, I
felt like I'd lost almost a decade of my life.

For the first few days, all I wanted to do was sleep. I've always
been an early riser but Susan would nudge me at 10 or 11 A.M. and
say I should probably get up. Once I did, I didn't know what to do
with myself—I didn't even feel like opening my laptop. It meant
facing all those unread emails and the past I wanted to put behind
me, and I wasn't ready to deal with decisions like buying a new
phone. Just about the only thing I wanted to do was eat.

The first time I went to the store by myself, I wandered the
aisles staring at all the choices—cheese, ice cream, cereal, fruit,

fancy chocolate bars, different types of coffee. I had no idea how long I walked around thinking, *I can have any of this whenever I want.* By the time I got home, I could tell Susan was anxious—I'd been gone for almost an hour. She said she didn't think I'd run off to the projects to buy drugs, but I could tell it was going to take a while for her to trust me.

I get why, but I was never really tempted to use—not even when I ran into a dealer and he pressed two bags of dope into my hand, telling me, "You know where to find me." He took off before I could give them back, so I just stood there for a minute with those familiar glassine bags in my palm—then I dropped them in a trash can, hoping no one saw me. I knew in my heart I was done.

I'd go to AA meetings and people would talk about how they thought about drinking or using every day, but that was the furthest thing from my mind. Maybe the reason I needed drugs was gone—I didn't feel that crushing emptiness anymore, I wasn't depressed and lonely. And Walker was right: I *was* getting too old for that shit. But mostly, I wanted to show everybody that I could put that life behind me, especially Liam.

The first time I saw him, about a week after I got out, I was so nervous I was having heart palpitations on my way to meet him. He was walking toward me with this big grin on his face, taller and with shorter hair than I remembered. I *was* trying not to cry as I hugged him. I thought I wouldn't know what to say, but it all just tumbled out as we walked. I could tell he was holding back a bit—it took a while for things to feel normal—but every time I tried to apologize he'd cut me off, which was really humbling. He was trying so hard to make it easy on me, the worst thing I could do was let him down.

With my friends it was tough in a different way. I wasn't sure what rumors they'd heard, so I was hesitant to reach out at first. Then one night I was out with Susan and saw someone I'd known for almost twenty years—she was with her son, and I was too embarrassed to say hi. When I told Susan, she said I was being ridiculous so I caught up to them, shouting my friend's name. She turned around and gave me a big hug, saying she'd heard I'd had a rough time. I didn't tell her everything right then, but we made plans to get together and eventually it all came out. That was sort of a turning point for me—I realized I had to be honest about what I'd been through.

Most people were really supportive, but I think some of my friends felt bad about what had happened to me, wondering if there was anything else they could've done. One friend told me that someone I'd known for years had discouraged him from trying to do an intervention—telling him I was beyond help. Hearing that was really painful. I know I pushed everyone away, but I still can't believe that anyone thought there was no hope for me. I spent a lot of time thinking about what I would've done if it had been the other way around.

Probably the hardest part was going to see my family a few months after I got out. Susan kept calling our trip "The Apology Tour," joking that we should get T-shirts printed up listing all the places we went. I remember getting off the plane in Edinburgh and being shocked by how much older my mum and dad looked, and feeling like shit about how much I'd contributed to that. We went to a pub for lunch and it was pretty uncomfortable at first, so I was glad Susan was there to keep the conversation flowing. My dad opened up more when I was alone with him, but my mum didn't seem to want to talk about what I'd been through. I think the fact that they both liked Susan eventually put them at ease. My mum made Susan steak pie—complaining about what a picky eater I am—and my dad showed her pictures of me growing up. I'd never seen them get attached to someone so quickly. By the time we left, I could tell they felt a lot better about me.

After that we flew over to Dublin and saw my brother and sister and their kids, who treated me like I was some long-lost uncle who'd just come back from years at sea. My nieces and nephews didn't know what had happened to me—although they probably guessed something was up. The initial awkwardness with my brother and sister didn't last very long. Pretty soon we were cracking up playing cards with the kids and they were joking that now that "the number one son" had reappeared they'd have to take a back seat. As great as it was to feel like part of the family again, it made me feel worse about all the times I wasn't there.

One morning, my sister and I went for a walk along the waterfront and she told me how glad she was that I'd pulled through, but didn't hold back about how hard it had been for all of them. It was sort of like her letter—she had to get it off her chest, but once she did she could let it go. My brother just kept saying, "It's all behind you, Graham—time to move forward," which was sort of the same attitude he'd had about his divorce. He wasn't bitter or angry, and he hadn't lost his sense of humor—teasing me about how puffy I'd gotten and telling me I should start running again. But he did put me on the spot about getting back to work.

That was weighing on my mind, too. I still had enough money left that I didn't have to take any job I could get, but with a criminal record, my reputation trashed, and not having done a photo shoot in years, I had no idea what I was going to do. I tried scrapping cars with Jimmy, but that wasn't really my cup of tea, so I finally bit the bullet and started emailing everyone I'd ever worked with. That wasn't easy, but like one friend told me, "*Suck it up and write them, Graham. You were a fucking dope addict, you can do this.*" He was right—I'd fought so hard to get clean and win my case, I couldn't let my insecurities hold me back.

But it was still pretty discouraging to send hundreds of messages and get so few replies. Even a client who wrote a letter to the judge for me wouldn't return my calls. I was starting to wonder if I'd always be a fuck-up in some people's eyes, but I kept at it and slowly things started coming together. I got little assignments here and there and it was brilliant to be taking pictures again. Then a friend offered me a part-time job teaching photography, which I jumped at—until I saw that the application asked, "*Have you ever been convicted of a misdemeanor or a felony?*" Luckily, I still got the job and it turned out I really loved it. I felt like I had something to offer and the students motivated me to embrace how photography had changed—not resist it.

A lot of people ended up opening doors for me, so it was tough to see many of the friends I was locked up with get thrown back into the same mess they'd left. Marco managed to stay clean for a few months, then got busted for possession, and Jimmy got arrested for driving without a license—even though the tow truck was parked, and he was just waiting for the guy who was helping him. Walker was doing well for a while, but he's young and all his friends are still partying, so he did what I used to do—think it was alright to just drink *less* or use drugs *occasionally,* which landed him back at York County Prison.

Actually, out of all the people I knew from those years, Tracy was one of the few who got her shit together and stayed clean. For a while I'd see her at AA meetings—she had really embraced the program and stuck with it—but after about a year I went less and less often. I definitely got something out of sharing and hearing other people's stories, but once I started running again, that became a more important part of my recovery. It was a way for me to put what I learned in the Freedom Program into practice: stepping back, thinking more rationally, not overreacting. It's hard to explain, but running gave me that release. And once I started sharing my story with people outside of AA, I found that more inspiring than talking to people who'd heard similar shares hundreds of times. It was a lot tougher to tell a colleague or an old friend what had happened to me, but I felt like I opened a door for them to have a conversation they wouldn't normally have had. They'd often tell me about someone they knew who had a problem, and those exchanges were really uplifting. It helped me get over the shame I'd been carrying around.

The biggest challenge for me was not beating myself up over the past or getting overwhelmed by everything I needed to tackle. There were many times when I got discouraged, but Susan really helped me keep a positive frame of mind. She was patient with me, but she also pushed me, encouraging me to step out of my comfort zone when I was reluctant—like when she suggested I look for a workspace. I was worried that renting a studio would be too expensive or inconvenient, but one night she and her friend opened up Craigslist, we started scrolling through listings, and within a week I'd found a place. It sounds crazy, but I was so out of the habit of doing things for myself, I just needed that little nudge to be more independent.

At first I'd thank Susan constantly for everything she'd done for me, but she went out of her way to make me feel like I didn't owe her some big debt. I thought things might be more fraught between us, especially living together, but she was way more laid back than she used to be. I'd go to my storage space and bring back some of my stuff—old running trophies, a photo of Johnny Rotten, vintage belt buckles—and she'd just roll her eyes and tell me we didn't really have anywhere to put all of my quirky knick-knacks. She'd get frustrated that I never screwed the lid on a jar of peanut butter tightly or I'd forget to pick up milk, but I did keep my promise to help with the chores and I was pretty good at fixing things.

I think Susan had gotten used to dealing with a lot on her own, so I tried hard to be supportive of her in the same way she'd been there for me. I'd pull her out of a funk when work got frustrating, suggesting we hop on the subway and go out to Coney Island or visit friends upstate, and we did eventually take that trip to Japan I suggested back in 2006. We ended up doing a lot of traveling, even cashing in some of those frequent flier miles I'd been hoarding, so I'd like to think I made up for some of the shit I put her through. I still send her pictures of love hearts I find painted on sidewalks or buildings, and I tell her all the time how glad I am that she's in my life. Relationships aren't easy when you're in the early stages of recovery, but I don't know how I would've managed if I'd had to do it all on my own.

I'm sure a lot of people thought Susan was crazy for taking me in, but that made me even more determined to prove I was worth it. I wanted to be everything I hadn't been for her the first time around. In one of her letters, she talked about what I needed to do to find the love that I wanted—get drugs out of my life and deal with my insecurities—and I did those things, but in the end, I think we both found the love that had been missing from our lives.

EPILOGUE

January 2016
Cobble Hill, Brooklyn

Graham and I are sitting next to each other on our couch, looking at my laptop. There are piles of paper all around us, marked up with edits—my comments in blue pen, his in green.

"I would never say that," he tells me, pointing to a line of dialogue on the screen.

"Well you wrote it," I answer, reaching for one of the many pages of handwritten notes he's given me.

"Okay, but looking at it again, I'm realizing that's not how I would've said it."

I exhale, slowly. "So how would you have said it?"

"I don't know . . . just not like that. It doesn't sound like me."

This is probably the fifty-ninth time we've had some version of this conversation, but we're too tired to argue about it—or fix it. I just highlight the line and we move on to the next page.

Writing a book with your partner, about the worst years of your life together, is not something either of us would recommend. There have been times when I felt like I was subjecting Graham to some sort of prolonged exposure therapy—forcing him to reexperience painful events again and again. As a therapeutic treatment, the goal is to reduce the negative impact of those memories, but in Graham's case, I'm not sure that desensitization ever happened.

"I need you to describe what it's like to smoke crack," I'd tell him, "And don't just say it's 'brilliant.' What does that hit *really feel like*? You've got to explain it with more detail—but not the same way you described shooting up."

Graham would get this pained look on his face, trying to remember how it felt to get high—then a couple of nights later, he'd wake up traumatized by yet another drug dream. After he finally fell asleep, I'd lie awake next to him, wondering if I was pushing him straight into a relapse. As much as I agree with Joan Didion, that it's important to remember the people we used to be, I'm not sure spending *so much time* inside our former selves was a good idea—for Graham or for me.

So why did we decide to do this? We've asked ourselves that question almost every day for the past year and a half.

At first I was just going to write about my experience, from my perspective: loving someone who's an addict and making a difficult choice about helping or walking away. But as I drafted an outline, picturing courtrooms and jail time, I realized that it would be a much richer book if Graham told his side of the story, too. I wasn't there when he was doing drugs or getting hauled off in handcuffs, so I knew he could capture what he went through better than me—with some help polishing the writing. It turned into an unusual collaboration, with debates over phrases and details and what to include or leave out, but we've tried to reveal as much as we and our families could bear.

Even at its worst, our experience was not as ugly or desperate as life can be for a lot of the people Graham knew, and our happy reunion isn't how many of these stories end. But it's the truth. Graham didn't relapse. We stayed together. It didn't take that long for me to trust him. After he got out of prison, I realized that our relationship wasn't going to work if he felt like he was still on trial, or if I was constantly suspicious. We had to move on with a clean slate.

When things were tough, especially that first year, many of the lessons Graham learned in the Freedom Program ended up giving us both the tools to address problems. Sadly, his bed-making skills lasted about seventy-two hours, and so did that habit of wiping up the bathroom sink. Even off drugs, he still sometimes walks out the door without his phone or his keys. But I've learned not to say "You need to pick up your awareness" in that smug way that drives him crazy—just like he's learned to let me be mad for at least a little while after we've had a fight, because I can't just get over it *instantly*.

Graham is better than me at saying he's sorry (he's had a lot of practice), and I think anyone who knows him would say he made a huge effort to make amends to the people he hurt. I can't imagine what else he could've done to prove that he deserved the chance the judge and everyone else gave him—which is why it's so frustrating that in some ways, he's *still* being punished for his mistakes.

Graham was lucky that his criminal record didn't prevent him from getting a teaching job he loves, but I'm sure there are many landlords who wouldn't approve his application as a tenant. He can't travel to Canada, unless he wants to pay a lot of money and go through a lot of hassle to get a waiver for his drug conviction. Whenever he returns from a trip abroad, he's usually taken into another room by immigration, while I wait with our bags—worried they'll find some reason not to let him back into the country. He finally applied to become a U.S. citizen, submitting glowing letters of support, but the woman who interviewed him said she couldn't approve his application—it had to go through a legal review. Almost six months later, as this book is going to press, Graham is still waiting for an answer.

These are all minor problems compared to the barriers many recovering addicts and former inmates face, but they make me wonder if we as a society really believe in rehabilitation. During the time he was in custody, Graham was primarily defined as a drug addict, a criminal, and an alien, and those identities can be tough to escape.

But if certain people hadn't seen beyond those labels and made even a small effort to help him, Graham probably would've ended up in a much darker place. If the woman at York County Prison hadn't given him my phone number, or his CO hadn't suggested he apply to the Freedom Program, or the judge had decided that Graham shouldn't be allowed to stay, our lives would be very different today. Just like what I did for Graham ultimately had a much bigger impact than I could've imagined—which is what I wrote about in my notebook almost five years ago, after Armen called to tell me that Graham won his case.

It's January 14, 2011 and this ordeal began—for me—on August 24. Even though I was confident things would go Graham's way, neither of us knew until now. I picture him in the courtroom, probably closing his eyes as the judge gives the verdict, then maybe fighting back tears (a little) because that's what he does when he's emotional, especially when people say nice things about him. That's the side of him I love—the guy who can be so grateful, and push so hard when he sets his mind on something. He'll go back to his dorm, have lunch—a last crappy baked potato—start packing and giving his things away.

When people say I saved Graham's life, I feel that's not quite right because in the end Graham chose to save himself. But I did change the course of his life and right now that feels pretty incredible. That everything he does from today on will be different than it would've been if I hadn't helped him, if he'd signed the deportation order and been banished from the U.S. Maybe he would've done ok, but in my heart I think he would've ended up giving in to drugs, and probably died of an overdose—maybe intentionally—slumped in a corner of some dingy room or stairwell. Who knows what will happen with us, but at this moment that almost doesn't matter. As painful and stressful as this has been, it was worth it.

That was the last time I wrote anything personal in my notebook. I'm not sure why, but maybe I didn't need that outlet anymore; I had Graham to talk to when I was anxious. But I can honestly say that even if we hadn't ended up together—or stayed together—it still would've been worth it, because I got to see all these people who love him get him back.

When I hear Graham on the phone with his dad, even when they're just talking about the shite weather in Scotland, I know what it means to his parents to have those Sunday calls, without the weight of the worry they lived with for so many years. Seeing him laughing with his brother and sister, or hanging out with friends—telling some story with that same passion I saw in Montauk, without the alcohol or drugs. And watching him hug his grown-up son and tell him he loves him, then hearing Liam say it back—maybe a little embarrassed, but no longer burdened by his dad's addiction.

I used to tell Graham that saying "I love you" is easy—the hard part is *showing* it. But I've come around to understanding that it's important to say it, too, because sometimes people don't make the leap from what you do for them to knowing how you feel about them. You have to tell them. And you also have to find the courage to "say things that are difficult to say," like David once told me, because if you don't, they fester and become much bigger problems. I think those two things are the glue that have kept Graham and me together—and hopefully, will keep us together over the long haul.

In a few weeks, it'll be too late to change any of the things we've tried to say in these pages, and I'm sure some of them will make us cringe later. We'll wish we said it better, or maybe not said some things at all. We'll realize we missed things we should've included.

All we can hope is that what we've written helps other people talk more openly about their own lives—that it gets easier to tell a friend that they're struggling with a drug problem, or admit that their child is using heroin, or say at a dinner party, "My brother is in prison." And maybe it'll change how some people think about addicts, and people with criminal records, and immigrants.

That's why we wrote this book, and right now, anxious about what's going to happen once it's out in the world, we hope that it will have been worth it.

ACKNOWLEDGMENTS

For a book as personal as this one is, we would not have been able to tell our story without the support and encouragement of many of the people who appear in these pages. Most of all, we're grateful to our friends and family for their input, especially when that meant discussing experiences that were difficult for them to revisit. Besides sharing their memories, letters, and email messages with us, many of them read drafts of the manuscript and offered feedback that helped make it a much more nuanced memoir. Chiemi Karasawa and Sam Douglas in particular gave us much-appreciated criticism and advice.

We'd also like to thank our editor, Jennifer Tung, and everyone at Ballantine Books for taking on a complex, two-person memoir and supporting us with patience and enthusiasm as it evolved. We're especially indebted to our agent, Will Lippincott, who championed this book from the beginning and always believed we could pull it off.

Finally, a nod of appreciation for each other. When we first realized that writing a memoir together was going to be tougher than we'd expected, Graham said that the most important thing was making sure we still loved each other once we were finished. We do, and we're grateful for that, too.

ABOUT THE AUTHORS

SUSAN STELLIN is a reporter and frequent contributor to *The New York Times*, where she worked as an editor for several years. She is the author of *How to Travel Practically Anywhere,* a travel planning guide, and has a B.A. in political science from Stanford University.

GRAHAM MACINDOE is a photographer and adjunct professor of photography at The New School's Parsons School of Design. Born in Scotland, he studied painting in Edinburgh and earned a master's degree in photography at the Royal College of Art in London.

In 2014, Stellin and MacIndoe were awarded a fellowship from the Alicia Patterson Foundation for their series American Exile, documenting the stories of families divided by deportation. They live in Brooklyn.

susanstellin.com
grahammacindoe.com

ABOUT THE TYPE

This book was set in Sabon, a typeface designed by the well-known German typographer Jan Tschichold (1902–74). Sabon's design is based upon the original letter forms of sixteenth-century French type designer Claude Garamond and was created specifically to be used for three sources: foundry type for hand composition, Linotype, and Monotype. Tschichold named his typeface for the famous Frankfurt typefounder Jacques Sabon (c. 1520–80).